Pacific Northwest Guide to
HOME GARDENING

Ray A. McNeilan
&
Micheline Ronningen

Illustrated by Micheline Ronningen

TIMBER PRESS
Portland, Oregon
1982

TIMBER PRESS
P.O. BOX 1631
Beaverton, Oregon 97075

Library of Congress Cataloging in Publication Data

McNeilan, Ray A.
   Pacific Northwest guide to home gardening.

   Includes index.
   1.   Vegetable gardening — Northwest, Pacific. 2.   Fruit-culture —
Northwest, Pacific. I. Ronningen, Micheline.   II.   Title.
SB321.M393   1982   635'09795   82-10701
ISBN 0-917304-39-X

CONTENTS

Chapter 1: INTRODUCTION

by Ray A. McNeilan

Overhead, perched on the limb of a lofty beech, a jay scolded with a raucous call. He sat above my garden, announcing himself King of all he surveyed and made it clear he resented my intrusion into his domain. I couldn't help admiring him. Clearly I was more delighted to share my garden than he was.

A quick survey of the garden showed once again the night had spawned a dozen small miracles of life. On the raised beds a seeding of radishes were pushing their way through the soil. Tiny slivers of carrot stems were popping up, almost invisible unless you caught the morning light glinting off their birth-clean stems.

Amid the signs of growth were telltale signs of the struggle with disease and predators . . . a few holes in some of the potato leaves, indicating a feast for some flea beetles . . . a little mildew on inner leaves of the grape trellis. The ladybug crew was already at work and empty husks of aphids showed Mother Nature's crew was effective.

Time for me to go. A job a hundred miles away awaited my presence. I retraced my footsteps through the morning dew. The sun was out in all its glory, leaves were turning to soak in its rays. The jay called his triumph at having driven off the intruder and sped off, a flash of blue between the firs.

Once upon a time it seemed all the exotic and interesting places in the world were far away. Then, little by little, it occurred to me there was a kingdom in my garden as exotic and exciting because in so many ways it was as unfamiliar in its intimate detail as the polar bears' range or the elephants' savanna.

When I belatedly realized the backyard was so interesting, I made two promises to myself and my garden. First I would try to understand it better and second I would improve it for those who come after I depart. Your garden is an adventure we invite you to share. In this book we will explore the mystery and beauty and conflict of our Northwest gardens and help you to make the most of it.

The first thing one should understand about the garden is there is nothing natural about it. Vegetables and fruit plants in their native state would be considered weeds today. The rambling blackberry that keeps trying to choke out my apple tree is a prime example. It is hardy, competitive and yields a moderate crop of seedy fruit. Contrast this with the row of hybrid strawberries that yields many pounds of delectable fruit but that also needs a lot of care and help to remain alive. Through years of research and breeding, the more desirable crop qualities of wild food plants have been selected, combined and enhanced. Unfortunately, in all this effort, some of the natural hardiness and competitiveness has been lost and today's hybrid food crop plants must be given special environmental care to flourish.

A garden is a human creation and not a natural entity so you will have to learn how to compensate for climate and soils and how to utilize cultural practices to make your fruit and vegetable garden the productive and enjoyable place you have visualized in your plans. The growing season and seasonal temperatures may not be exactly right for the plants you plan to grow without special planning and care. The soil may need to be changed a little to give your flavorful, but somewhat delicate, plants a chance to grow properly. Your particular brand of insects, diseases, weed or animal pests may find your garden the most delectable and exotic thing around and they will spend great amounts of time in it.

Whether you are a beginning gardener or one with considerable gardening experience, you will find there are challenges almost daily to stimulate your interest. Mysteries you have never suspected await your enthusiastic spring preparation of the ground and planting of seeds.

But gardening is not all fun and excitement. Successful gardening is really the wise management of resources. You may not have thought of it in this way but the resources in our gardening places are priceless. We have the soil that came to us through millions of years of rock weathering. We have the climate, a boundless mixture of sunlight, rain, and moderate temperatures, that is ours for the using, compliments of the ocean and mountains and valleys. And we have all kinds of plants to select in our try at feeding ourselves fresh fruits and vegetables.

Our job of managing these resources involves more than simply watching the rain fall on the soil and the sun light up the foliage. We must manipulate some environmental factors and perhaps, even make our own microclimate to fit the plants we want to grow.

We must also supply and adjust the factors available to us for growing our plants. At hand will be such things as fertilizers, water, and the tools of pest control. To these natural and physical things, we need to apply planting techniques, pruning practices and learn when and how to harvest the product of our work. Over a period of several years we will have to become acquainted with crop rotation and cover crops, grafting and exposure. In so doing we will find that our limited gardening information has grown into mature ideas on which we can build yet another year of gardening experience.

Gardening is a learning process. It is an experience in which ignorance is not bliss. You will also find it nearly impossible to keep from discovering some new bit of information each time you venture among your fruit trees or through rows of cabbages and corn. Gardening has been praised with many useful attributes; it pays, it gives you exercise and tastier food, it can be enjoyed by all ages, and is a way to fight pollution. Also, it gives some security and doesn't require a large outlay of money. Above all, we submit that gardening gives you a chance to do your own thing with your own plants, test your abilities and reasoning powers and to do your own bit to make your environment more enjoyable and healthy. It was with this tenet in mind that we prepared this book to give you some of the basic facts and management tools needed. If you are already gardening perhaps it will help you solve some of the problems encountered along the way.

To get you started, consider what you could do with the patch of spare ground in your yard. Let's consider what could be grown on an average space of 20 x 50 feet.

EXAMPLE: A 20 × 50′ FRUIT AND VEGETABLE GARDEN

House

Patio

Perennials:
A. Blueberries
B. Trailing Berries
C. Rhubarb
D. Asparagus
E. Strawberries
F. Espaliered Apple Trees

Annuals:
1. Radishes & Carrots
2. Head Lettuce & Beets
3. Tomatoes
4. Swiss Chard
5. Kohlrabi
6. Cabbage
7. Kale
8. Cucumbers
9. Celery
10. Summer Squash
11. Peppers
12. Green Beans
13. Onions
14. Potatoes
15. Sweet Corn
16. Broccoli or Brussels Sprouts
17. Peas

Miscellaneous:
Containers on patio for additional fruits or vegetables, herbs, flowers.

Scale: ☐ = 1 sq. ft.

We give this illustration to challenge your planning abilities. This book is not for the casual gardener but is written for the dedicated, dirt-under-the-fingernails person who is ready to learn how to use the land and climate and his or her abilities to produce food. It is not a specialty book about cabbages or apple growing, but is basically a do-your-own-growing book for any and all food crops adapted to the Northwest. Heretofore the Northwest gardener had no single source to locate information on growing Northwest vegetables, small fruits or fruit trees. We have tried to provide such a single source with this book.

We believe there is a solution to any Northwest gardening problem: soil drainage, fertility, climate, pests, fruit varieties, frost, etc. However, as in other undertakings, one of the major hurdles is identifying the problem itself. With a well defined problem one can usually proceed to a solution. This book is designed to help you identify the problems associated with vegetable or fruit growing and then to help derive solutions.

In this book we tell of the techniques useful in growing plants.   There are so many, and they are adaptable for the many different gardening situations in the Northwest. By understanding and using our suggested ways of gardening, we hope you will discover the joys of gardening and the satisfaction of exploring the exotic and exciting kingdom of your own garden.

Chapter 2: CLIMATE

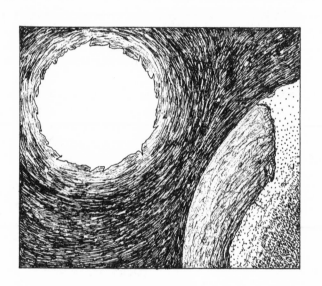

Introduction

The adaptability of a food crop to a specific environment is essential to fruition and precedes in importance any soil, irrigation, nutrient or pollination requirements. Under less than ideal climatic conditions, time-to-maturity is either lengthened or impossible to meet. Some areas of the Northwest have such moderate temperatures that fruit trees cannot bear properly because their bud chilling requirement is not met during the winter season. Other areas experience such rapid changes in temperature and rainfall amounts that a gardener can be hard pressed to get a decent crop of radishes.

Diversity is an appropriate description for our climate. Growing seasons vary from sixty days in the mountainous regions to 290 days in the coastal valleys.

Rainfall in Yakima, Washington may be ten inches in a year while Newport, Oregon has counted nearly seven feet. Rain is a resource for which the Northwest is noted, but a gardener soon finds that the supply is not uniform or particularly timely. For example, in 1976, downtown Portland, Oregon received 28 inches of rain while Gresham (just twelve miles east) received 40 inches.

Most of our rain falls in the winter and because of our soil types we usually have to begin irrigating the day after the rains quit. Much of the soil nitrogen is leached away each year by the heavy winter rains. Here nitrogen is usually the most needed soil nutrient.

Sunlight in the Northwest is adequate to grow numerous food crops, when we get it. In spring the western half of the region may not see the sun for a week or more at a time. Light filtering through the clouds is enough to sustain the perennial plants, but without the heat from direct rays of the sun the soil remains cold and wet. Some soils may not be warm enough for cool season vegetables until April. Warm season crops such as tomatoes may have to wait until June to be transplanted.

Soil and air temperatures are the most influential elements in gardening. To some degree the impact of low temperatures may be blunted by microclimate adjustments. But to some degree they must simply be recognized as unchangeable and so plants must be selected that are adapted to our situation. Later in this chapter we will detail some of the climatic conditions of the Northwest as they relate to growing food crops and suggest ways to develop a suitable microclimate.

The Macroclimate

The Cascade Mountain range that extends the length of the Northwest region causes dramatic climatic differences between the eastern and western parts of the Northwest. The east side receives much less rain because the clouds are usually wrung dry in crossing the mountains. The eastern part receives much more sunlight, is hotter in the summer and colder in the winter, temperatures are more extreme, and the growing seasons are shorter.

As a result, the standard "frost free days" indicator has to be adjusted for various areas. Thus Salem, Oregon and Yakima, Washington have about the same total number of frost free days in a year. However, Salem warms very gradually to an acceptable garden planting temperature. Yakima, on the other hand, with fewer clouds and more solar radiation, experiences a rapid and definite warming to suitable temperature. As a consequence, planting schedules in these two cities are very different.

The macroclimate of the entire Northwest is mild, despite its latitude, due to the influence of the Pacific Ocean. Oceans absorb solar radiation and hang onto it. The deep stirring action of water currents maintains the overall temperature fairly evenly, day and night and season to season. Our predominantly western winds carry this warm, moisture laden air over the region. The twin factors of moderate temperature and high rainfall basically characterize our climate. In short they create the macroclimate that generally governs our greenery.

Temperatures, though generally moderate, vary considerably due to elevation differences, amount of associated sunlight, or interactions with wind, rain and snow. For the most part, we are relatively free of temperature extremes and rarely experience the cold, dry Arctic winds which our more Easterly colleagues beyond the Rocky Mountains endure. In most

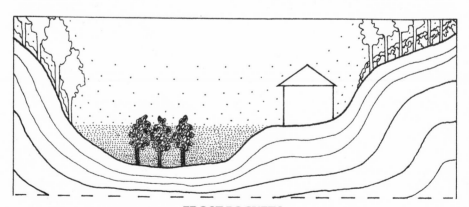

FROST POCKETS
Cold air settles to the lowest part of the terrain. Low areas will be most subject to late spring and early fall killing frost.

parts of the Northwest a zero degree (Fahrenheit) reading is rare. On the west side of the Cascades the influence of the Pacific may allow entire winters to pass with temperatures never dropping below 32°F.

However, on a local basis, the lay of your land and its surroundings can make a world of difference. The Northwest is marked by a diverse topography of valleys, hills, mountains and bench lands. Local terrain may funnel strong winds or decrease wind velocity. Cold air moves down into a valley. Valleys are usually warmer in the summer than the surrounding slopes, but they frequently harbor cold air pockets.

The region has two distinct patterns of moisture. The west side is characterized by wet winters and dry summers. The east side receives some snow in the winter and minimal precipitation during the summer. But both parts of the region must rely upon irrigation for growing fruit and summer vegetables.

The rain that falls during the winter west of the Cascades is a mixed blessing and poses extra problems for gardeners. Heavy rains erode unmulched gardens, compact the soil, cause root problems in poorly drained areas, and leach away valuable nutrients.

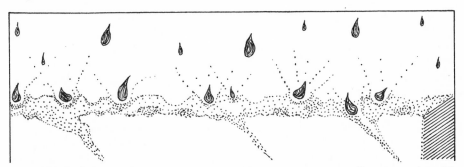

RAINDROPS ON SOIL: Effects erosion (loss of fertile topsoil), compaction (air spaces in soil are reduced or eliminated), and leaching (minerals are washed away). Plant roots need air, fertile soil and minerals; before winter rains begin, place a 1—2″ organic cover (a mulch) over your garden area to lessen impact and soil/mineral losses.

To gain a better feel for the climatic ranges and extremes in your area, get acquainted with your local weather bureau. Oregon has 286 weather stations, Washington 218, and British Columbia has 465. You can find weather data for almost any place you might want to garden. Knowledge of growing season, rainfall amounts, and temperature ranges are essential to a gardener, and this data is available. Gardening zone maps will only provide a general indication of temperature extremes so consult the specific information for your specific area. The following *Weather Summary Data* indicates some of the variance within our region.

WEATHER SUMMARY DATA

	Total Annual PRECIPITATION		Last Spring FROST		First Fall FROST		Frost Free Days	
	'74	'79	'74	'79	'74	'79	'74	'79
Oregon								
Brookings	63.2	70.8	3/8	2/2	12/23	none	290	332
Newport	80.7	72.7	4/16	4/7	10/6	12/7	173	244
Seaside	78.5	72.7	4/13	3/24	11/2	11/11	203	232
Corvallis	50.7	42.0	4/12	3/22	10/8	11/14	179	237
Eugene	56.7	51.2	4/12	5/29	10/7	11/8	178	163
Wilsonville	42.4	40.9	3/24	3/21	10/5	11/8	195	232
Portland	40.2	35.7	3/18	2/21	11/28	11/11	255	263
Salem	45.9	37.9	5/13	4/19	10/5	10/17	145	181
Roseburg	34.0	35.5	4/13	2/3	10/6	none	176	331
The Dalles	12.8	12.7	3/22	3/10	10/6	11/19	198	254
Bend	11.6	9.8	6/26	6/20	7/2	7/2	6	12
Pendleton	14.3	16.0	5/31	5/30	9/13	10/9	105	132
British Columbia								
Vancouver	49.1	39.4	3/23	3/28	11/3	11/8	225	225
Washington								
Aberdeen	92.0	77.1	4/13	3/1	12/22	11/27	253	271
Mt. Vernon	37.3	24.9	4/13	3/24	10/5	10/31	175	221
Port Angeles	23.3	23.2	3/20	3/2	11/22	11/19	247	262
Bellingham	33.7	30.4	4/13	4/20	10/6	10/31	176	194
Seattle	33.7	28.4	3/20	2/25	11/28	11/21	253	269
Tacoma	38.4	36.5	3/8	3/16	11/29	11/20	266	249
Longview	50.0	36.5	3/22	4/10	—	11/13	284	217
Richland	4.5	7.0	3/20	3/21	10/6	11/1	200	225
Yakima	8.2	6.8	5/16	4/20	10/3	10/17	140	180
Spokane	16.0	14.3	5/16	4/21	10/5	10/30	142	192
Pullman	20.0	20.3	5/16	4/20	9/27	10/28	134	191

Information for this table was derived from National Oceanic & Atmospheric Administration climatological data, annual summaries for 1974 and 1979 and from the Meteorological Service, Vancouver, B.C.

NORTHWEST TEMPERATURE & PRECIPITATION AVERAGES BY MONTH

	J	F	M	A	M	J	J	A	S	O	N	D
Oregon												
Brookings												
Precip.	13.6	10.1	9.0	5.6	4.6	1.6	0.6	0.9	1.9	7.2	12.2	13.2
Temp. F.	47.0	48.3	48.7	50.6	54.1	57.5	58.5	58.9	59.6	55.8	51.8	48.5
Roseburg												
Precip.	5.9	3.8	3.2	1.8	1.8	1.2	0.2	0.4	0.9	3.1	5.1	6.1
Temp. F.	40.9	44.6	46.9	51.3	56.9	62.4	68.2	67.9	63.4	54.7	46.9	42.5
Eugene												
Precip.	7.5	4.6	4.4	2.3	2.0	1.2	0.2	0.5	1.2	4.0	6.5	7.6
Temp. F.	39.4	43.5	45.9	50.3	56.4	61.4	66.9	66.1	61.0	53.2	45.6	41.5
Salem												
Precip.	6.9	4.8	4.3	2.2	2.0	1.3	0.4	0.5	1.4	3.9	6.1	6.8
Temp. F.	38.8	42.9	45.2	49.8	55.7	61.2	66.6	66.1	61.9	53.2	45.2	41.0
Bend												
Precip.	1.9	1.0	0.7	0.5	1.1	1.7	0.3	0.5	0.3	0.9	1.6	1.9
Temp. F.	30.2	34.8	37.1	43.2	49.8	55.8	62.8	61.3	55.5	46.7	38.1	32.7
Portland												
Precip.	9.0	4.8	6.4	2.6	2.2	0.8	2.3	0.1	0.1	2.2	7.1	6.9
Temp. F.	38.1	42.8	47.1	51.4	55.2	64.6	67.5	68.4	69.1	56.6	48.5	44.0
Seaside												
Precip.	12.1	9.4	8.2	5.4	3.1	2.5	1.2	1.6	2.9	7.3	10.5	12.3
Temp. F.	42.2	45.7	45.9	48.8	53.0	56.9	59.7	60.1	58.9	54.4	48.5	45.0
The Dalles												
Precip.	2.4	1.7	1.4	1.1	1.2	1.0	0.2	0.4	0.6	1.5	2.3	2.4
Temp. F.	31.6	38.0	42.7	49.4	56.7	63.2	70.1	68.6	62.0	51.4	40.7	35.1
British Columbia												
Vancouver												
Precip.	8.6	5.8	5.0	3.3	2.8	2.5	1.2	1.7	3.6	5.8	8.3	8.8
Temp. F.	36.3	41.0	42.8	47.4	53.4	59.9	62.8	62.9	57.4	50.2	43.3	38.5
Washington												
Longview												
Precip.	6.3	5.8	4.3	3.1	2.4	2.0	0.8	1.4	2.0	4.6	6.4	7.3
Temp. F.	38.2	42.3	44.6	49.4	55.0	59.8	64.4	64.3	60.7	52.9	45.1	40.5
Pullman												
Precip.	2.8	2.1	1.8	1.5	1.6	1.6	0.4	0.6	1.1	1.9	2.6	2.7
Temp. F.	28.0	34.1	38.3	46.0	53.3	59.2	66.8	66.0	59.2	49.3	37.9	31.8
Tacoma												
Precip.	5.5	4.0	3.4	2.3	1.5	1.2	0.7	1.1	1.8	3.7	5.5	5.7
Temp. F.	40.0	43.6	45.2	50.0	55.9	60.5	64.8	64.2	60.1	53.0	50.0	41.9
Aberdeen												
Precip.	12.4	9.7	8.3	5.5	3.2	2.4	1.2	1.9	3.5	8.1	11.2	13.3
Temp. F.	39.7	42.9	44.1	48.1	53.2	57.4	60.5	60.8	59.1	52.6	45.6	41.5
Port Angeles												
Precip.	4.0	3.0	2.0	1.3	0.9	0.9	0.5	0.7	1.2	2.7	3.8	4.0
Temp. F.	38.5	41.4	42.9	47.1	52.1	56.3	59.4	59.0	56.6	50.2	43.9	40.6
Seattle												
Precip.	5.1	3.9	3.2	2.3	1.7	1.5	0.8	0.8	1.7	3.4	5.3	5.3
Temp. F.	39.7	43.4	45.5	50.5	56.7	61.4	65.9	65.4	61.1	53.8	46.1	42.1
Yakima												
Precip.	1.3	0.7	0.5	0.5	0.5	0.7	0.1	0.2	0.2	0.5	1.1	1.2
Temp. F.	27.5	35.7	41.8	49.5	57.9	64.5	70.7	68.6	61.3	50.1	38.4	31.3
Spokane												
Precip.	2.4	1.6	1.5	1.1	1.5	1.3	0.4	0.6	0.8	1.4	2.2	2.3
Temp. F.	25.4	32.2	37.5	46.1	54.7	61.5	69.7	68.0	59.6	47.8	35.5	29.0

Climate and Plant Growth

To get a feel for the importance of the various elements of the climate relative to plants, let's look briefly at each. Sunlight, temperature, precipitation, and air movement each do something to or for a plant.

Sunlight is needed by all green plants. It is the energy source in *photo-synthesis*. Photosynthesis is the physiological process which permits green plants to make their own food from the basic elements. A green leaf, in the presence of light, uses carbon dioxide from the air and water from the soil to make carbohydrates (starches and sugars). Light is the trigger and provides the energy but the rate at which the starches and sugars are formed depends on temperature and light intensity. Some photosynthesis occurs around 40°F with about 500 foot-candles. (One foot-candle is the amount of light from one candle illuminating a square foot surface a foot away.) A peak rate is reached at around 75°F and 3500 foot-candles intensity. Beyond this point the process slows due to the physiological limits of the plant.

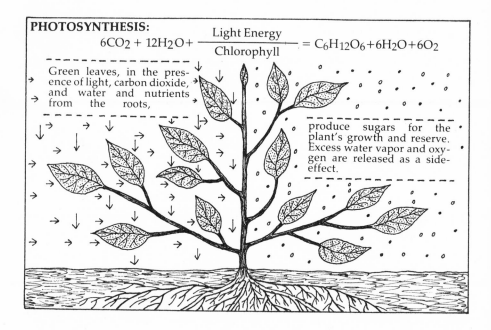

PHOTOSYNTHESIS:

$$6CO_2 + 12H_2O + \frac{\text{Light Energy}}{\text{Chlorophyll}} = C_6H_{12}O_6 + 6H_2O + 6O_2$$

Green leaves, in the presence of light, carbon dioxide, and water and nutrients from the roots,

produce sugars for the plant's growth and reserve. Excess water vapor and oxygen are released as a side-effect.

Photosynthesis is a material creation process. It is through this working system that the plant can make its own food for growth, storage, and fruit development. Stored food reserves are sometimes eaten by us (root crops) or serve perennial and woody plants as a food and energy supply through the winter and spring seasons. There is a counter process that takes place as the plants use these food reserves. This process is called *respiration* and takes place both day and night as the plant develops. During the respiration process the carbohydrates previously made by photosynthesis are broken down to release energy; the plant takes in oxygen, and gives off carbon dioxide (another of Nature's recycling efforts).

For a green plant to stay ahead of its respiration requirements it must receive enough sunlight to produce the plant food needed to function and store reserves. With only a few hours of daily sunshine or filtered sunlight, food plants cannot keep up. Vegetables, small fruits, and tree fruits planted in shady areas will be spindly and weak and not productive simply because they lack the light needed to make their own food and produce fruit. It must be noted that there are a few food plants that can grow in partial shade. These are mentioned in the food crop chapters.

Temperature and light effects are hard to separate because the sun is the sole supplier. So, until our clouds thin out in the spring, our soils remain too cold for many plants. Fortunately for avid gardeners, there are vegetables that can tolerate cool weather. These can be planted a month or so before the final frost and help extend our gardening period many days beyond the recognized growing season.

We encounter a unique problem in growing fruit trees due to our moderate climate. Fruit trees require a certain amount of cold in order to properly prepare flower buds to enter and break dormancy and so set good flowers in the spring. Winters so mild that the temperature never dips below freezing fail to fulfill this requirement. Consequently, in the spring following a mild winter, apple trees frequently get only a sparse set of flowers and these may bloom over a period of a month with only a few flowers available for fertilization at any one time. These conditions make it tough for proper pollination to occur and so a poor crop of fruit results. Don't get excited unless this happens year after year in your orchard. If it does, change to species a little less demanding of cold, like filberts. Fulfilling chilling requirements are manifestly beyond a gardener's capabilities.

Hot midsummer weather marks the end of cool season, spring planted vegetable crops. This gives the progressive vegetable gardener a clearly marked stopping place for early crops and a starting place for fall crops. There are the odd years of eccentric weather when this dependable pattern is disrupted. But the norm is what we must plan for.

Cool season vegetable crops respond to hot midsummer temperatures by flowering and making seed (bolting). Sometimes cool season crops will bolt as the result of an unusual sequence of marked temperature changes — late February planting in cool soil and low ambient temperatures, followed by a month or so of warmer than normal soil and environmental temperature, followed by cool temperatures until the middle of May. Following such a weather abnormality, gardeners are dismayed to find their hoped-for crop of cauliflower blooming or the lettuce going to seed instead of growing leafy things to eat.

Growing seasons in the Northwest are adequate, if not ideal, for nearly any plant we care to try growing. We may need to extend the season a bit to gain some growing time for certain vegetables or we may need to select varieties that will develop and mature under our local conditions. We can skirt the handicap of climate for tomatoes and other long hot season crops by using month-old transplants to decrease the time needed out-of-doors. We can skirt the handicap of spring frosts by selecting fruit trees whose blossom periods come after danger of frost is past.

The long mild period of spring and early summer, broken by a month or so of midsummer temperatures in the high eighties and nineties, followed by a long mild period into the fall gives the ardent vegetable gardener a chance to grow at least two and maximally three different kinds of vegetable crops. Cool season crops can be grown from late winter until hot weather causes them to bolt. They can be planted again in late summer to ripen in the cool days of fall. Warm season crops can be planted in late spring, overlapping the late spring vegetables, to develop in the heat of summer and ripen in late summer. Successful vegetable gardening results from learning which vegetables are suitable for each temperature period. Warm season crops must be selected to fit the time available from soil warming to a temperature of 50°F to the first fall frost. If they do not fit the temperature period don't plant them. In short, don't plant tomatoes requiring 120 days of hot weather if your typical climate pattern never reaches temperatures in excess of 75°F.

An important guide for vegetable gardens is the number of frost free days. This number can guide you to those kinds of vegetables which will do well in your area as well as those which need substantial protection or nurturing if they are to produce. Bend, Oregon, for example, seldom experiences more than a dozen days in sequence without frost. Gardening in such a climate with less-than-hardy crops obviously involves providing good night protection.

Frost free dates, as reported in climate records, vary by as much as two weeks from one year to the next. This variance commonly depends on the overall spring weather pattern, so the wise gardener will base his plantings on close observation of the weather pattern preceeding the planting schedule he has in mind rather than fixing rigidly upon a specific date. The significant element to observe is the cloud layer as frost is most likely to occur during cloudless nights following a warm spring day. If you have already planted and observe these conditions in late April or early May, give the young vegetable transplants or seedlings some protection.

Another important guide to plant selection is number of "degree days." This number is calculated as the total temperature range averaged for a number of growing seasons. Every plant must have a minimum number of degree days to develop properly. Thus, it is useful for selecting vegetable plants in general and is particularly significant for the person wanting to grow grapes in finding the grape varieties that will do well in a specific area.

By utilizing the climatic factors favorable to our adapted plants we can enjoy year-around gardening, but to do so takes planning. Planning is necessary not just to make sure the ground is prepared in the fall before rains begin in order to plant perennial fruits or early vegetables, but also to select those varieties of plants which will prosper in the climatic conditions available to us — "frost free" days, "degree days," etc.

Beyond the planning involved in selection, planting, and harvest, planning must be done for tree pruning and pest control, and to provide time for all the kinds of interference with which any human enterprise is beset from rain to unwanted distant relatives. We have stressed the paramount role of planning for the garden but these plans must be viewed as flexible within certain limits to accommodate the variability of the natural world. Thus, one of the problems facing the home orchardist or small fruits grower is finding a time free of rain to undertake dormant season pest control measures. Rain in the Northwest continues into the early spring, just at the same time when new foliage and flower buds are opening and growth on fruit plants is initiated. Resultant moisture, accompanied by favorable temperatures for the multiplication of disease organisms, not only stimulates cherry brown rot and strawberry botrytis, but also prevents the effective use of controls. Flexible advance planning, accompanied by constant readiness to respond when temporary climatic conditions permit, is needed during wet and mild periods to prevent plant disease.

The heavy rainfall west of the Cascades, coupled with the clay soils typical of the area, forces the home gardener to carefully consider the matter of drainage to provide for the long-term needs of berries, perennial vegetables and fruit trees. If you are among the minority possessing well drained soils count your blessings. Many gardens require drainage facilities before plants can be expected to grow to maturity. Raised beds, container gardens, and supplemental drainage systems are more commonly used by Northwest gardeners than gardeners in other parts of the country.

Erosion from winter rains is another factor with which Northwest gardeners must contend, particularly if using raised beds or uneven ground. Raised beds that are not mulched or covered with compost will erode badly and gardens on steep slopes may be washed to the bottom of the hill by spring.

Leaching of mineral nutrients also occurs as the rainwater passes through the topsoil on its way to the subsoil or nearby stream. A good deal of the soil nitrogen is lost each winter. The loss is particularly marked in the top six to eight inches of soil where the feeder roots of most vegetables and fruits grow.

Despite the problems presented by our climate, the canny gardener can benefit from the natural precipitation and work a deal with Mother Nature to carry soil building materials into the soil with the rainwater. Limestone applied to the soil between the caneberries or in the dripline of fruit trees will be carried downward during the winter rainy season. Manure mulches spread across the vegetable garden will trickle minerals into the soil and increase fertility.

Soil moisture is needed by all plants but in the right amounts. Too much is as detrimental as too little. Most leafy, succulent vegetables are nearly 90% water and if they don't receive the correct amount their quality and growth suffers. Because most vegetable plants are grown during our dry summers, we must irrigate to get the most from our vegetables. To get an idea of what would happen to the garden if soil water needs were ignored, take a look at the native grasses around your area. In the spring when abundant water is being supplied by rainfall the grasses are vigorous and lush. In the summer, when rain has stopped, they toughen up, quickly flower and go to seed; they remain in a semi-dormant state until fall rains pick up again. Fall rains initiate a flush of growth as the grasses put out a final effort to build up their reserves before temperatures drop and growth ceases. This is the natural sequence which the home gardener must deal with in managing his unnatural creation, the garden, by irrigating and conserving soil moisture.

All gardens need air circulation in moderate amounts. Air movement helps prevent disease by keeping the plant foliage drier. Air movement is also necessary for those trees and vegetables that depend on wind pollination to develop fruits.

Just as with temperature, moisture, and light, extremes of air movement must be managed. We seldom have periods with absolutely no air movement. Usually a light breeze is present. But, occasionally the air moves too forcefully or comes from the north or east and is too dry, hot or cold. If the native evergreens in your area have branches growing on one side, expect strong winds from the other side.

High winds cause plant reactions similar to stress. Researchers have found that when corn is exposed to hard wind, it stops growing and will take several hours to recover its composure and continue growing. Corn planted in an area subject to frequent hard wind may take all summer to get knee high.

High winds also accelerate the loss of water through evaporation, both in the plant and from the soil surface. Rapid loss of water from the growing plant withers and sears leaves which inhibits their photosynthetic abilities; causes flowers on beans and squash to drop; kills young plants or seedlings; prevents the normal development of berries; and causes developing small fruits to dehydrate and lose quality.

If your area is subject to hard winds, consider growing the lower bush fruits instead of fruit trees or planting a shelter belt. You must do more irrigating during summer to keep your plants in prime growing condition.

On the other hand, too little air movement means poor air circulation through foliage. Poor air circulation can lead to even more disastrous results than high wind. Fungus diseases can build up rapidly in poorly ventilated gardens and destroy most of the plantings.

Cold winds kill foliage and new twigs. Such winds are of particular concern in growing trailing berries and trellising them in the fall. In areas marked by cold wind, it is better to leave the trailing vines on the ground during the winter and trellis them in the spring.

Humidity of the air has a bearing on how well our vegetable and fruit plants grow and yield. When humidity levels are high, leaf transpiration is slower and the plant's tissues remain full of water. In the Northwest where high air humidity is common during spring and early summer, crops grown for their sweet fruits (strawberries, raspberries) or for their crisp succulence (lettuce, cabbage, green onions) are outstandingly better than those grown in drier climates. In this respect we have a uniquely gracious climate for home gardening. But no blessing is without its penalties as high humidity also provides a happy environment for plant disease organisms. High humidity accompanied by warm temperatures produce ideal conditions for many of the fungus diseases that disfigure or kill horticultural crops.

The observant gardener can get a handle on what sorts of plants do well in his area by looking at the surrounding native plant life. Wild relatives of some of the vegetables we plant in the garden — mustard, radish, carrot, cucumber, the nightshade and onion may be found. Wild blackberries, elder, and huckleberries indicate good berry growing conditions. Wild seedling trees of cherry and apple that have escaped domestication tell us that the fruit trees will do well. There is an old farm saying that "If weeds won't grow, it's darn poor soil," to which might be added "and the climate's not so great either."

The best single practice for living comfortably with your garden is to use only locally adapted plant materials. Vegetables, small fruits, and tree fruits that are adapted to the Northwest climate will give you the highest and best return on your efforts. Not all varieties of all vegetables do well in every part of the country. Unfortunately, national advertising touches every reader, radio listener, or television watcher. Beefsteak tomatoes, Iowa corn, Texas dewberries, almond trees and pistachio nuts do not do well in Northwest conditions. Strawberries are specifically bred and selected for a certain light intensity and growing season; varieties brought from the Midwest where temperatures are warmer in the summer and the light more intense never live up to their nationally advertised features in our more moderate climate.

Exotic plants, or varieties not adapted to the Northwest, exact a price in terms of care higher than any possible yield. Try something different in the annual vegetable garden every year, but stick to the varieties bred for our climate as food standbys. Perennials take a longer time before becoming fruitful so definitely stay with the Northwest recommended varieties if you're planning on sustenance.

After years of research effort the agricultural colleges, Extension Service, and Experiment Stations have developed strains of all the common mid-latitude vegetables, fruits and trees which are specifically suited to the soil, climate, light quality, and growing season typical of your general area. Research continues and assures that the best strains of plants for our area are found locally.

The Microclimate

While the concept of *microclimate* recognizes its imbedding in the general sunlight, temperature ranges, air patterns, rainfall and growing season typical of the region it specifically focuses on the conditions in one's own gardening space. A gardener soon realizes that the judicious placement of a seed or transplant, the nourishing application of fertilizer, and careful attention to watering are all for nought if the conditions in his garden patch won't cooperate. Whatever your plans for your garden, you must first spend some time getting aquainted not only with the local weather but also with the way the climate in your own yard differs from the local pattern, no matter how slightly.

Plant growth is affected by almost anything in the immediate vicinity, including buildings, walls, driveways, screens, trees, etc. in addition to soil, climate, etc. The plain recognition of these influences leads one to understand that small adjacent sites can possess radically different microclimates. Thus, a specific microclimate can be very inhospitable to good plant growth despite the fact that the general local climate is benign.

Now it must be remembered that just as buildings, etc. may have created an inhospitable microclimate, adjustments in features or practices by the gardener can convert inhospitable microclimates to ones suitable for good plant growth. Luckily, most plants have some range of tolerance and in many cases only a single factor is responsible for peak growth. By the rational adjustment of the microclimate most garden patches can be managed to grow a garden successfully. In short, microclimate adaptation permits the gardener to adjust heat, light, water, and air to provide the mix of factors which encourages plant growth.

It must be recognized that the microclimate is not a fixed entity. Any change in the garden's surroundings causes microclimate changes. The amount of sunlight changes as nearby trees grow larger; air circulation will increase or decrease as hedges grow or are pruned; temperatures are affected by the addition or loss of ground covers, mulches, etc. Paving the driveway will cause more heat to be generated in the areas immediately adjacent and change the soil water supply by diverting the flow of subsurface water. Building a solid fence or planting a row of tall shrubs changes air flow, shadow patterns, and temperatures. Painting a house or any other structure white will increase air temperature by reflection.

Use your imagination, ingenuity and resourcefulness to find ways of making subtle or drastic changes in the microclimate of your garden spot. Sometimes the smallest, seemingly insignificant, change in the garden's surroundings can make the difference between success or failure. Often it will take a year or two of gardening for you to find the shortcomings of the garden area. Keep records of the problems encountered, what treatment or control you used, and dates of extreme temperatures. This will provide you with data on how your microclimate differs from any other. One of the satisfactions of gardening is learning how you can influence the growth of a plant. Much of the action or regulation comes through your efforts at building your microclimate in such a way that it is more suitable to the food crops you like to grow.

The growing season of any area has its natural sequence but, it is also what the gardener makes of it. If full advantage is taken of the natural climatic factors and if the microclimate is regulated, garden crops can be grown even though climate records show the season to be too short. In Bend, Oregon for example, even though records show that frosts may occur at anytime during the summer, with only about 12 days between frosts, people still grow tomatoes, sweet corn and bell peppers. How? By altering their microclimate to supply the needed warmth, providing frost protection, and taking full advantage of sunlight for plant growth.

The gardener, no matter where he is, truly does not grow a plant. Instead, he provides the right factors at the right time, so that the plant can follow its inherited program of growth. Sometimes the gardener will provide shade if the plant shows signs of scorching. If a plant starts getting spindly and weak, some of the overhead shade might be pruned away to give it more sunlight. Albeit, certain weather conditions (frost, drought, heat) can be eased by some adjustments (hotcaps, water systems, shading), some adjustments may be too demanding to warrant their use with any degree of economy.

The severity or extremes of the climate determine how resourceful you must become to grow the garden plants you like. Tomatoes can be grown in Bend or watermelons in Aberdeen; how successfully depends on how ingenious the gardener is at manipulating the plant and the microclimate to overcome the deficiencies imposed by by the overall climate.

The home gardener, noted for having a green thumb, is probably the person with a sense of microclimate management. He is the person who seems to know instinctively the exact climatic situation needed for plant growth. Some of us have more trouble than others in knowing what to do to assist our plants. The plant care expert will know how to adjust the amount of heat a plant receives, how to provide more or less sunshine as plant requirements are noted, and how to re-direct air or water.

The microclimate is all-important to the gardener who likes a challenge of growing something out of season or growing something which has a longer growth period than the growth period tables indicate. Here is where the seasoned gardener can excel, a beginner can discover the intricacies of plants as they are affected by the environment, and where a plant hobbyist learns of all the climatic factor interactions and of the changes he can make to grow his favorite plants.

The hobbyist who wants to be the only gardener in his neighborhood with ripe watermelons by early August will amend his microclimate accordingly. He may supply lots of sunny heat (direct and reflected), and special protection from cold soils in the spring.

The beginning gardener learns that hot, dry wind in midsummer can make all of the bean blossoms drop off; that new transplants may require shading during their first days in the garden, and that a lack of air circulation around the fruit tree allows mildew and mold to develop. These are learning situations and the next time he will develop ways to change the microclimate to better fit the plants.

A seasoned gardener uses his experience of growing food plants, along with an understanding of his local climate and microclimate. He may use hotcaps to protect new transplants, black plastic mulches to warm the soil sooner, make screens for protection from summer wind or to provide shade, prune out some overhanging limbs for more sunlight, or mulch the roots of vegetables and berries to conserve water. These are all simple methods of adjusting the microclimate to the needs of garden plants.

A good gardener knows that a climate cannot be made perfect for growing everything, but that it can be modified and improved. If you want to grow orange trees in Port Angeles, Washington, the modification of your microclimate may involve building a greenhouse. We are not suggesting this sort of drastic climate modification but rather we plan to show you a few simpler ways to extend your own yard climate-wise. Some buildable aids are covered in "Beating the Odds."

Gardening on a northerly slope is similar to gardening on the north side of a tall building — you have to select plants that are a little hardier and that can get by without as much sunlight. North slopes are slow to warm in the spring. A valley floor soil could warm up to 50°F by early April while northerly sloping land might be several weeks behind. Solar radiation will be greater on south and west facing slopes or on south and west sides of nearby structures. These are the places where vegetable gardens, berry crops, and fruit trees will have a better chance of growing and fruiting successfully.

CARDINAL POINTS: For the gardener seeking the warmest site for fruit and vegetable growing, look to an unshaded southern exposure. Next would be a western exposure. The east side of things gets the morning sun, but the west side gets the hotter afternoon sun. A northern exposure is pretty tough — cold, little light.

Sunlight Adjustments

Excessive amounts of light and heat are seldom a problem in the Northwest. Sunscald may affect the bark of newly planted filberts or heat pockets may exist in a yard that may pre-cook your vegetables by mid-August. Some other situations that might warrant reducing heat involve protecting bare soil and shielding new transplants in their first few days after planting. Here are some additional points to consider:

1. Shading will usually be a temporary thing so don't plant your vegetables under a shade tree on the off-chance that the garden might be too hot. Vegetables and most of the fruit plants need all the sunlight available. Shading is commonly needed for new transplants and can be supplied with paper, an umbrella, some cloth, plastic netting, fir boughs, or whatever is handy. Give the young plant some screening from the hot midday sun for 4-5 days following transplanting. A shingle stuck in the ground on the sunny side will often provide enough shade, and also protects from drying wind.

2. On rare occasions in the Northwest, fruits of tomatoes and pepper may sunburn if exposed to a week or more of direct, hot sunshine. Sometimes this happens after we have pruned away excess foliage in order to increase air circulation. Sheets of newspaper or any other lightweight, easily moved material can cover and protect the fruits until they are harvested or the weather changes.

3. Organic mulches serve several functions, one being to moderate the temperature of the upper soil levels. A layer, 1–2" deep, of sawdust, barkdust, straw, grass clippings or any other organic material will act as an insulation layer and keep the soil below cooler than nearby bare soil. In the spring this effect can work against the gardener but once the soil has warmed to 50 or 60°F, mulches moderate soil temperature.

Many home gardens are located in places where nearby buildings, trees, large shrubs or hills block part of the sun. In these areas some adjustment of the microclimate may be necessary to gain the light needed. Here are some ideas:

1. Get 'em up off the ground. Many of the vine crops that are normally allowed to scramble around on the ground can be trained upward on trellises, fences, A-frames or poles to stronger available sunlight. This also gives you more ground space to plant, mulch, cultivate or more easily care for the plants' other needs. Trees that would normally produce excess shade on nearby beds can be espaliered to grow out of the way and still remain functional for fruit or aesthetics.

2. Plant in containers to make "movable" gardens. Vegetables and certain small fruits (strawberries and blueberries) can be grown in tubs, wooden boxes, barrels or pots. One of the advantages gained is mobility. As the seasonal sunlight pattern changes, shift the containers to catch more light. For large containers a dolly will add greatly to mobility. Placing the

containerized plants next to a sunny wall will gain light and added calories of heat.

3. Plan ahead to place tall growing types of vegetables or trellised berries on the north or east side of shorter plants. Most plants are growth compatible but the tall ones can rob sunshine and unless you have planned for this and planted shade tolerant vegetables alongside, you may be disappointed in the results.

4. Sometimes sunlight may be increased by reflection. Aluminum foil or some of the new reflecting polyethylene sheetings can be put on a frame to send light into areas that do not have their needs met normally. Foil, laid on the ground alongside a row of warm season vegetables, will also help to increase light and ripen fruits.

5. Prune. Nearby trees have a beautiful way of gradually growing larger and more dense while intercepting the light that could be reaching your garden. Get out the pruning saw and do some selective branch thinning. Tall shrubs should also be thinned to allow more sunlight into the garden area.

Wind Adjustments

All gardens need air circulation and sometimes just a few minor adjustments can mean the difference between healthy plants and diseased or uprooted ones. If you live in an area noted for its windiness, especially during the growing season, a permanent windbreak planting would be the best solution. If your wind is funneled into the garden area by buildings, hills or other topographical features, a few strategically placed screens will divert it elsewhere.

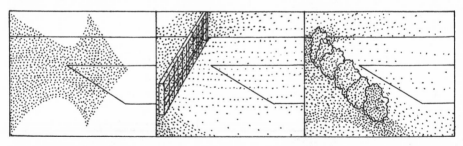

WIND PATTERNING: If the force of your local winds exceeds the strength of your plants, adjustments can be made using fences or shrub plantings to redirect the air flow. Screening for this purpose is aimed at lessening the impact of the wind without seriously reducing air circulation or sunshine in the garden.

Here are some further points on reducing wind velocity:

1. Windbreak plantings of trees, shrubs or vines more tolerant of forceful air than the tender vegetables or fruits could be placed along the windward side of the garden. Some planted windbreaks may themselves be damaged by wind, so consider whether your plant selections can tolerate the expected wind. Unless you have a half-acre or larger garden, most

windbreaks do not need to be more than 5—6' high. Evergreen shrubs (juniper, yew, laurel) or a row of Dogwood trees are examples of greenery wind barriers. Some vining plants, such as English ivy or the faster growing Virginia Creeper, are easily trained on a fence. To make a double duty, summertime barrier, why not plant a row of grapes that can be trellised to help divert wind?

2. For the small garden area, various kinds of baffles or obstructing devices can be made and arranged to suit the air flow management needed. Baffles of board fences can be permanent parts of the garden landscape or can be designed to be removed at season's end. Shade cloth nailed to wood frames can be placed on the windward side of wind-susceptible plants. If your garden spot seems to be a wind tunnel, a few well placed tall shrubs or fences will baffle the wind force. New transplants are easily damaged by forceful wind. These can be protected long enough for them to start growth, with a shingle or piece of stiff cardboard stuck in the ground four inches to the windward side.

3. Build the surrounding landscape with an eye to designing a microclimate for tender vegetables or small fruits. Berms, if they fit your landscape scheme, can act to moderate wind patterns. Find out where your strongest winds will come from during the summer growing season. Build a berm on that side of the garden, making sure that plants that are to grow on it will not cause excessive shading. Plants should only be tall enough on the berm to divert strong winds. Use your imagination and knowledge of local air movement. Consider that most of the damaging wind will come as the new warm season transplants are being set into the garden. The next critical time will be in hot, midsummer days when fruit is being formed on tomatoes and beans and when fruit is ripening on the small fruit plants (red raspberries, boysens, etc.). When selecting plants for your berm, remember that deciduous ones will work.

4. Should all else fail, put an enclosure around your choicest or most tender crops. Ring them with fine mesh screen or shade cloth. Don't close the screens so tightly that no air can move in or out of the enclosure, but just enough to prevent whipping and too-rapid evaporation.

In some gardens it may be necessary to increase air circulation in order to reduce incidence of fungus diseases or aid in wind pollination. In these situations, the gardener must amend the microclimate by pruning surrounding plants, by growing plants up on trellises or stakes, or by selecting plants known for their disease resistance. Bushy vegetable and small fruit plants will need some pruning of their foliage during the summer to allow more air and light to enter. Tree fruits may need to be pruned to remove interior brushy growth to allow better air movement through the tree.

Temperature Adjustments: Warming the Air

Often the enthusiasm of gardening or boredom with winter overcomes the precaution of waiting for spring frost threats to pass. If air temperatures remain too cool, or there is a possibility of a late spring frost, here are some suggestions for warming the air:

1. A plastic tent over a row of tomatoes or peppers, open at the ends for air circulation, supported by wire hoops, can keep warm season plants alive through nightly temperature drops to 28°F. A simpler method is to bend fiberglass panels into a quonset hut shape to give frost protection.

2. Place tender plants alongside a wall or fence that absorbs and re-radiates heat, or plant near the south or west side of a building to take advantage of the microclimate temperature boost from these structures.

3. Reflectors of aluminum foil or shiny metal can be used between rows of vegetables wanting more heat during the summer. This microclimate adjustment also has merit in controlling or preventing some insect pests.

4. Sometimes it is helpful to create a sun pocket for certain vegetables such as melons, okra, sweet potato or others that require lots of heat. This is also helpful for growing grapes, but one needs to supply air movement and do some extra pruning of foliage to prevent serious mildew infestations. A sun pocket can be created by simply surrounding a plant, or plants, with a fence of polyethylene as tall as a mature plant, supported by stakes, open at the top, with black poly on the north and clear poly on the remaining sides. Sun pockets naturally exist in many yards where solid walls screen the north and east sides, or along the west or south sides of hedges and windbreaks, or along the west or south side of tall crops such as corn and sunflowers. A sun pocket's drawback is reduced air circulation, but the enterprising gardener can find ways to overcome this shortcoming.

5. Old tires can be used to circle vegetables and small fruits to supply nighttime warmth by re-radiating the heat absorbed during the day. While they may not be aesthetically acceptable to everyone, to the gardener whose plants need some added heat this can be one of the less expensive and most functional devices.

6. Rock pathways or stone mulches work in the same manner as tires. Rocks absorb heat during the day and radiate it at night, keeping nearby plants warm enough to grow.

Temperature Adjustments: Warming the Soil

In the Northwest we must sometimes find ways of making the garden soil drier and warmer. If your situation demands increased soil temperature, here are some suggestions:

1. Black or clear polyethylene film mulches. A sheet of clear poly placed over ground beds will warm the soil as much as 15°F. Black film will warm the soil about 8–10°F and will also prevent weed growth by denying sunlight to the weed seedlings under the plastic. (Though clear polyethylene warms the soil more it also allows the growth of weeds underneath.) Vegetable or strawberry transplants set in through poly mulches establish themselves much faster and develop their edible crops much quicker than those without the advantage of additional soil warmth.

2. Remember that wet soils remain cold much longer in the spring. Draining away excessive water or elevating the row of food crops above the wetness will provide soil warmth. Tile, plastic or rock drainage systems will repay their cost many times over by keeping plants healthier and more vigorous. Raised beds are also a way of manipulating the microclimate for plants needing drier and warmer soils.

3. One cause of cold and wet soils is shade from overhanging trees or from evergreens which block the morning and/or afternoon sun. Pruning or total removal may be the only way to assure enough solar radiation on the garden spot.

4. Increasing the ventilation of the garden spot will help dry the soil. Here again, pruning may be needed to allow more air to circulate.

5. Should none of the above suggestions fit your needs, how about growing vegetables, small fruits or dwarf fruit trees in containers? Containerization allows the gardener practically total control over soil, light, and air needs for a plant.

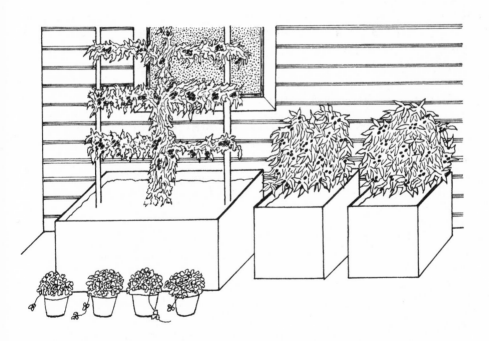

Beating the Odds

It is said that everyone talks about the weather but no one does anything about it. To the extent of casually changing the macroclimate this is true. We can't change the seasons, nor the cold of winter, but we can take advantage of what we know about our plants and devise ways to fit them into our growing seasons and our microclimates. Following a careful and well thought out strategy it is possible and practical to beat some of our weather odds.

While the temperature regime of the Pacific Northwest is moderate it still includes extremes of summer heat, cold spring nights and early fall frosts. They are more important to the home planting than are temperature averages.

No matter what the climatic shortcomings, there are ways of overcoming them. The gardener who is determined to grow okra or peanuts in the Northwest can find a way to do it no matter what the cost or hassle. Even though there are plants adapted to our climate that make few demands, we think it wise to provide information on some easily built aids that can extend the growing season. Though their construction and operation will require additional time of the gardener, they will also markedly increase annual yields in our area.

Coldframes, Cloches, and Tents:

One of the most commonly used means of extending the growing season for annual crops is some sort of structure where seedlings can be grown to a larger size before being set out in the garden. If built large enough, semi-hardy plants can be grown throughout the winter. Coldframes, cloches or plastic tents are some of the most frequently used structures to extend the growing season and to protect tender plants from adverse weather conditions.

Coldframes are essentially greenhouses without heat, built low to the ground and used to grow hardy seedlings and protect new plants from cold and wind. Their sole function is protection of tender plants, either for short periods in the spring or through the winter for growing small batches of cool season vegetables. You can use a coldframe to start seedlings of vegetables a month or six weeks before weather permits seeding them outdoors. They are especially effective for starting transplants of tomatoes, peppers, egg-plant, or other warm season crops. For the person with a limited space for gardening, a coldframe can become a garden in itself where lettuce, chives, radishes, green onions and parsley can be grown nearly year-round. In most gardens the coldframe is only used from January to May, however it can be a constant source of new plants or freshly harvested produce.

Coldframes depend on solar radiation for their heat source, accumulating warmth during the day and retaining it to protect the plants through the night. To be effective a coldframe should be placed where it will be in full sunlight and protected from the wind. Coldframes are built right on the ground and use the soil floor as the growing area or as a base for placing flats or pots of plants. Soil can be banked up around the sides for added insulation. The tops are made of glass or clear plastic to catch full sunlight and are removable (or hinged) so they can be opened for necessary ventilation during calm, sunny days and shut at night.

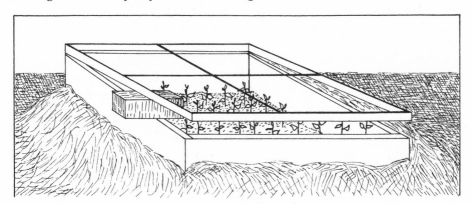

Coldframes can be built with wood or metal sides. If wood is used, preserve it with copper napthenate so the wood that is in direct contact with the soil will not rot out quickly. Sidewalls should be tall enough to shield any of the plants you plan to grow inside the structure. A convenient height that will handle most seedlings or winter crops uses a front wall of 12" and back wall of 18". The sides should be sloped to hold the cover at an angle to the sun.

Cloches are a sort of movable coldframe designed to be placed over a group of tender plants for cold protection. The idea is to make a portable, lightweight structure that can be moved around the garden as needed. Cloches can be made with a wood or metal frame covered with polyethylene sheeting or fiberglass. Young, new transplants could be covered for three days or longer while they begin their life in the garden, then the cloche can be transferred to another group of baby plants, or be shifted to protect tomato plants from expected frost. The cloche works best for small row or block plantings.

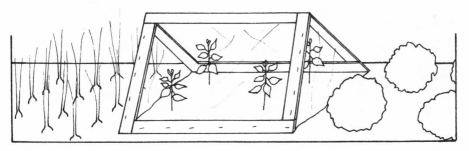

A structure that has evolved from the cloche is the tunnel or tent placed over an entire row of plants. The only items needed for the protection tunnel are some stiff material for hoops to hold the cover and some 4-mil clear or translucent polyethylene for the cover. Hoops can be made of wire, willow branches or any other stiff, but bendable, material. Stick the supports into the ground, lay the poly across and anchor it down by burying the edges. Leave the ends open so air can circulate through the tunnel. At night close the ends by either tucking them inside or tying. The tent or tunnel makes a dandy place for getting vegetables or strawberries off to a good start in early spring. They are cheap to make, easily placed, and when all danger of cold weather is passed they are easily removed and stored.

Hotcaps are simply cones of paper, usually of translucent waxed paper, that are placed over young tomato, pepper, eggplant, squash, and melon plants. The base of the cone is covered with dirt to hold it in place. Hotcaps can remain in place until the plant crowds the cone and the danger of frost is passed. Cheaper versions of the hotcap can be made of newspaper sheets folded into triangular forms to fit over a plant. Newspaper cones should be removed during the day so the plant can receive sunlight. The same protection can be supplied by milk cartons (with one end cut out so the carton can fit over a plant) or from large food cans, buckets or cardboard boxes. Placing these protective devices over the plants in the evening and removing them the next morning becomes a bit of a chore and you will likely decide to wait until *all* danger of frost is gone before planting warm season crops again.

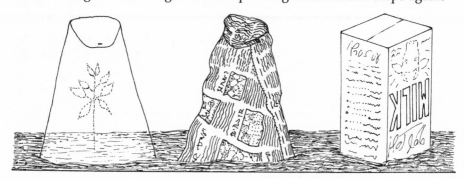

Hotbeds and Greenhouses:

Going a step further in providing better places for growing plants, or in providing them enough protection to stretch the growing season, we come to greenhouses of various types and hotbeds. Both are designed to provide artificial heat. Some are quite expensive while others are economical enough to easily justify their use for home vegetables. The expense involved depends on size, materials used and sophistication of equipment used in watering, heating, and ventilation.

The hotbed is essentially a coldframe with a source of heat. From the outside they are identical, with the same dimensions and materials used for walls and cover. The advantage of the hotbed is that it can be artificially warmed rather than depend solely on solar radiation. Hotbeds can be multipurpose structures used for propagation, growing transplants or for growing mature, ready-to-eat crops. Because they are heated by sources other than sunlight, continuous attention must be paid to ventilation. This generally involves propping the cover open an inch or two. Small, thermostatically operated fans can be installed to circulate the air when conditions warrant.

Hotbeds are usually heated by either electric soil heat cable or hot water (perhaps from solar equipment). Old-time hotbeds were heated with fresh animal bedding and manure buried about 2' deep in a pit below the hotbed frame. Decomposition of manure does generate heat but the temperature is hard to regulate, and so is not dependable through a cool period.

Soil cable is available in various lengths and wattages so a little shopping around will give you any combination needed. In order to provide a temperature between 50 and 70°F, place the soil cable so it is supplying 10–15 watts of electric heat per square foot of growing area. To help insure a constant temperature, many soil cables come with thermostats. Make sure that any wiring you use is weatherproof. Line the inside walls of the hotbed with waterproof insulation to help contain the valuable heat and decrease the cost of operation. Wood used in the sidewalls should be treated with copper napthenate to prevent rot.

A step beyond the hotbed is a pit greenhouse. Pit greenhouses look like ordinary greenhouses that have sunk halfway into the ground. An advantage is that it is more heat effective than a regular greenhouse because it takes advantage of earth insulation. By being sunken, or below the soil grade, it can also be built at less cost than can a standard greenhouse with side walls. A disadvantage is that it is wetter inside and may be difficult to drain properly. So find a well drained site, in a sunny location. Walls can be of earth, or for more permanence, make them of concrete, cement blocks or rock. The upper half of the house is covered with polyethylene, glass or fiberglass.

Ordinary greenhouses make good places to start and grow cool season crops, produce transplants of warm season crops, propagate woody ornamentals, and in general have a big time playing with plants. Greenhouses are a lot of work however, and plants growing in them require a lot of care. In reality greenhouses are usually dutifully used for a year or two and then become a storehouse for junk. This is not to say they are not worth considering, but only a simple warning. In most cases a hotbed will be more useful and less costly.

Greenhouses should be placed to receive full sunlight during the fall, winter, and spring months. During the summer months the roof will need some shading to keep plants inside from suffering heat prostration. An ideal place in the yard is near a deciduous shade tree which will allow sunlight to reach the greenhouse in the winter and shade the house in the summer. Many gardeners build greenhouses with the idea of growing their own tomatoes, cucumbers, and melons during the winter. A great idea, but costly. Northwest winters are dark and dreary and the days are too short for these plants to produce their fruits. Consequently lighting systems must be added to make the plants perform. By the time the first cucumber is produced, the light bill far surpasses the cost of a bushel from the nearest store.

When planning your greenhouse, plan for a permanent, properly covered building with sufficient heat supply, watering capabilities and ventilation. Each factor has equal importance in the successful use of your greenhouse. Structures can be of wood or metal. Wood should be copper treated to last longer and should be painted white to reflect light onto the plants. The covering can be glass, polyethylene or fiberglass. Glass is best and the most expensive. Polyethylene sheeting is cheapest and the shortest lived. Generally 4−6 mil poly, clear or translucent, is available for covering greenhouses and will last from six months to three years depending on the grade. "Ultraviolet resistant" poly is the longer lasting. Fiberglass should be greenhouse grade and as clear as possible for light transmission. Cheaper grades of fiberglass generally are good for about ten years before they become brittle and the fibers loosen and collect so much dirt that they cannot be cleaned. The more expensive types, sometimes coated with a polyfilm to prevent fiber erosion, may last twenty or more years.

Heating sources in the greenhouse must be able to provide 50°F at night. To arrive at an approximation of the size of equipment needed requires some calculations by your nearest heater supply house. Heat can come from solar energy, from gas or electric heaters, or from soil heat cable.

Watering is a frequent task in the greenhouse so make sure enough water outlets are installed at the beginning. Some new automatic watering systems are available from greenhouse supply companies to take some of the drudgery out of this chore.

Ventilation of the greenhouse is essential in disease prevention and if not properly planned for in the original design can be very troublesome, especially in the spring when you are trying to grow that special crop of transplants. Cooling may be done with electric fans (select one with enough capacity to completely exchange the air in your greenhouse in one minute), or by adjusting windows, vents or doors to allow outside air to rapidly circulate inside.

The climate rules the garden. It determines the number of days when growth can occur, imposes rain and sunlight restrictions, and dictates the temperature variables under which we may garden. By studying the locally effective climate and by circumventing its bad parts with microclimate changes, it is possible, and practical, to beat the odds.

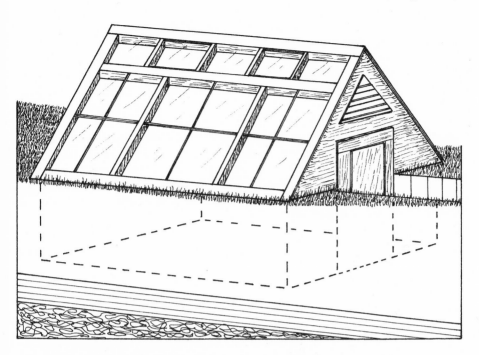

PIT GREENHOUSES date back to the 18th century and are still considered one of the most energy efficient greenhouse designs in use due to the insulation value provided by the earthen sides.

A primary consideration in construction cost is the winter water table and soil composition. *Water table* is the depth at which water saturates the ground. Your local Soil Conservation District should be able to provide information for your particular site.

Chapter 3: SOIL

Introduction: Origin & Composition
Top, Sub & Types
Water: Drainage & Irrigation
Maintaining Soil Heath: Fertility & Deficiency & Excess
Soil Afflictions: Insect & Disease
Containers: Alternative Growing Space for Food Crops

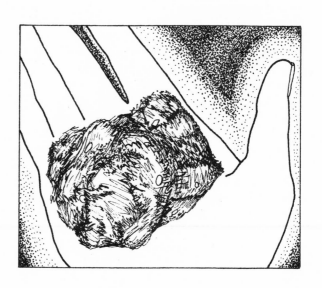

Introduction: Origin & Composition

The soil in your yard is a priceless commodity. It has evolved through a succession of rock deterioration episodes, and the long-term effects of plants and animals. The parent rock of our planet has undergone some drastic transformations to give us the soil we now use for gardens, berry plants, and fruit trees.

In the Northwest it takes 1,000 years to create one inch of topsoil. A detailed account of how our soils developed is too complicated to be dealt with here. We may not care that cracks have expanded from plant roots, acids have developed from plant decay, and freezing and thawing, wind and rain and glaciers have worked their effects on the original rock to make just a fraction of an inch of soil in our lifetime. We may not care that the differences in soil we casually note in passing may have been caused by changes in water deposition or wind direction ages ago which brought soils from an entirely different region rather than from the layer below. Or we may not care that differences in soil types may be due to some minor differences in weather, exposure or elevation eons ago that are reflected today in soil texture, consistency or structure differences.

Practically, most gardeners only consider whether the soil in their yard will grow plants and if it will not grow plants perhaps why and how to fix it. However, we feel that the importance of this soil we so casually walk on, dig into, sweep up, tamp down, plant in, erode, and sometimes even conserve, warrants a word about its source.

The original particle of sand or clay was a product of weather on the bare rock of our planet. Wind, rain, freezing and thawing started the process of soil making. Those first particles of sand and clay provided a place for early plant life to snuggle down and get some anchorage and nourishment. Then, in the presence of a variety of climatic conditions, those early forms of plants interacted and gave us different types of soil. In a very tiny nutshell, this is how our soil was developed. It is not complete by any means, but for the gardeners who worry more about why plants turn yellow and become stunted, or wonder why raspberries die, our explanations of how to deal with these problems is more meaningful.

Soil predates gardening. In fact it predates the growth of anything other than a few simple life forms of algae, moss, and lichens. Soil is a biological entity. It is alive, or at least it should be to be called a fertile soil. A gardener must recognize this biological life of soil in order to appreciate the suggestions we will offer on soil management. Biologically alive means that the soil is more than grains of sand, a few clods, or simply a mass of stuff that is sticky when wet and cracked when dry.

Soil is composed of many kinds and sizes of particles of clay, silt, sand, and organic matter. These are the parts that are easy to recognize and accept as soil. Also, and equally as important to a gardener's success, are the vital organisms which aid the gardener in many ways or challenge his plants in some other ways. These microscopic organisms include fungi, bacteria, and parasitic nematodes. They each exist to survive in their own right, but in so doing they perform certain functions. Fungi and bacteria (soil microflora) reduce minerals to their simplest forms to be taken in by our vegetables, small fruit plants or fruit trees. Indeed, when you fertilize your garden you do not fertilize the plants in that soil but furnish food for the microflora that convert the nitrogen and change the phosphorus and potassium into soluble forms that the plants can use. This is why we stress the idea that soil is a biological being that must be carefully managed to remain healthy. Nematodes we could probably do without, although they exist in a balanced ecology with equal numbers of parasites and predators. It is only when this balance is upset and the predator population diminishes that we have the problems with the parasitic types.

Many other things dwell in our soils which make it a crucial part of our world. Earthworms, grubs, scavengers of various sorts, moles, and gophers all will be found in a soil and help to keep it alive and fertile. Some of them may not be perceived as being beneficial to gardening efforts, as when mole mounds appear in the strawberry bed. Others are perceived as useful — the earthworms that help aerate the soil, and the scavengers that decompose large bits of organic matter.

Man's treatment of the soil determines whether the soil remains healthy and fertile or becomes compacted, eroded, worn out and dead. Proper management using organic matter amendments, nutrient balancing with fertilizers (chemical or organic), and maintenance of tilth and structure by careful and thoughtful cultivation will keep a soil healthy. Failure to attend to these practices will change even the best of soil into a non-productive pile of worn out dirt.

Management of garden soil begins with an evaluation of what is there. Soil exhibits certain characteristics that give you a clue as to its fertility and makeup. Such things as weed growth, color, cloddiness, surface cracks, algae growth and erosion can tell you something of what to expect from your soil. They will also indicate some things that you must do in order to grow the best crops in your ground.

The fact that weeds will grow tells you that the soil has some fertility. Additionally, the type of weed will tell you something about soil depth, drainage and aeration factors. Pull several weeds and look at the roots. Deep rooted weeds are a good sign that the topsoil extends downward at least a foot or two. Weeds whose roots remain in the top several inches of soil will tell you there is a problem with drainage, soil aeration or depth of topsoil. If the weeds are those that normally grow in a swamp you will have a serious challenge in getting rid of excess water. No weed growth usually indicates problems so serious that you probably must spend several years solving soil problems.

The color of your soil tells you something about its drainage and organic matter content. In upland soils where drainage is good, gray or white soils indicate low fertility. In low ground though, gray soils usually indicate poor drainage. Commonly, a brownish-black color indicates sufficient organic matter content. In hill or upland areas where the surrounding soil is mostly brown, black colors on the surface in low spots indicate mucky conditions resulting from poor drainage. Well drained soils in valley floors that have developed under tall native grasses are often black from the organic matter than has accumulated over the years. Solid red colors generally suggest good drainage. Yellow colors suggest leaching and a low supply of soil nutrients.

Clods of dirt and cracks in the soil surface can tell you that the soil is tight and sticky when wet and easily compacted. The cracks indicate a tight, massive type of soil that swells when it is wet and shrinks when dry. Spading, tilling or plowing this type of soil when it is wet is disastrous. All you make is more clods. Such soil needs lots of added organic matter to separate the soil particles in order to adapt it for growing plants.

Algae or cushion-type mosses growing on the surface tell you the soil is moist for long periods of time. Wetness may be caused by poor drainage, lack of air circulation to dry the surface, or because the soil is a tight, clayish texture that hangs onto the water. Cushion mosses will grow wherever the soil is shaded and damp but reflects an environmental condition rather than a soil problem. If algae is growing on the surface do some digging to see what lies below and plan on adding organic material for aeration.

Erosion refers to the displacement of soil by wind or water. In Northwest gardens, erosion usually results from water movement across the soil surface. Hillsides erode and raised beds wash into the pathways unless means are used to slow surface runoff. If you are gardening on sloping land make plans to divert water from driving rains. Diversion ditches, grass planted in strips across slopes, mulches, and winter cover crops all help prevent erosion.

The soil in your garden is a unique mixture of many things. It results from several billion years of rock decomposition, shifting by glaciers, water and wind and is the product of countless chemical, biological, and physical actions. Now it is also subject to your efforts to help keep it fertile, productive and alive.

Top, Sub & Types

The soil visible to you is only the top side of a layer that may extend from several inches to several feet downward. This is the topsoil and too frequently it is the only part of the soil that a gardener considers. Below the topsoil are other layers that extend, in various thicknesses, down to bedrock. These layers are referred to as the subsoil. The subsoil has a profound effect on root growth and subsurface water. There may be substantial differences between your soil and the neighbor's across the street.

These differences are called *soil types* and are caused either by natural or manmade changes resulting in varying amounts of sand, clay or silt.

A SOIL PROFILE

A Horizon: topsoil.

B Horizon: subsoil.

C Horizon: soil material.

D Horizon: parent material.

A Horizon: topsoil. Accumulates organic matter and the semi-decayed forms called "humus." Most biologically active layer and primary root nutrient area.

B Horizon: subsoil. Accumulates soluble materials from the "A" horizon through water soaking into the ground. Contains some microscopic life and root growth. Usually finer and more compact than "A".

C Horizon: soil material. Results from the disintegration of lower rock formation. No biotic activity.

D Horizon: parent material. The bedrock area; primary cause of local differences in soil type.

Soil scientists have developed soil profiles for over 70,000 different soil types. Knowing the profile of your gardening area will aid in selection of plant material, watering routines, and fertilization programs. Horizons are identified by changes in color and texture though not all horizons are part of all soils. Differences in depth per horizon play a major part in crop production. If you dig a hole 5–6′ deep you should be able to identify the depths of several layers.

Soil is too often taken for granted by the gardener. At first glance the soil seems to hold all sorts of promise. Later, as the digging starts, he finds problems in handling, spading, weeding and watering. Still later he begins seeing differences in the growth and vitality of his plants. To help understand the importance of soil management let's look at topsoil, subsoil, and soil types.

TOPSOIL:

Topsoil is an often misunderstood term. It is vaguely understood to be a rich, mellow, fertile sort of soil that can be purchased and spread across the garden and will automatically insure the growth of plants, solving any soil problem. Not so. It is simply a term used to name the top layer of soil. It may be fertile or it may be barren. The label itself carries no guarantee.

Topsoil is the most active part of the earth as it is in this layer that bacteria and fungi and other organisms live which contribute to the soil fertility. This is also the layer in which roots of plants will grow to take in the minerals needed for growth, water to stay alive, and obtain the anchorage needed to stand erect.

The topsoil can be manipulated. If done wisely you can build and enrich what you have, if unwisely you will diminish its growing value or lose it to erosion. Your topsoil is your most valuable gardening possession. Wise use of this resource will give you years of successful plant growth and yet leave it in better condition for following generations. Misuse leads to a soil that can hardly grow weeds.

Soil has certain characteristics, some of which can be described by words like texture, structure, tilth, and friability, along with others that refer to drainage, acidity, fertility, and contamination.

The *texture* of a soil refers to the ratio of sand, silt, and clay particles. This ratio infuences the ease with which soil can be worked, the amount of air and water it will hold, how quickly water can move into and through the soil, and how easily roots can penetrate the soil layers. The texture also gives you a clue as to how adequate the supplies of minerals used by plants might be.

Coarse textured soils are sandy, feel gritty, hold little moisture, and are usually low in plant food. Fine textured soils are made mostly of clay particles. They hang onto lots of moisture during our wet winters and may stay too wet to garden until early summer. When dry, fine textured clay soils crack, and when wet they swell.

Structure refers to the way the soil particles hold together to form natural aggregates or chunks. A shovelful of sand has no structure, each sand particle does its own thing. A shovelful of a clay loam has aggregates of various sizes and may be described as granular, blocky, platy or perhaps even cloddy, all of which show various degrees of structure. Structure affects the growth of roots. Soils with a "good" structure have many pore spaces between the soil particles which allow air and water to enter and permit easy root growth. An ideal garden soil will have at least 50% pore space in the top 8". Soils with a poor structure, usually those of fine texture (clay), tend to hold water, be poorly drained, and are difficult for roots to penetrate.

The structure of a soil is changed by weather and management practices. Plowing, tilling, spading or walking on the garden soil when it is wet can destroy a soil's natural structure. Heavy, pounding rain on bare soil will have a similar effect. Adding organic materials will improve soil structure. Growing a winter cover crop after the garden is finished will help make a better soil structure. The effect of freezing and thawing during winter loosens the soil. By staying off the ground until it dries in the spring, soil which has frozen and thawed during winter will be in mellow shape for planting.

Tilth refers to a general combination of physical and chemical characteristics and usually indicates a degree of fertility as well as a desirable soil structure. A soil is said to be in good tilth when it approaches a loam texture and when the inclusion of organic matter, fertilization and cultivation have built the soil to its peak of perfection. *Friability* is equally as vague to most gardeners and refers to a soil's consistency. A soil is said to be friable when a handful will hold together with gentle handling and with a little pressure the soil will crumble.

Topsoil may extend from several inches to several feet or more downward. Differences in color and structure usually indicate where the topsoil stops and subsoil begins. To learn what you need to know about your garden soil,dig down several feet and look at what's there.You may find it harder to dig as you get down a foot or so. This indicates increased compaction, perhaps from a different soil type containing more clay. In a garden that has been spaded or tilled to the same depth every year you will find a compacted layer of soil just below the normal tilling depth. This layer is called a hardpan or plow sole and will hinder root growth and restrict drainage. Often the subsoil layers will be a different color and their texture will feel different from that of the topsoil. They will likely have more of a slick feel and may be dark red, yellow or perhaps even blue.

SUBSOIL:

The roots of growing plants spread through the topsoil and subsoil in search of moisture and minerals and in so doing, anchor the plant. The surface soil serves as a banquet table for the plants growing in your garden, the subsoil serves as the pantry for moisture and plant food minerals. If conditions permit, the roots of perennial plants, such as fruit trees or rhubarb will penetrate to a depth of twenty feet or more. The roots of many annual vegetable plants may go three feet deep, and if there are no restrictions, the roots will draw moisture and plant nutrients from the total depth.

The subsoil generally can be penetrated by roots of growing plants, but penetration is not the most significant aspect of subsoil. It may contain restrictive things like hardpans, gravel, sand, or compacted layers that affect the movement of water and so effect drainage. One of the most common problems with subsoils in the Northwest is that they restrict drainage and suffocate the roots of deep growing perennials and woody plants.

A good way to learn more about your subsoil is to dig a hole five or six feet deep and take a look at the layers beneath your garden. One of the easiest ways to do this is with an auger which can bring up samples from below for your inspection. The color of the subsoil gives you a clue as to what to expect in the way of drainage capacity.

A brown or reddish colored subsoil without mottling usually indicates the subsoil has good natural drainage. The deeper this coloration extends downward, the better chance you will have growing food crops free of problems caused by too much moisture in the root zone.

A subsoil which is black or dark gray in color indicates an accumulation of organic matter accompanied by poor drainage. The organic matter will be an asset if the drainage problem is solved. Often the black subsoil will have a disagreeable odor which tells you there's an urgent need to correct the drainage.

A mottled subsoil is almost a guarantee that water movement under your garden is so slow that drainage is poor. Mottled subsoils will be marked with red, yellow or gray streaks or spots. Usually these soils have a fine texture. A blue subsoil is almost a sure bet that you will need to do something about your drainage. The blue color comes from iron in soils that are continuously saturated.

Subsoils have the same measurable textural and structural qualities as topsoil. They can be identified and managed. This is fortunate because sometimes we have to use it to grow gardens. In many areas of new subdivisions where the topsoil has been covered with excavated subsoil, completely removed or compacted during grading operations, the damaged soil is all that is left to work with. The gardener's first inclination when considering this situation is to buy loads of topsoil. This tack is all right but you may do better working with what you have. If you bring in new topsoil, work at least half of it into the soil below. This makes a transition layer between the new top and old subsoil and prevents a barrier interface between the two distinctly different soils that could restrict water and root movement. Purchased topsoil sometimes comes from the bottom of a hole so check around before you buy. Oftentimes the addition of organic matter, fertilizers, and lime or gypsum is sufficient to build a subsoil to the point where it will grow plants. As gardening progresses through the years, your own good management can make the subsoil topsoil.

TYPES:

Soil types are named on the basis of their major constituents. Some types are clayish, some are sandy. The ideal soil has almost the same percentage of sand, clay, and silt. Everyone would like to have a loam type but few of us are that lucky. Most of us in the Northwest have what is called a silty clay loam. This is a neat way of describing a soil that with a little careful management will grow almost any plant adapted to the Northwest. It will not dry as fast in the spring as a sandy soil but neither will it stay as wet as a clay soil.

A way of determining your basic soil types is by the "feel test." Wet a sample of soil to a dough-like consistency and rub it between your finger and thumb. Sandy types have a gritty feel and crumble easily when wet. A balanced mixture of sand, silt and clay, possibly a loam, will have a smooth feel, like flour, when dampened. Loamy soils can be molded when wet and will hold their shape without being sticky. Clay soil types are fine textured and can be rubbed into thin sheets and ribbons that will hold their shapes and resist breaking when dry. The feel test is only one of several ways to learn more about your soil. The jar test, described in Chapter 5, is another.

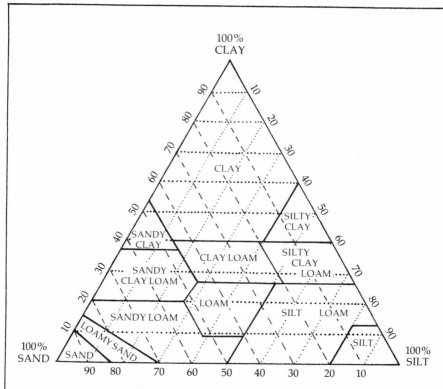

The soil textural triangle is a diagram which can be used to determine the textural name of your soil. Begin with a mechanical analysis using the jar test on page 131 to determine the approximate percentages of sand, silt and clay. Read the clay percentage going up and across from the left side of the triangle, the silt percentage going down and across from the right side, and the sand percentage going across and up to the left from the bottom. If, as a result of the jar test, your soil is found to be approximately 85% sand, 10% silt, and 5% clay, yours is a loamy sand. A loam soil might have 45% clay, 25% silt and 30% sand. Figure out your own soil.

Sand is the largest of the particles. Sand supplies aeration to soil because the sand particles lie together like a jumble of miniature rocks leaving air spaces between. A sandy soil is low in fertility because the sand particles cannot hang onto mineral elements needed by plants. Plants can be expected to send their roots deep and far in sandy soil, partly because they must grow an extensive root system to find any food and partly because the aeration supplied by sand permits vigorous root growth. A sandy soil needs organic matter to act as blotters for food minerals. Sandy soils erode easily.

When gardening in sandy soil your management plans must include winter cover crops or mulches to prevent erosion, annual applications of organic matter to build fertility, and frequent watering during the summer to maintain soil moisture.

Silt particles are smaller than sand and are the sort of things that are carried along by water when floods occur. Silt is made of various sized and shaped particles and is a balancing material between the extremes of sand or clay. Silt by itself makes a tight, impermeable soil but is apt to be rich in minerals. Silty soils generally have a poor structure and poor drainage characteristics.

Clay particles are the smallest of all but have more of an impact than any other particles on soil management activities. Soils in which clay is the major constitutent have particles so tightly packed that nearly all air and water movement is stopped. This sort of soil is so poorly drained that it may remain too wet for successful vegetable and fruit production.

A soil with so much clay that the water stands for several days following a heavy rain and then cracks when it finally dries should have organic material worked into it to loosen or separate the clay particles. Some people try working sand into clay to make it more penetrable but unless you add as much sand as you have clay you will only create a soil resembling cement. Organic matter in the form of rotted manure or compost, leaf mold, peat moss or straw is better for amending clay soils.

Dig, feel, and sample the layers of soil in your garden to get a better picture of the things you must do to grow the best and most productive food crops.

Water: Drainage & Irrigation

Water is critical to the life and vigor of all food crops. We need enough to supply the plant fluids necessary for health and succulence. If we have too much for too long, however, we have a problem equally as serious as too little. Too much water in the soil fills the pores and spaces where air should be found. If soil conditions or management practices cause the soil to stay waterlogged and airless, roots die. There must be a balance between air and water at the roots to support plant growth. In this section we will discuss how to get rid of excess and how to supply needed water.

Water removal is one of the most critical needs in many of our garden soils. Due in part to the types of soils in the Pacific Northwest, but more commonly because of previous mishandling of the soil, drainage problems severely limit gardening success. Raspberry plants dying two or three years after planting, green beans succumbing to molds, and fruit trees never making it past their third birthday all are grim reminders that poor drainage is our single most serious problem in this region.

When we speak of drainage problems we are not referring to surface water that runs downhill or stands in puddles after a hard rain. We are talking of the unseen water that lies below the surface. This soil water should move downhill also and it will, if nothing hinders its movement. But things such as man-caused compacted areas, layers of tight soil including a hardpan or plow sole, or deep layers of clay do hinder proper movement of the water. Anything that stops the normal movement of soil water can cause drainage problems.

How do you recognize a drainage problem in your soil? First, look at the trees and shrubs growing in the vicinity, secondly check for marshy spots, thirdly, dig a 5–6′ auger hole looking for the subsoil characteristics outlined earlier, and finally give the potential garden spot a simple perc test.

Willows, birch trees, rushes, sedges, cattails, are bog loving plants tolerant of wet conditions and will thrive in some of the poorest of soils. The absence or presence of these types of plants gives you a start in detecting water problems. Junipers, maples, oaks, and other dry land plants commonly used in Northwest landscapes will not tolerate poor drainage and will die within a few years after being planted in soil that stays wet.

Marshy spots are bad news to the person wanting to grow food crops. Not only does the continuing presence of water prevent root development, the area stays so wet it is impossible to prepare for planting. Soils that squish beneath your feet need radical drainage measures.

A test commonly used by land developers to determine the drainage capability of an area is the perc (percolation) test. Basically this involves digging a hole, filling it with water and checking to see how long it takes for the water to disappear. Complete drainage in two hours means you have a soil that drains well. If half the water remains in the hole three hours later you have a drainage problem and must plan accordingly. Dig several holes, one a foot deep to see how the topsoil drainage goes, and another three feet deep to check the subsoil.

How do you correct drainage problems? There are several ways, including growing plants on raised beds, installing drainage pipes, or growing plants in containers. The best and most permanent method, if you have ground with a slight slope, is to install drainage lines to carry the water away to a natural outlet of some sort. If your ground is soggy and perfectly flat, look into using raised beds or growing your garden in containers.

Subsurface drainage pipes are usually made of clay or concrete tiles, or perforated plastic. The pipe should be around four inches in diameter and whatever length is convenient. Clay tile generally comes in one-foot lengths, plastic in various lengths. The drain lines need to be buried deep enough to draw water from a wide area. Here is a rule of thumb to use in determining how deep to bury the drain lines: for every one-inch deep (soil over the tile) the line drains an area one foot wide. If your vegetable garden area is 30 feet wide, a single drain line through the middle buried 30 inches deep will suffice. Better drainage will result from two lines fifteen feet apart, thirty inches deep, resulting in a wider and deeper drainage field for growing vegetables and small fruits.

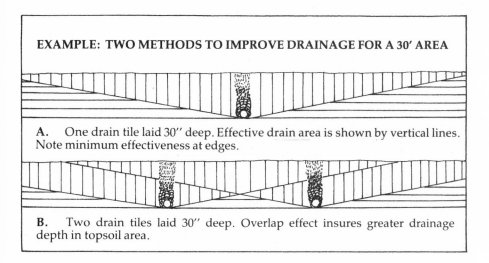

EXAMPLE: TWO METHODS TO IMPROVE DRAINAGE FOR A 30' AREA

A.   One drain tile laid 30" deep. Effective drain area is shown by vertical lines. Note minimum effectiveness at edges.

B.   Two drain tiles laid 30" deep. Overlap effect insures greater drainage depth in topsoil area.

When planning drain lines, keep in mind two important points. First, the drain line must slope downward. A fall of one foot in 100 feet of line is sufficient to move water. Second, the drain line must open to an outlet of some sort. Storm drains, curb drains, streams or other natural waterway will carry away the water once it is moved out of the soil. When placing drainage lines, place six to twelve inches of gravel, coarse sand, sawdust, or straw around the drain pipe. If enough coarse backfill material is available, fill the trench to within a foot of the surface then finish by filling the top with topsoil. Drain lines are a lot of work to install, but the result of a properly installed drainage system will be obvious and it will pay for itself with many years of productive gardens.

On sloping land excessive water can also be controlled with diversion ditches. Dig a ditch across the upper part of your yard between the garden and the arriving water to direct the water elsewhere. To be effective the ditch should be dug deep enough to reach a restricting layer of soil (hardpan, clay layer). Usually the water problem on slopes occurs when the downward percolation of water is stopped by an impermeable layer of soil or rock. The water runs downhill, on top of this layer, arriving in your garden to saturate the ground. The diversion ditch can be left open or be filled with rocks (thus making what is called a "French"drain).

Sometimes a dry well can solve drainage problems. A dry well is a hole, five or more feet deep, backfilled with rocks. Excess water will move into it and from there seep downward thru a layer of sand or gravel. A dry well should be dug deep enough to reach a natural layer of sand, gravel or other coarse textured matter that will carry the water. A dry well dug in a deep layer of clay simply becomes a bathtub, holding water for a long time and keeping the area as wet as before. If you're in doubt about the depth of impenetrable soil on your site, contact the local Soil Conservation District before settling on a dry well construction.

Two other methods of growing food crops are used to overcome drainage problems. These are raised beds (which is discussed in Chapter 5) and container gardening, discussed later in this chapter.

We have discussed drainage before irrigation because it is one of the most common problems encountered by Northwest gardeners. Drainage is often the factor that prevents the successful growth of vegetables, small fruit plants and fruit trees. Its seriousness and wide extent warrants a lot of digging and study of your soil before planting anything.

Once the problem of standing water is solved, water must be supplied for plant growth. Irrigation of garden soils becomes a critical part of gardening in the Northwest once the spring rains have stopped. An odd feature of the Northwest, especially to gardeners arriving from elsewhere, is that the day after the rains stop we have to begin irrigating.

Irrigation must be timely — sufficient to replenish and infrequent enough to keep the plants busy extending their roots downward to find moisture. Many gardeners water too little and too frequently. This leads to battling molds and mildews because the plant foliage and upper soil surface are constantly damp. Furthermore the plants grow poorly because the soil is not dampened deeply enough for good root activity.

Timeliness of irrigation is important in maintaining vigor and in obtaining the best production from plants. Whether you supply the water or it falls from the sky, there are certain times in a plant's cycle of growth when water needs are critical. The first time is right after transplanting or planting seeds. The new plants must have moisture to keep the roots alive and begin growth. Seeds must have moisture in order to initiate growth and keep the new cells of roots and shoots alive. The second critical time is when the food crop approaches the harvesting point. Vegetables and fruits are mostly water so to obtain the best quality the plant must have adequate water to achieve the best quality.

How much and when to water depends on the type of soil. Sandy soils drain and dry quickly and may need to be watered several times a week during the warmest and driest part of the growing season. Soils with a large percentage of clay will hold onto water longer and may need to be replenished only half as often as a sandy soil. While a sandy soil dries out much faster than a clay type, it requires only a third as much water to replenish the top eight inches as the clay requires.

Practically speaking, we need to apply the amount of water to fit between the extremes of saturation and drought. Depending on soil type, it may take from one inch (sandy) to nearly four inches (clay) of rain or irrigation water to replenish soil moisture when plants begin wilting. Need for irrigation should be based on how fast water is being used by plants or lost to evaporation. A good way to estimate need is by feeling the top inch of soil or by digging into the top several inches. If it is dry, better irrigate; if it is damp, let it go for another day. Watch the health of your plants — if the spinach wilts or the corn leaves roll, the soil needed water yesterday.

There are many ways to put water on the garden. The best way is whatever puts the water on at a rate the soil can absorb. Sandy soils absorb water quickly, others like clay or silt absorb water much slower so the water more readily runs off. Further, level beds absorb water faster than those on sloping ground. The best watering practices will keep the soil damp, yet not wet, during the entire growing season for annual vegetables and through the ripening period for berry plants. Trees, once they have become established, seem to do quite well without much extra care, providing the soil is deep and moderately retentive of moisture.

To meet these criteria, the system must obviously be selected for the type of plant. Soaker and drip systems are the most effective and efficient for gardens and small fruit crops. These systems supply water slowly, continuously, and mostly to the row of plants. Less water is wasted between rows so fewer weeds are watered. Another advantage is that dirt is not splashed onto the foliage or fruit plants.

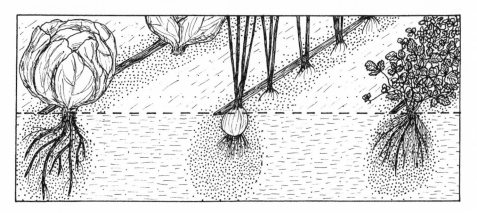

Overhead sprinkler systems are less efficient but work as satisfactorily for getting water onto the garden area. Overhead sprinklers should be used in early morning so the foliage can dry quickly before molds and mildews start growing or sun causes leaf burn. Also, less water is lost to the atmosphere by evaporation with early morning watering.

A handy way to water large individual vegetables such as tomatoes, peppers and vine plants is to bury tall juice cans alongside the plant. Punch holes in the bottom for the water to enter the soil six or eight inches below the surface. When the plant needs water, simply fill the can. In this way the water goes to the plant's roots, rather than to weeds growing between the rows. Fertilizers can also be supplied to the plant in this way.

Few areas in the western part of the Northwest use flooding as an irrigation technique. Flood irrigation between vegetable rows does not work effectively in our relatively porous soils.

One last point on watering. Do it infrequently but put lots on when you irrigate. Depending on your water system, water pressure, and size of pipes carrying water to your yard, it may take an overhead sprinkler three or four hours to apply an inch of water to the area covered. Soaker hoses, drip systems and various forms of these systems may take six hours or more to put an inch of water into the soil. The point is, it takes time to get the water on in enough quantity to do the plants any good. Hand watering may or may not be effective. If you hand water each plant individually with the hose, the plant will probably get enough to grow. If you sprinkle the area with a spray nozzle all you are doing is washing the foliage. Few gardeners can stand still long enough to give a deep soaking irrigation.

Here is an easy way to measure water. Set a flat-bottomed container under a section of the soaker hose or in the pattern of the sprinkler. Let the water run for an hour or two and measure how much the container has caught. How little has actually come from the sprinkler may surprise you but will indicate the need to increase the amount of time you irrigate.

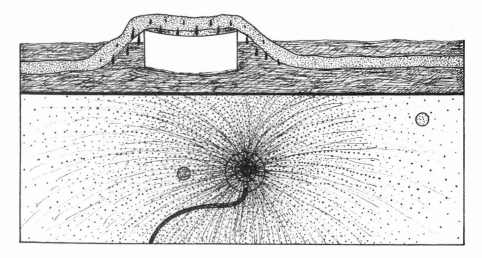

Once you get the soil damp, conserve the water with mulches and by pulling competing weeds. Some mulches, hay and straw for example, bring weeds to the garden. Bark and sawdust are weed free. Newspaper is cheap and makes a good mulch although it may be considered unsightly. Grass clippings are okay but they melt away quickly. Don't use grass clippings from lawns treated with weed killers for at least two clippings after the herbicide treatment. Plastic mulches do an excellent job of conserving moisture and can be of black or clear polyethylene. Plastic mulches warm the soil below, organic mulches insulate the soil surface. Wait to apply organic mulches until the soil has warmed.

Maintaining Soil Health: Fertility & Deficiency & Excess

To successfully grow a vegetable garden, a crop of strawberries or a fruit tree one needs to know a few things about what makes a soil fertile. All soils are not equally fertile. Some, like the black river bottom soils, we can look at and feel certain they are fertile. Others, like the fine-textured, densely packed subsoils exposed during housing development, leave us with the feeling they might be lacking something that constitutes a part of fertility. Soil fertility comes from a mixture of things — mineral nutrients, organic matter, water and air and clay.

There are at least sixteen elements that a plant takes from the soil for growth. Some are needed in large amounts while others are needed in such small amounts that a normal soil will have enough for our gardening lifetime. The major nutrients are nitrogen (N), phosphorus (P), and potassium (K). These are needed in the largest amounts. Each supplies a key element for plant growth. These three are not needed in equal amounts in all soils by all plants.

The three major plant food elements are the basis of "complete" fertilizers blended to supply varying amounts of the nutrients and fit the needs of various plants. When you purchase a complete fertilizer you will find numbers prominently displayed on the label. The numbers refer to the percentage of nitrogen, phosphorus and potassium. For example:

5 - 10 - 10
5%N - 10%P - 10%K

N, nitrogen: needed to stimulate shoot growth and leaves, develop chlorophyll for green color and for photosynthesis.	P, phosphorus: needed for flower bud growth, root growth and is the main energy supply for new plants.	K, potassium: needed for resistance to insect and disease enemies, for root development and is a balancer of N & P.

Not all plants need all three of these. Phosphorus and potassium needs should be determined by a soil analysis. As a guide, leafy plants need mostly nitrogen. This could be supplied by a fertilizer such as ammonium sulfate, 21-0-0; ammonium nitrate, 33-0-0; or in a complete fertilizer such as a 15-5-5- mixture. Flowering plants and those whose edible parts are seeds or fruits need a little nitrogen and a lot of phosphorus (which could be supplied in a 5-10-10 mixture or something in a similar ratio). Seldom is potassium needed by itself. If a soil analysis shows potassium to be low, for leafy crops it can be supplied as potassium nitrate (13-0-44), for fruiting crops it can be supplied in 5-10-10 or something similar.

Recommendations for fertilization are often given in terms of *actual* amounts of a particular element needed. Nitrogen, for example, is often recommended at one or two pounds *actual nitrogen* per thousand square feet of area. This may be confusing if you have forgotten your high school math. The fertilizer label lists percentages of the main mineral elements, nitrogen, phosphorus and potassium. To figure out how many pounds of fertilizer are needed to give actual amounts of nitrogen or phosphorus or potassium, divide the percentage figure (for the element being recommended) into the pounds actual element being recommended. For example, you have a bag of 5-10-10 fertilizer on hand. You are told to use one pound actual nitrogen per thousand square feet of fall cover crop planting. To find out how much of the mixed fertilizer is needed divide one pound by 5% ($1.00 \div .05 = 20$). Result: 20 pounds of 5-10-10 fetilizer is required to supply one pound of actual nitrogen.

Nitrogen is needed for foliage and stem growth. This is the element that is needed to grow leafy chard and spinach, lettuce and sweet corn. It is needed for growth of berry plants and for annual growth of fruit trees. Emphasis is given to nitrogen feeding not only because of its function but for another important reason — nitrogen is a soluble element so is carried away in water. Heavy rainfall or irrigation carries nitrogen downward and beyond the reach of annual vegetables or shallow rooted berry plants.

Nitrogen can be supplied in several ways, the choice being one of how fast the effect is needed, how much you are willing to pay, and how long the nitrogen is expected to remain. Chemical forms of nitrogen are fast-acting and cheapest. Organic forms give a slower response, remain effective over a longer time and cost more per unit of nitrogen.

Commonly used chemical forms of nitrogen are ammonium nitrate, ammonium sulfate, and calcium nitrate. These forms give fast response and are valuable for side-dressing in early summer to make leafy vegetables grow.

Common organic forms of nitrogen include blood meal, tankage, fish meal, guano and materials from other protein sources. The organic forms are slower to react because they depend on bacterial and fungal activity to decompose the fertilizer to its elemental constituents. These soil inhabitants require optimal soil temperature and moisture in order to decompose organic materials effectively. Organic fertilizers applied to early spring vegetable gardens are slow in giving any responose because the soil is too cold for bacteria and fungus organisms to release the nitrogen from the organic particles rapidly.

Nitrogen should be applied carefully to make a food crop plant do what you want. If the plants need to be encouraged, use it. If they are making adequate growth and leaf color is deep green, don't. When we discuss fruit trees we will advise looking at the amount of annual growth to judge nitrogen needs. Tomatoes fertilized with too much nitrogen will grow gigantic vines, but no fruit. Corn without enough nitrogen will remain short and spindly and set few ears. Most of the annual vegetables and berry plants need about two pounds of actual nitrogen per thousand square feet of area per year. Fruit trees, because of their greater root extent, may only need nitrogen during the first several years of development.

Phosphorus is needed primarily as an energy source for new plants. Seeds germinating and transplants beginning growth need phosphorus. Because the root systems of new plants are small, phosphorus must be placed near the plant's roots. Phosphorus is nearly insoluble so it should be worked into the soil at planting time or placed nearby as a side-dressing soon after planting. Later, after the young plant has passed adolescence, phosphorus is needed to develop flower buds and to form seeds necessary to form fruits.

Phosphorus is most easily supplied as phosphate fertilizer or as a part of a complete fertilizer mixture. The important point to remember about phosphorus is that it needs to be placed in the soil near the roots of your plants. As a general rule, one pound of actual phosphorus per thousand square feet of garden space is sufficient. From a practical standpoint one cupful of superphosphate spread alongside a fifty foot row will supply all the plants' needs for the season.

Potassium needs are not well understood. We know it is needed as a balance between nitrogen and phosphorus to permit the proper use of these elements by plants. It also is helpful in giving the plant some hardiness, tolerance, or a bit of resistance to disease and insect pests. Potassium is somewhere between nitrogen and phosphorus in solubility. It can be flushed out of soil with lots of water but it will build up in soils that are not well drained. Potassium can be supplied to garden soil in potassium nitrate, muriate of potash, potassium magnesium sulfate or in any of the complete fertilizers such as 5-10-10. Generally, one to two pounds per thousand square feet per year is sufficient.

Increased use of wood stoves and consequent dumping of ashes on the garden, will increase potassium to very high levels after several winters. Wood ashes contain potassium and calcium, so care must be used to not overdo the ash bit. Only a soil analysis can tell you if the potassium level is getting out of bounds. Plants may refuse to grow because of high potassium levels, but this is only one reason in hundreds for poor growth.

Calcium, magnesium, sulfur and boron are the secondary minerals needed for food crops. Calcium is needed for building cell walls in the plant. A deficiency of this mineral in tomatoes prevents the formation of the base of the fruit and results in a condition called blossom-end-rot. Calcium is usually supplied as ground limestone or wood ashes. A single application of 50–80 pounds per thousand square feet usually remains effective for several years.

Magnesium is needed for green color. It is used in forming chlorophyll, the green stuff in the plant cells which, when it receives light, makes plant food through photosynthesis. Deficiency symptoms usually occur in older, lower leaves which become yellow between the green veins. Magnesium can be supplied with dolomite limestone or epsom salts.

Boron is an element that is very important but only in very small quantities. It is easy to use too much of this element and make the soil toxic to plant growth. Boron deficiencies are described in the vegetable and tree fruit chapters. Boron can be supplied by various forms of borax or with borated fertilizers. Use them cautiously!

Sulfur is needed in leafy crops for green color and will often give the same greening response seen from a nitrogen application. This is because sulfur is one of the principle nutritional requirements of various soil bacteria and so steps up their decomposition activity. Sulfur comes in many of the complete types of fertilizers. A specific sulfur deficiency is seldom seen.

Calcium and sulfur play another important role in gardening, that of controlling the pH. The pH of a soil is a measure of its acid or alkaline reaction. Calcium will raise the pH, making soil more alkaline while sulfur will lower it making the soil more acidic. More on this later.

SUGGESTED APPLICATION RATES FOR COMMONLY USED FERTILIZERS PER 100 FEET OF ROW CROPS

To Supply:	Fertilizer	Row Spacing: *cups to use		
		1 foot	2 feet	3 feet
N	Calcium nitrate	2	4	6
N	Ammonium nitrate	1	2	3
N	Ammonium sulfate	1 3/4	3 1/2	4 1/4
N	Urea	2/3	1 1/3	2
P	Superphosphate	1	2	3
P	Treble superphosphate	1/2	1	1 1/2
N-P	16-20-0	1	2	3
N-P-K	5-10-10	2	4	6
N-P-K	12-12-12	1 1/2	3	4 1/2

* cup measurements are approximate, based on density of fertilizer, broadcast application.

The other mineral elements needed by plants are called minor, or trace elements. They are needed in very small amounts and are normally present in all Northwest garden soils. Iron, zinc, manganese, copper, molybdenum, chlorine, aluminum, and sodium are included in this group. While each is important to plant growth, general garden fertility maintenance programs will keep the soil supply high enough to satisfy plant needs. Deficiency signs will seldom be seen for any of the minor elements.

Organic matter is the seat of biological activity in soil. It is with organic matter that bacteria, soil fungi, earthworms, and various other forms of beneficial soil life work to make the tilth, texture and structure of good garden soil. Organic matter generally adds little mineral fertility but serves to give the soil wildlife something to chew on to make humus. As soil bacteria and fungus organisms decompose organic matter particles they use soil nitrogen for energy. Few organic materials carry enough nitrogen to support their own decomposition so you should add some extra nitrogen whenever you work a batch of strawy manure, wood chips, leaves or barkdust into the ground. Here is a general rule of thumb to use in estimating the nitrogen needs imposed by organic matter additions; for every one-inch layer of organic matter add one pound of actual nitrogen per thousand square feet of area.

ORGANIC MATTER ADDITIONS AND NITROGEN NEED

For every one inch of	Add:	per 100 sq. ft.	per 1000 sq. ft.
matted leaves	Ammonium nitrate	2/3 cup	3 pounds
	or		
straw	Ammonium sulfate	1 cup	5 pounds
	or		
barkdust	16-16-16-fertilizer	1¼ cup	6 pounds
	or		
wood chips	Calcium nitrate	1⅓ cups	6½ pounds
	or		
sawdust	Urea	½ cup	2½ pounds

The addition of organic matter should be a continuing activity. Some types of organic material seem to melt away quickly while others will influence the soil for a year or more. Green materials such as fresh lawn clippings, young weeds and vegetable scraps from the kitchen are mostly water and while they do encourage the activity of earthworms they do little for the soil's texture. Mature plant parts have cellulose fibers which are slow to decompose and so help change the soil structure and allow air to circulate or water to move through. Any organic material placed in a soil with air, water and warm temperatures will eventually decompose into beneficial humus, the mainstay of life in the ground. The important thing to remember is, keep the supply coming.

A good way to add organic material during the off season is by planting fall cover crops, also called *green manure* crops. For larger gardens or where other forms of organic matter are not easily obtained, green manuring is the most economical means of building soil. Cover cropping means seeding a fast growing grass, grain or legume in late summer and plowing it under in early spring. Cover crops should be sown by mid-September. The cover crop also protects the garden soil from erosion during the winter. If it has grown too tall for easy incorporation by late winter, mow it before spading or tilling. Annual ryegrass, Austrian field peas, garden peas, winter oats and barley are good soil improving winter crops in the Northwest. Here are suggestions for seeding winter cover crops:

Cover Crop	Pounds of Seed to Sow per 1,000 sq. ft. of Area
Alfalfa	1
Austrian Field Peas	2
Barley	2½
Crimson Clover	1
Garden Peas	2
Oats	2½
Rye (winter)	2
Turnips	½
Vetch	1½

Compost is an excellent organic soil amendment; it is not hard to make, and is a way to recycle nature's leftovers. When tilled in, it adds to the moisture-holding capacity of soil and improves tilth. It is also a first-class mulching material. Any of the garden wastes such as weeds, lawn clippings, leaves, vegetable or kitchen scraps, etc. can be used to produce the rich, humusy material recognized as finished compost. The only garden wastes unsuitable for composting are diseased plant parts which should be burned.

The breakdown of raw organic materials into compost is carried on by microbes. For this work they'll need air and moisture in addition to plant debris. There are numerous designs and home remedies to make composting convenient. The simplest way to get started is with a pile in some out-of-the-way spot. Make it however large you need, but a pile higher than 6' may not receive enough air. The pile can be enclosed with boards, cement blocks, wire fencing or whatever is handy to contain the pile and also allow air circulation.

After you have stacked the materials, keep the pile damp but not soggy. Summer watering will be easier if the top is dish-shaped. In winter the pile should be covered to reduce runoff and consequent leaching of nutrients.

The pile must be turned from bottom to top to hasten uniform decomposition. In the summer, turn the pile at least once a month or every week if you want even faster results. In the winter, the pile is fairly inactive because cooler temperatures slow microbial activity so it only needs to be turned once or twice. If you notice a strong ammonia smell or other offensive odor, turn the pile immediately. A healthy compost pile will generate heat but no odors. The length of time required to break down the materials will vary with contents, size, time of year, and management. As a rule of thumb, when the pile of compost is about half the size with which you began, the compost is ready to use.

If stacking compost is not your bag, here is an equally effective way to

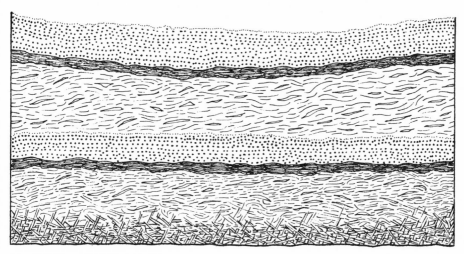

MAKING A COMPOST PILE

Begin with a six inch layer of grass, leaves, young weeds, or any organic matter available. Put the coarsest materials on the bottom. (If tree branches and pruned woody materials are to be included, chop them up first or they will take forever to break down.) Cover this layer with an inch of manure. If manure is not handy, sprinkle one cupful of complete fertilizer over the plant residues for every 25 square feet of top surface area. Next place a two inch layer of soil or sod and a cupful of lime over the layer of leaves and fertilizer or manure. (The soil contains the microorganisms needed to start the decomposition process.) Now continue building the pile with alternating layers of organic matter, fertilizer and soil until the pile is four or five feet high. ⎯⎯⎯⎯⎯⎯⎯⎯⎯⎯⎯⎯⎯⎯⎯⎯⎯⎯⎯⎯⎯⎯⎯⎯⎯

use leftover plant material for soil improvement. Simply dig a trench in the garden, twelve to eighteen inches deep, and fill it half to three quarters full with leaves, peelings, twigs, corn stalks or whatever. Sprinkle a cupful of complete fertilizer and a half cupful of limestone for every twenty feet of length. Cover the trench by digging another alongside. By the time a year has gone by you will have trench composted your way across much of the garden area. Trench composting can be carried out during the summer between the rows of vegetables and through the entire winter season.

Another critical factor in soil fertility is the clay content of the soil. That's right, this is not a typographical error. Clay content is important because clay particles store and exchange minerals in the soil. Each clay particle has a negative electrical charge that allows it to hold onto mineral ions having a positive charge. So, when you fertilize the garden, you first replenish some of the elements held by the clay and secondly stimulate bacteria and fungi to release more elements from the fertilizer material. The clay particles hold onto such things as hydrogen, potassium, calcium, magnesium, and ammonia nitrogen.

This holding capacity of clay is called the cation (cat-EYE-on) exchange or base exchange capacity. It can be measured by laboratory analyses. Exchange capacities of soils vary due to difference in type and amount of both clay and organic matter (which also carries an electrical charge and exhibits exchange or holding capacity).

As a root grows through the soil it exchanges the mineral ions held by clay. A soil having a low cation exchange capacity (CEC) does not hold much mineral wealth for plants. On the other hand, a soil with a high exchange level has not only lots of reserves but also lots of storage ability to feed plants.

CEC levels are stated in millequivalents per hundred grams of soil. A sandy soil might have a CEC of 7 meq/100 gms. A loamy soil might have a value of 40 meq/100 gms. Humusy or muck soils might go as high as 200 meq/100 gms. Clay soils can have 200−400 meg/100 gms. The higher the CEC the more minerals the soil can supply to growing plants. To convert this measuring system to an understandable one, one millequivalent of calcium is equal to 400 pounds of calcium per acre, one millequivalent of potassium equals 780 pounds per acre, one millequivalent of magnesium is equal to 240 pounds per acre.

Soils with a high CEC have greater capacity to absorb and retain calcium, potassium and magnesium. Several implications flow from this. One is that a high CEC soil, adequately fertilized, will maintain high levels of calcium, potassium and magnesium from one year to the next. Another implication, important in effective fertilization programs, is that these elements are not mobile in a high CEC soil. This means that surface applications tend to be tied up in the surface clay or organic matter. To get these minerals into the root zone of food plants they must be physically worked into the ground. High CEC values indicate that your soil has good potential for growing crops, if you manage that potential properly. But if your soil has a low CEC reading do not give up, but simply apply the above minerals more frequently to maintain soil fertility.

Two soil amendments should be mentioned here to sort of round out the mineral nutrient information — gypsum and wood ashes. Gypsum is composed of calcium and sulfur. Calcium is alkaline, sulfur is acidic. As a result, gypsum applied to soil supplies these two minerals without affecting soil acidity or alkalinity. It is usually used to loosen clay soils through a process called *flocculation*. Flocculation is a clumping process, whereby the particles of clay are changed from a normal flat platelike configuration to roundish clumps of particles. In this process, air spaces form between the clumps thus making a clay soil looser, better drained and aerated. The process takes time and most gardeners give up long before results are evident. If you have a clay soil apply gypsum annually at 60 pounds per thousand square feet worked into the soil. Don't expect results for three or four years.

Wood ashes contain calcium, potassium, magnesium and a little phosphorus. The following table illustrates the average percentages available in fir and oak ash. Generally the hardwoods (deciduous trees) yield higher amounts of minerals than do the evergreen.

Mineral	Percentage in *Fir*	*Oak*
Calcium	14.0	25.0
Potassium	10.0	15.0
Magnesium	2.4	3.0
Phosphorus	2.0	3.0

As a rule of thumb, an annual application of 1—1½ pounds of ashes per hundred square feet of garden area will take care of the calcium, magnesium, and potassium needs of growing plants. Do not use ashes around blueberry plants as they cannot tolerate the high levels of calcium and consequent high pH values. The elements in ash are water soluble. If ashes are to be stored for later use, put them in a dry place. Do not use ashes in gardens with high potassium levels, else this element may become so high that growth is adversely affected.

How do you determine the mineral levels in your soil? There are several ways. The best is to send a sample to your nearest soil testing laboratory. State land grant universities provide soil testing services in their soils departments. In addition, several excellent private soil testing labs offer their services to gardeners as well as farmers. Check with your local county extension agent for soil analysis labs in your area.

When taking a sample for testing, collect a number of representative subsamples that can be mixed together to represent a single soil type or soil condition. Soil samples should be taken from the top 6—8" layer. Use clean sampling tools and avoid contaminating the sample during mixing and packaging. Local extension offices can advise you on taking and mailing samples to soil laboratories.

A soil analysis should be made when new ground is being prepared for gardening. This will help you determine what the ground needs to grow your plants. After four or five years, or whenever you suspect a soil mineral imbalance, take another test to see how things like calcium and potassium and phosphorus are holding up. A soil analysis will show where deficiencies exist and help prevent excessive buildups of things like potassium or boron.

Another means of assessing the mineral content of your soil is to watch for signs of deficiencies as displayed by your plants. Plants will tell you when they are not getting the elements they need by differences in foliage color and size. The following table lists some of the most common deficiency symptoms to watch for.

DEFICIENCY SYMPTOMS

Mineral	*Vegetables or Berries or Fruit Trees*
Nitrogen	Growth retarded, leaves fade to yellow-green color, foliage smaller than normal, reddish and purplish colors develop in severe cases.
Phosphorus	Stems, slender and woody; leaves, small and often darker green than normal, undersides of leaves may develop reddish-purple cast, old leaves often mottled with light green areas developing between dark green veins, veins may eventually become purple.
Potassium	Symptoms first on older leaves which become ashen gray-green, leaf margin becomes brown, leaves develop bronze and yellowish brown color, foliage may be crinkled, dead areas develop in leaf centers.
Calcium	Stems thick, vegetative growth retarded, terminal buds die, immature leaves die back from twig tips, fruits are malformed, leaves may be distorted.
Magnesium	Yellow or reddish colors first appear between veins of old leaves while veins remain green, leaves brittle, margins curled upward, light colored areas on leaves die, defoliation common leaving only the newest leaves on ends of twigs.
Boron	New leaves light in color, brittle and often deformed, terminal buds may die, root crops may be hollow, plants severely stunted, new growth may be nearly leafless, fruit malformed.
Sulfur	Lower leaves yellowish green, new leaves smaller than normal, leaf margins turn almost black on some plants (strawberry).
Iron	Newest leaves affected, turning light yellow color, veins may remain green, plants stunted in severe deficiency.
Zinc	New leaves abnormally small and mottled with yellow, with dead areas in the leaf, twigs will be slender and with very short internodes near the tips, forming a ring of leaves near the end of the twig, leaves drop, starting with older leaves then moving toward the youngest.

Now, what about the soil pH? Soil pH is a measure of the acid or alkaline reaction of the soil. Most garden soils range from 5.0 (acid) to 9.0 (alkaline). A pH of 7 is neutral, neither acid nor alkaline. The lower the pH number the more acid or sour the soil and the higher the number the more sweet or alkaline. Soils west of the Cascade Range are natively acid, east side soils are alkaline or neutral in reaction.

The pH level of your soil is important as it governs the availability of minerals for plants. Most soil minerals are optimally available at a pH level between 6.0 and 6.8. The chart below shows what happens as pH ranges beyond this optimum.

PLANT NUTRIENT ACCESS BY SOIL pH

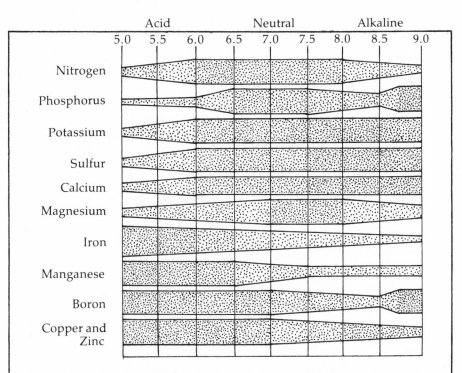

The width of the band indicates the availability of the element. The wider the band the easier the plant can obtain the element from the soil, the narrower the band the more difficult it becomes.

When ailing plants fail to respond to fertilizer, soil pH is probably wrong. The best pH range for Northwest gardens and orchard soils is 5.5–7.5. As pH values drop below, or rise above this range, most minerals are bound into insoluble compounds that cannot be used by plants.

Soils differ in their capacity to retain nutritional minerals. Likewise, soils differ markedly in the amount of calcium or sulfur required to alter the soil pH. A sandy soil, low in organic matter, will not require as much lime to raise the pH level as will a clay soil or one high in organic matter. The difference is due to the different holding capacities of the soils.

The pH of a soil can be determined either by a soil test or a home-type pH meter. Sometimes, plant growth may indicate something is out of line. When you have applied the right amount and types of fertilizer, but plant growth remains poor, investigate the pH level of your soil.

The pH level of soil can be changed by adding lime to acidic soils raising them toward neutral or adding sulfur to make alkaline soils more acid. The table below tells you how.

ADJUSTING SOIL pH TO APPROXIMATELY 6.5

pH from:	*Material Used	Pounds to Apply per 100 sq. ft. by Soil Type		
		Sandy Loam	Loam	Clay
7.5	sulfur	1½	2	2½
7.0	sulfur	¼	½	¾
6.0	calcium	3	4	6
5.5	calcium	5	8	11
5.0	calcium	7	11	15
4.5	calcium	10	13	20
4.0	calcium	12	16	23

* Sulfur can be applied as garden sulfur, flowers of sulfur or dusting sulfur. Iron sulfate or aluminum sulfate can be used in place of sulfur but will take about 2½ times more material to make an equivalent change in pH. Calcium can be applied as ground limestone, dolomitic limestone or hydrated lime. Generally ground limestone and dolomite will give a more gradual and longer lasting effect. Wood ashes can also be used to raise the pH but they will also increase levels of potassium and may carry other elements that are nonessential or possibly damaging to plants.

Ideally you should not apply more than 1½ pounds of sulfur or 8 pounds of limestone per hundred square feet in a single application. If larger amounts are required, split the applications, putting on half in the fall and the remainder the following spring. Such a program will induce a gradual increase or decrease in the pH. Work the materials thoroughly to a depth of six to eight inches.

Soil Afflictions: Insect & Disease

No matter how accurately you measure and apply fertilizers; how faithfully you add organic matter; how well you correct drainage problems; and how carefully you adjust pH levels, unexpected developments may come along to interfere with your gardening process.

Soil problems are usually of a physical or chemical nature, relating to water, soil types, nutrients and pH. But occasionally biological problems can develop in your soil, affecting growth adversely and in exteme cases killing plants. These biological intruders include such things as symphylans, nematodes and certain diseases that we would prefer not finding in the garden. A few of the culprits can be seen but for the most part they are invisible. Often the only signs of their presence are dead or stunted plants; dead roots, or root abnormalities. Usually these pests show up only in limited areas of the garden but may, if allowed to get out of hand, occupy the entire site. In this section we will give you some tips on what to look for to detect biological problems before they get out of hand.

Probably the most common culprit in vegetable gardens and small fruit plantings is the garden symphylan. Symphylans are tiny critters that move rapidly through spaces in the soil. When full grown they may measure ¼" in length, although most will be smaller. They have twelve pairs of legs when mature. They hatch from egg clusters laid in the soil. The eggs are so small you can hardly see them. Symphylans reach a population peak in late summer. August and September are the best months to control excess populations by soil fumigation.

Symphylans or "symps," are native inhabitants of most Northwest soils and subsist on native vegetation. In a natural setting, populations remain relatively static. However, when we grow garden crops their population explodes thanks to the abundant and nutritious food supply we provide. Suddenly we have a problem on our hands. Often the existing population is augmented by bringing symps into the garden via manure.

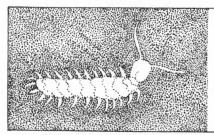

GARDEN SYMPHYLAN, *Scutigerella immaculata.*

Habit: Soil dwellers. Usually found in the top 10–12" of soil. In hot, dry weather symps move down to subsoil layers.

Populations: Many generations per year. Eggs laid spring through summer, as many as 20 per mass. Hatching takes place about 10 days later; adult stage is reached 45–60 days after hatching. Winter is spent in soil as adults.

Symps are general feeders which attack germinating seeds, plant roots and any plant parts laying on the soil surface. How do you know they are present? Examine the soil and observe young plants. Dig a shovelful of soil and sort through the particles and clods. Look for the small, white, fast-moving symps. They are not more than ¼ inch long, will have from six (babies) to twelve (adults) pairs of legs and will move quickly away from the light. Don't confuse them with the garden centipede (slender, 15 or more pairs of legs, brownish or tan color, an inch or so long), or the millipedes (hard-shelled, many legged, an inch or more in length, slow moving) that are commonly found in rich garden soil. (These two inhabitants of the soil are usually beneficial.) Sample a number of areas throughout the garden. The best time of the year to investigate is at their peak population period in August or September. The best place to look is in damp soil, but a careful spring inspection will also give you a clue as to their presence, and so give you an opportunity to develop a control strategy for new plantings. If you find only one or two symps per shovelful, you probably will not experience any damage. If you find ten or more in each shovelful of soil, you are going to have difficulty growing food crops. Often they live in specific areas in the garden, so by identifying and treating those spots you can avoid a general invasion.

Young plants planted in soil infested by symps remain small and stunted, eventually lose their color and die. The symps nip off and eat the young tender roots. The plant sends out more roots which are also eaten away so the plant is never able to take up the water and minerals necessary to live. If you dig a plant attacked by symps you will find a root system consisting of a mass of short stubs — evidence of where the pests have feasted.

Manure stored in an old pile is a favored breeding place for symps. When we spread this nice, well rotted organic material on our soil to increase the organic content of the soil, we may also be seeding a crop of symps. Look at your manure carefully before hauling it home to enrich your ground; you may be bringing problems.

Now, what to do? The possibilities range from trying to live with them to eradication. One method is to keep the soil between the planted rows stirred up. Thorough pulverization of the soil just before planting will scatter and destroy many symps. Symps do not make their own tunnels to move through the soil, instead they travel through existing cracks and crevices in the soil and through the spaces left by clods or organic debris. If you break up their pathways by frequent tilling or deep cultivation you make it harder for them to reach your plant roots.

There are several insecticides that can be used to protect some crops. Check with your local extension office or experiment station to see what is legal in your area.

If your soil is badly infected and you are really serious about ridding yourself of the symphylan, you will have to resort to soil fumigation. Soil fumigation, done properly, can keep your garden free of symps for three or four years, providing you don't carry them back in via manure or infested plants. Plan ahead for fumigation. The ground must be warm and damp enough for the symp population to be in the top layers of soil. It must be done in soil free of plants, plant debris or trash. The best time is in mid-spring after the soil has warmed to at least 50°F. Late summer in an inconvenient time for most gardeners because it coincides with the ripening of most summer vegetables. Mid-spring fumigation on the other hand simply means delaying planting until the process is completed.

To fumigate the soil, first loosen it by tilling or spading eight or more inches deep. The fumigant can then be applied in various ways depending on the type used. The fumigant most commonly available to the home gardener and the safest to use is *Vapam* (also known as VPM, SMDC or sodium N-methyldithiocarbamate). This product is a liquid that can be applied on the top of the soil with a sprinkler can or hose applicator, or into the soil by injection. Once applied the soil is covered with a sheet of plastic. The liquid Vapam becomes a gas on entering the soil and penetrates as deeply as the soil has been loosened, killing any symps encountered. Leave the soil covered for at least a week then rework the soil to allow any remaining vapors to escape. Lastly, let the soil air for a week and the soil is ready to be planted.

Another soil inhabitant that is even harder to see and more difficult to forecast is the nematode. Nematodes are so small that it takes a microscope to see the ones that bother the garden and small fruit plants. Nematodes are native inhabitants of Northwest soils and seem to reside in some sort of harmony with native plants. But when we develop a garden full of tender roots for them to feed on they frequently increase their population to the point that they seriously inhibit plant growth.

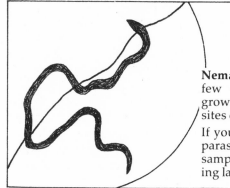

Nematodes: microscopic worms. Only a few species are detrimental to plant growth; other species are important parasites of pests.

If you suspect an overpopulation of plant-parasitic nematodes, take a soil and root sample from the problem area to a soil testing laboratory for analysis.

Nematodes are so small that they have difficulty moving from one place to another without our help. An infested spot that developed in the garden because we planted a tasty host, will enlarge only a few inches a year if the nematodes have to move themselves. Unfortunately, nematodes are usually carried from one place to another by people bringing infested soil into gardens or from one spot in the garden to another on shovels, rakes, and cultivation equipment (tillers or plows) carrying soil particles from place to place. They can be brought to the garden in topsoil from an infested field or on the roots of plants given you by a neighbor. They can also be carried by water washing across infested areas and into your garden.

There are basically two types of nematode. The first, bores into plant roots, while the other chews holes in the outer parts of roots. The first cause root knots to form, while the latter make lesions in the skin of the root. Both affect the plant by interfering with water and mineral uptake, making holes for disease organisms to enter and both spread virus diseases from plant to plant.

How do you know if they are present? Watch your plants, dig up a few that are looking sickly and see what the roots are doing, or send a sample of roots and soil to a testing laboratory specifically for a nematode count. Symptoms of a nematode infestation are not clear cut so it is difficult to positively identify stunting by nematodes without a lab analysis. Similar symptoms can be caused by any one of many other factors. An infestation of nematodes usually builds gradually in one area of the garden. Plants in that area will be dwarfed, poorly colored and never amount to much, even though you give special care to fertilizer and watering needs. The presence of an area in the garden that simply refuses to grow healthy plants gives you a clue that something is amiss in the soil. That something could be nematodes.

The only sure way to identify a nematode probem is by sending a soil and root samples to a testing laboratory. Land grant colleges and universities have nematode detection laboratories in conjunction with Botany and Plant Pathology departments. Private labs may also offer these services. Check with your local extension agent for advice on where to send samples.

Control of nematodes in the home garden is the same as for control of symphylans: soil fumigation. Rotation of crops is not the answer because the nematode can remain dormant for several years, awaiting a crop that it likes. Marigolds planted in the garden may deter nematodes for a while, but they cannot eradicate this pest.

Other biological soil problems that may plague the garden include soil-borne diseases that kill the roots of desirable plants. Most of these are carried into the garden on seeds and plants. Potatoes brought from the supermarket bin may carry several diseases, not harmful to the consumer of the spud, but which, when planted, will introduce bacterial ring rot disease, fusarium wilt or scab. Strawberry plants offered by a friendly neighbor may carry a disease or two to your soil. Fruit trees often carry nematodes to their new planting site. In all cases, when planting perennial plants or plant parts, make sure the plants are certified free of disease. Your first line of defense in keeping your garden free of disease problems is to buy plants which are certified disease free from a reputable dealer.

In addition to soil fumigation there are several other methods of combatting soil insect and disease infestations. The oldest, and still one of the best, is by changing the planting area for vegetables and small fruits — called crop rotation. Crop rotation simply means not planting the same crop, or relative of it, in the same spot each year. Potatoes, strawberries, root crops and tomatoes should be planted in different sites each summer.

Solar heat can be used to pasteurize the upper four to six inches of garden soil. This can be done very simply in midsummer. Cover the ground that needs treating with a clear plastic sheet. Cover the edges of the plastic with soil so wind doesn't carry the sheet away. Do this in mid-August when the summer sun is the warmest. The sun warms the soil and the plastic traps the heat. On a sunny, clear day the soil temperature can reach 140°F, hot enough to kill soil inhabitants — bugs, diseases, and nematodes. Leave the cover on for several sunny days, then uncover and plant.

Biological soil difficulties are hard to identify and harder to control. The time spent preventing or properly identifying and planning control measures will be repaid by healthy, productive gardens.

Containers: Alternative Growing Space for Food Crops

If the soil in your yard is not suitable for a vegetable and fruit garden, or if garden space is limited, or if you want to grow some exotic plants not adapted to the Northwest climate, you can turn to growing in containers. Container gardening has many advantages over conventional gardening. Soil problems are simply bypassed — poor drainage, late-warming soils, and soil diseases. Advantage can be taken of sunlight by moving the containerized garden into the most sunny parts of the yard, deck, balcony or patio. Perennial weed problems are virtually non-existent for the container is separated from weed infested ground. Soil insects are not a problem when the roots of your plants are boxed and far removed from the soil source of the nematodes and symphylans.

However, all is not beer and skittles, as container gardening demands close attention to certain plant management practices. Because the soil mixture in a pot, box or tub is removed from Mother Nature's soil storehouse, the continuing supply of water and minerals must be furnished by *you*. Container soil warms and dries faster in the spring to give you a head start on gardening, but as the season progresses this rapid drainage and drying means you must water more often. During the hot, dry days of summer you may need to supply water several times per day, every day. The mineral nutrient content of most soils provides plants with a continual supply which need be augmented only occasionally while the soil in a container must be re-supplied frequently to replenish the minerals lost through irrigation.

Almost anything that will hold soil can serve as containers for your garden. Nursery pots, tubs and buckets, wood or metal boxes, cement blocks, barrels or clean food cans are just a few of the kind of containers which are used to grow plants. They should be substantial enough to hold plants for at least one season for vegetables and for ten or more years if you are planting berry plants or fruit trees. Containers made of wood should be built of redwood or cedar if possible, as they last longer. Other woods will not last as long but their life can be extended by painting the wood with copper napthenate wood preservative. Do not use pentachlorophenol or creosote as these compounds damage plants.

Containers must have sufficient capacity to hold enough soil for normal root growth of your proposed planting. Naturally small plants, radishes and parsley for example, can easily be grown in small and shallow pots. The larger the plant, the bigger the pot must be to allow it to grow normally. Obviously, a fruit tree needs a planter large enough to hold fifteen or twenty cubic feet of soil.

Most important, when choosing a container make sure it has drainage holes in the bottom or sides to permit excess water an easy escape. Containers that will sit on a flat surface should have drainage holes in the sides near the bottom. Containers set on balconies should have a drip pan under them to keep your irrigation water from raining on the folks below.

CONTAINER SUITABILITY

Size	Plants Best Suited
4-inch	chives, onions, radishes, parsley
1-gallon	bush beans, strawberry, lettuce, chard
2-gallon	peppers, beets, kohlrabi, carrots, eggplant
5-gallon	sweet corn, blueberry, tomato, cucumber, cauliflower
box: 24" depth (× 24" wide min.)	canefruits, elderberry
box: 36" depth (× 36" wide min.)	grapes, dwarf fruit trees

The soil used in a container must be fast draining yet provide enough water retention to keep the soil evenly moist throughout the root zone. A mix that drains too fast won't hold enough moisture to keep plants alive. One that drains too slowly will cause roots to die and rot. Soil dug from the yard and placed in a container simply will not work. It is too heavy, usually drains too slowly and packs too tightly into the container to provide natural aeration.

Soil mixes can be purchased or you can make your own. A mixture made of equal parts of clean sand, fertile garden soil and barkdust or peat moss works well for most plants and can be made inexpensively. Supply the necessary minerals by adding to a 5-gallon bucketful of soil mix, ¼ cupful of dolomite lime and ¼ cupful of bone meal or single super phosphate (0-20-0) plus a rounded tablespoonful of a complete fertilizer such as 12-4-8 or

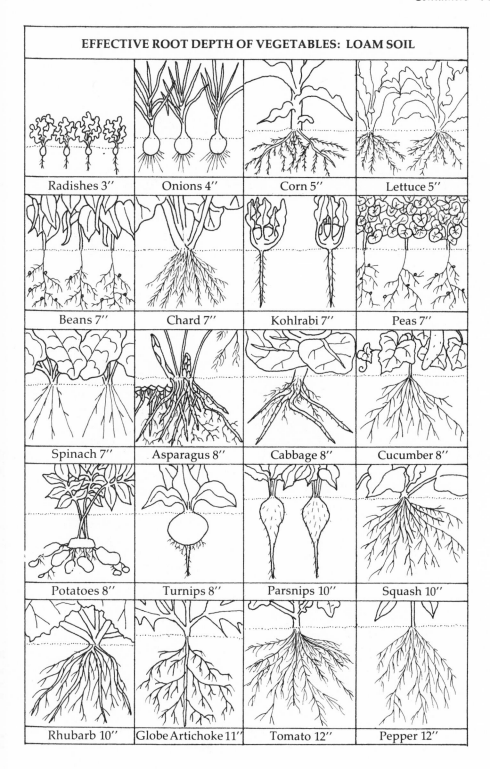

EFFECTIVE ROOT DEPTH OF VEGETABLES: LOAM SOIL

Radishes 3"	Onions 4"	Corn 5"	Lettuce 5"
Beans 7"	Chard 7"	Kohlrabi 7"	Peas 7"
Spinach 7"	Asparagus 8"	Cabbage 8"	Cucumber 8"
Potatoes 8"	Turnips 8"	Parsnips 10"	Squash 10"
Rhubarb 10"	Globe Artichoke 11"	Tomato 12"	Pepper 12"

15-5-10 mixture. These minerals provide a basic nutrient supply to get the plants started.

Container drain holes should be covered with screen or netting to keep the soil mix from sifting out. Place a thin layer of gravel, rock or broken pottery in the bottom just to keep the drain holes unplugged. Fill the container with the prepared soil mixture and you are ready to plant.

Plant vegetables, small fruits and dwarf trees as suggested in their respective chapters. Vegetables are a natural for container gardening. All you need to do is provide a container large enough to accommodate the normal root growth of the plants. Do not crowd the plants. Vegetables need the same spacing in containers as recommended for garden planting.

When selecting varieties for your container vegetable garden, keep in mind that some varieties are comparably productive and more easily managed than the garden-planted regulars. Though "Patio Tomatoes" have been a container standby for years, more and more vegetables are being developed especially for the container gardener. For example, peas are available in dwarf form as is a variety of corn that is 4−5' tall at maturity. Cucumbers, beans and even watermelons are available as compact bush-types.

The very dwarf forms of tree fruits are suitable for growing in large sized containers. Containerization allows good tree fruit growth on any sunny patio, deck or balcony. Select a container that holds at least 15 cubic feet of soil mix, is well drained and sturdy enough to last for many years. Dwarf apples, grafted onto M-9 or M-27 roots, make ideal container trees for your patio orchard. Dwarf varieties of pears, peaches and plums also make good, manageable trees for the containerized garden. A marked advantage of growing trees in containers is that they can be moved to utilize available sunlight most effectively or to provide protection from extreme weather. Containerized woody plants (trees and berry plants) will require winter protection during severe cold spells to keep the soil temperature from making dramatic changes which kills roots. This can be done by wrapping the container with insulation material and mulching the top of the soil with a layer of bark or sawdust. Water the soil before freezes begin. Roots in dry soil will be damaged much more quickly by freezing weather than roots in damp soil. Do not bring pot-grown trees indoors for the winter because they require a period of cold to properly prepare flower buds for normal growth the following spring.

All of the berry crops are well suited to growing in containers. Strawberries are fun to grow in barrels, blueberries will do as well in containers as in the ground if they are taken care of properly, and canefruits thrive on the attention given them in containers.

Grapes will need about ten cubic feet of soil for root growth to support vine growth. Strawberries will produce crops growing in a six-inch nursery pot. Vining plants such as blackberries, logans and boysens can be planted in wooden tubs or boxes and trained onto arbors, trellises or across the sunny side of the house. In all cases, the amount of top growth and consequent berry crop will be proportionate to the amount of space allotted for root growth.

Strawberries are the easiest berry for container growing. They will grow, bloom, bear fruit, and grow new runner plants in almost any container. The larger the more productive. A reasonable way to grow strawberries as a container crop is in a strawberry barrel or growing column designed to grow them vertically.

Once your container garden is planted, you must supply water and fertilizer regularly to keep the plants growing normally. Saturate the soil when watering. Allow some water to run out the drain holes to prevent the accumulation of fertilizer salts in the soil. Light waterings cause a concentration of dissolved fertilizer minerals in the upper inch or two of soil. Concentrated fertilizer salts kill plant roots and eventually will kill the plant. Excess salts will be shown by a white residue on the soil surface or around the inside edges of the container.

Fertilizer may be added in a soluble form every three weeks or can be applied once or twice a year in insoluble, dry, slowly available forms. "Slow release" fertilizers that can be applied as a topdressing to the surface of the container soil will replace the need for continual feeding. Most of these slow release fertilizers remain effective for six to nine months and are valuable for long-term container plantings of trees, berry plants and other perennials. Sulfur coated ureas, resin coated soluble fertilizers, urea formaldehyde and organics such a blood meal and tankage are some of the slow release types available to home gardeners. Fertilize the containerized plants only while they are growing, not when they are dormant.

Soluble commercial fertilizers, such as 20-20-20, used at one tablespoonful per gallon of water, will supply all the minerals needed if applied on a 3–4 week basis during the growing season. If manure or compost is available, fertilizer needs can be supplied in a form of tea. Here is a suggested way:

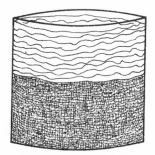

Compost Water Use one part finished compost to one part water. Stir and apply to root zone of plants. Add more water and use same compost several times. Afterwards compost can be used as mulch.

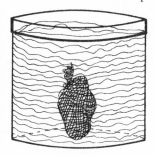

Manure Tea Tie fresh barnyard manure in a cheesecloth or other porous bag and submerge in warm water. Cover and let steep for 30–45 days. Remove bag and dilute mixture to color of weak tea. Apply to root zone of plants and water in well.

Chapter 4: PESTS?

Introduction

The three great natural hazards of gardening are weather, insects, and plant diseases. Weather is probably the chief hazard in growing food crops here in the Northwest, but the order of importance is not certain. The interrelation between all three is so close and so complicated that the real origin of trouble may be difficult to determine. While the problems in the garden less often relate to pests (visible or invisible) you'll need to be able to recognize plant conditions that may be pest-related.

Pests come in many forms. There are the insect and non-insect pests that crawl, fly or run to the garden where they suck, bore, chew or tunnel various parts of the plants you are trying to grow. Animals are common invaders — field mice, gophers, moles, browsing deer, and foraging raccoons can consume a lot of vegetables and fruits before they are surfeited. Birds are pests when berries are ripening or sweet corn and bean seedlings are coming up. Wandering dogs are pests when they trample the rows of vegetables. Weeds are pests by definition: "a plant out of place, or one which no one has found a useful purpose for." By this definition any plant could be a weed, but for practical reasons our "weeds" are the self-sown wild plants that can so easily overrun our carefully planted gardens, berry rows, and home orchards. There are three prime pests which cause disease — fungi, bacteria, and viruses. Almost every food crop is susceptible to a particular set of diseases, but whether or not they will strike depends on weather and plant growth factors.

Something qualifies as a pest when it adversely affects the plant you are trying to grow by either ruining the parts you would like to eat or by damaging the plant so badly it cannot function as a healthy organism. A single aphid sucking the juices from a snap-bean leaf would not qualify. But, the colony of offspring found on the leaf a week later keeps the leaf from feeding the snap beans you are looking forward to eating. A single fungus spot on an apple might not seem to warrant an all out effort to control scab, but it does tell you that the disease is present and if environmental conditions are right, the disease will spread to cover the tree. Some of us will tolerate infestations of bugs or invasions of diseases as long as we are still able to harvest something. If you are the sort of gardener who cannot stand to see a few aphids or speckled leaves, you will need to undertake the serious study of all the possible enemies to Northwest greenery. Our viewpoint is more easygoing. We will accept a few pests as long as they don't seriously affect the yield.

The basic line of defense against enemies of the garden is prevention through cultural practices outlined in the specific food crop chapters. These cultural pointers include sanitation, plant selection, site selection and plant growth management. Each of these is discussed in detail, not only to maximize your yield, but also to provide you with a valuable first tool to use in protecting your garden from pests.

A pest may become serious if there is nothing to inhibit its growth, or stop the expanding population. Powdery mildew is a typical fungus disease of food plants, but it does not become a problem as long as air circulation, sunlight, and humidity levels are right. However, when cloudy, warm days come along, the leaves will begin to take on the white cast symptomatic of the disease. Weeds, unless inhibited with a hoe, mulch or herbicide can quickly smother a vegetable garden or crowd out the berry plants. Aphids with all systems working and with plenty of soft juicy leaves to sip on, can quickly rise to a standing-room-only population unless you invoke adequate control measures or natural predators appear in sufficient number to help you control them.

How do you identify the appropriate line of defense? When do you become really serious? The seriousness of the pest depends on what sort of damage it causes. This is a matter of being able to identify the critical forces that attack plants. Diseases range from the serious viruses (for which the control is eradication of the host plant) to the less important mildews (which can be stopped by sanitation and air circulation). Insects range from the hard-to-control spider mites to the easily removed tomato hornworm. Weeds run the gamut from hoeable annuals to invasive perennials like quackgrass. Animals can be kept off with netting and fencing or you may have to mount a small scale war to evict moles or gophers.

Early detection of invading bugs, animals, weeds, and diseases is essential. Some pest problems are first seen at certain places on plants, some can be expected at certain times of the year while other pests (like slugs) are less selective. Leaf diseases usually begin on parts that are perpetually shaded, where air stagnates, or where the foliage remains damp for a long time. For example, late blight of tomatoes begins low on the plant, often in the interior where everything is tangled and air isn't circulating adequately. The flea beetles that chew pinhead size holes in potato leaves are giving notice that they are present and laying eggs for their young which tunnel into the skin of the developing potatoes. Moths and butterflies in the garden are laying eggs for a population of leaf-eating worms. The white butterfly dancing over the row of sauerkraut-on-the-hoof is forecasting a batch of green hungry worms and should tell you to prepare your control methods soon.

Leafrollers and gray mold botrytis appear in spring with new foliage and new plants. Spider mites and fruit rots are found in midsummer. Mildews and grasshoppers move in by late summer. In this chapter we deal with the more serious pest problems of home food growing and with ways to detect their signs.

Insects can be damaging or merely incidental. Diseases usually warrant treatment or removal of infected parts. Weeds are always there for you to pull because they are such keen competitors and sometimes harbor diseases and bugs. Animals are usually a transient worry, coming and going as something attracts them to your yard. Pest control (or perhaps management is a better word for we seldom control them) is a continual matter of recognition.

Pests can be managed using one or several techniques. Sanitation involves removing and destroying plants or plant parts that become infected. Prevention involves keeping pest problems away by eliminating weeds, providing the right environmental conditions for plants or by using chemicals to protect tender foliage. There are a lot of natural controls for the insects that eat your garden. Birds, predatory bugs, and parasites all do their bit and your efforts should assist theirs. Manually picking off injured parts, large insects, and in general keeping the garden clean will go a long way in keeping your plants healthy. Your pest management program will probably be a combination of methods which have proved suitable and effective for your own situation.

It is not entirely true that insects and diseases are less likely to attack vigorous and healthy plants. But it is certainly true that vigorous plants can survive pest attacks more successfully than can a sickly anemic one. The point is, if growing conditions are right for a plant it can withstand a few problems. If it is already under stress because of poor drainage, less than adequate sunlight or malnutrition, it may easily succumb to the added burden of bugs or disease spores.

Pesticide is a general term referring to chemicals that are lethal to specific pests. Included in this category are insecticides, fungicides, bactericides, herbicides, and rodenticides. Use of them can be a gardener's "ace in the hole" if other efforts to protect your crop fail. Pesticides will control a large number of pests but will not eradicate all of them. They are a tool to be used cautiously and only when needed to prevent or overcome destruction of your plants. Timely application is a must for these tools to work.

Insects are controlled or managed by use of insecticides, either chemical or botanical. Insecticides kill insects through ingestion, absorption, fumigation, or smothering. Many of them are specifically designed for a certain insect or for a certain type of insect.

Diseases are managed by fungicides and bactericides. Fungicides are used to protect plant leaves and stems from arriving disease spores. Bactericides are used to provide protection agianst bacterial particles once a bacterial infection has been sanitized. In extreme cases that involve soil diseases, fumigation with eradicants is employed.

Weeds are controlled by herbicides. Some herbicides are selective and will keep weeds from growing yet will not affect woody vines and trees if used properly. Some herbicides are non-selective and will kill or injure any plant they reach. Herbicides are difficult to use in vegetable gardens because of the varied plant population. Some vegetables are not susceptible to a specific weed killer while others curl up from fumes wafting by on a breeze.

Rodenticides are used to control small animals that might come to your garden. Mole baits and mouse poisons are the most commonly used materials in this category.

The single most important thing to insure your safety and that of others when using a pesticide is to study the pesticide label before each use and follow the directions explicitly.

Insects

Most garden insects are harmless or beneficial, only a small percentage develop into pests. A few chewed or curled leaves indicates normal insect activity. If invasions that call for use of an insecticide should develop, choose one registered for the crop needing protection and use it according to label directions.

The concept that calls for practical, common sense efforts in controlling insect pests is called *Integrated Pest Management* (IPM). IPM has been used by farmers for years and it is only recently that these traditional methods have been labelled "IPM." What the term refers to is the integration of cultural methods, natural predators, and/or pesticides to make a crop less attractive

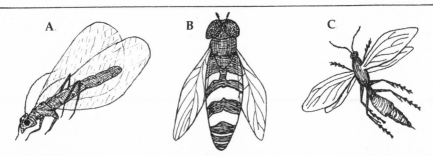

A. LACEWING: Greenish see-through wings and eggs stuck on inch-high filaments identify the presence of this aphid-eater.

B. SYRPHID FLY: Larva feed on aphids and mealybugs. The adult is identified by yellow or white bands across a black body.

C. WASP: Adults eat many garden insects; larvae of some are parasites in the bodies of insect hosts.

D. GROUND BEETLE: Adult beetles may eat slugs, certain caterpillars, root maggots, fly pupae and assist in decomposing organic matter.

E. SOW BUG: Rolls into a ball when disturbed. Its main diet is decaying organic matter.

F. MILLIPEDES: These many-legged animals curl into a spiral when disturbed. They may eat a few soil insects but basically they assist in the breakdown of organic matter.

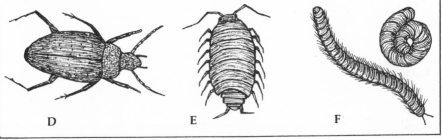

to injurious sorts of bugs. It relies upon identifying both beneficial and injurious insects and noting whether or not the "good guys" are present in sufficiently large populations to control the populations of harmful ones. If the balance between groups is proper, damage to plants will be minor. If, however, injurious insect populations are growing, the gardener must intercede with measures to restore a proper balance.

The most common beneficial insects found in Northwest gardens are ladybugs, lacewings, syrphid flies, wasps, and spiders. All are predators of crop eating bugs and so help to control them. Others are beneficial because they either eat other bugs or assist in the decomposition of organic matter in the soil. These beneficials include ground beetles, sow bugs, millipedes, and earthworms. (Some of these are not *true* insects but we will include them under a single heading of insects for practicality.)

Various classes of injurious insects not only have a unique way of feeding on plants but also prefer specific parts of plants. Some are chewers that devour leaves. Grasshoppers are the most notorious of this type and in a dry summer when native vegetation has died down they can easily chew a vegetable garden to the ground. Some are sucking types that extract the juices from plant leaves and stems. Aphids are the most common suckers. An overabundance of aphids on plum trees can curl the leaves so tightly that the tree has trouble setting and ripening fruit. Some insects are miners and bore their way into tree trunks or tunnel through foliage. A pernicious offender in this group is the peach root borer that tunnels its way into the crown of peach or apricot trees.

All insects develop through well defined stages from the time they hatch. This process of growth is called *metamorphosis*. A *complete metamorphosis* involves four stages from egg to larva (worm) to pupa (dormant cocoon) to adult bug. The other form of development is called *incomplete* (or *partial*) *metamorphosis* and proceeds from egg through several nymph stages to adult. During the nymph stages the bug looks like a miniature adult.

METAMORPHOSIS CYCLES:

Complete —

Egg	laid in various places singly, in clusters, or in masses.
Larva	worms, grubs, maggots, in all colors and sizes. Larva may eat leaves, mine into stems or bore into fruit. This is commonly the stage in which the insect does the greatest damage to plants.
Pupa	appear as lifeless, either hard-shelled case or cocoon housing the larva. At this stage the larva changes form dramatically, from a worm or grub to a winged adult.
Adult	main purpose in life is to reproduce and lay eggs for succeeding generation. Some adult forms are damaging and eat as voraciously as larval forms do — chewing holes in leaves, mining into trunks and stems or eating fruits. Some

common damaging adults are: asparagus beetle, cucumber beetle, root weevils, flea beetles. Some adult insects are not damaging as they confine their diet to nectar, pollen, or decaying organic matter. Included among the latter are: leafminers, cabbage and radish maggot adults, carrot rust fly, onion maggot adult, tomato fruitworm moth, cutworm moths, crown borer adults, codling moths, caterpillar moths and fruit flies.

EXAMPLE: COMPLETE METAMORPHOSIS
Tuber Flea Beetle

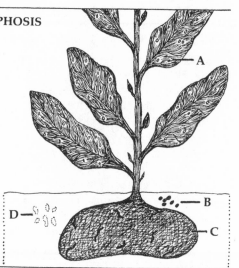

A. Adult emerges in May or June; eats small round holes in leaves; lays eggs.

B. Eggs are laid near the base of the plant and hatch in 5–8 days.

C. Larvae emerge and feed; tiny brown tunnels or trails in skin of potato evidence their feeding.

D. Pupa, dormant stage. In 10–14 days pupae will emerge as adults. Two or three generations usually develop in one season.

Incomplete or Partial —

Eggs   usually are less obvious and hard to find. Generally, egg masses will be tucked away at the base of leaves, under bark scales or buried in the soil. (Some, like aphids, may only have a single egg stage per year but are able to reproduce nymphs directly for the rest of the year. Others, like spider mites, keep a continual supply of eggs coming.)

Nymph   several nymphal stages occur. All stages are often found on a plant at the same time. At each stage the insect grows in size and adds more of the adult body parts. Nymphs are as hungry and voracious as adults.

Adult   the insect has reached full growth and is ready to reproduce and lay eggs. All adult insects characterized by incomplete metamorphosis are damaging to food crops in one way or another. Insects of this type include: aphids, spider mites, symphylans, scales, pear psylla, earwigs, slugs, grasshoppers, stinkbugs, leafhoppers, squash bugs, thrips, and spittlebugs.

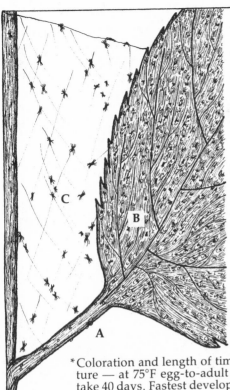

EXAMPLE: INCOMPLETE METAMORPHOSIS

Two-spotted Spider Mite

Adults are 1/50 of an inch or less.

Several generations develop per year and all stages may be present at one time.

*At 75°F:

A. Eggs laid over the leaf or stem and hatch in 2 or 3 days.

B. Nymphs
   1. Feed on leaves for a few hours to two days.
   2. Rest one or two days.
   3. Molt and feed on leaves.
   4. Rest

C. Adults
   5. Feed on leaves.
   6. Rest.
   7. Mate.
   8. Lay eggs.

*Coloration and length of time between stages varies with temperature — at 75°F egg-to-adult occurs within 5 days, at 55°F it would take 40 days. Fastest development occurs in hot dry weather.

The importance of metamorphosis to the gardener is in knowing when the best stages to destroy the pest occur and when controls will be needed and effective. Watch for signs that tell you of an insect's presence. Following are some of the common Northwest insect pests classed by their favored plant parts. Control measures should be utilized on the basis of actual, or understanding of potential, damage.

Mechanical methods include smashing, picking or washing off, or pruning out offending critters. Frequent close observation will give you ample time to destroy the early stages of infestations manually. However, if this method is to work for you, you must stay with it. We're talking about a daily effort to physically reduce bug populations. Pick off and remove early batches of worms, hose the foliage during dry weather to wash off mites and aphids, or cut away and destroy plant parts that are badly infested with bugs that got past you.

Biological methods are sort of "with Nature," but require some effort on your part to recognize the helpful insects and animals that eat destructive bugs and to give them a hand whenever possible.

INSECT DAMAGE KEY

Plant Part/ Symptom	Possible Insect	Food Crop Affected	Watch For:	Insect Stage/*Control			
				egg	larvae/nymph	pupae	adult
LEAVES **pieces missing, chewed from edge toward the midrib**	grasshopper	Vegetables	jumping insect		P-2, 4; M-1		P-2, 4; M-1
	slugs	Vegs. & Berries	slime trails	M-1	P-9; M-2		P-9; M-2
	asparagus beetle	Asparagus	red or brownish spotted beetles		P-2, 4, 6; M-1, 2		P-2, 4, 6; M-1, 2
	climbing cutworm	- All -	fat worms hiding in soil		P-3, 4; M-2, M-5		
	armyworms	Vegetables	striped brown worms near soil surface		P-3, 4; M-2 M-5		
	cabbage looper	Vegetables	white butterfly		P-6, 8, 10; M-2		
	tomato hornworm	Vegetables	3-4" long striped green worm w/black horn on rear		P-8; M-2		
	root weevil	Berries	circular leaf notches		P-2		P-2
	tent caterpillar	Tree Fruits	large webbed tents	P-13	P-1, 2, 3, 4 8; M-2, 4		
	currant worm	Berries	blossoms wilting, small, green spotted worm inside fruit		P-2; M-2		
hole chewed in middles	flea beetles	Vegetables	jumping, tiny dusty black bugs		P-3, 4, 6, 10		P-3, 4, 6, 10
	cucumber beetle	Vegetables	greenish bug with black spots				P-1, 2, 3, 4, 6; M-1, 2
	pear or cherry slug	Tree Fruits	exclamation point-shaped, wet looking larvae		P-1		
curling, sticky	aphid	- All -	colonies, usually on undersides or new growth	P-13	P-1, 2, 10; M-1, 3; B-1		P-1, 2, 10; M-1, 3; B-1
	whiteflies	Vegs. & Berries	flying dandruff		P-7, 10; M-3; B-1		P-7, 10
dry, dusty	spider mites	- All -	tiny webs, loss of plant color	P-11 P-13	P-1, 5; M-3		P-1, 5, 11, P-13; M-3
mined	beet leaf-miner	Vegetables	tunnel trail in leaf		M-4		
speckled	leafhopper	- All -	tiny white spots		P-2		P-2
	thrips	Vegetables	leaves (and flowers) dry and wither		P-1, 2, 6		P-1, 2, 6
cupped	spider mites	Berries	tiny spiders on underside	P-11 P-13	P-1, 5; M-3		P-1, 5; M-3
	spittlebug	Berries	froth		P-4, 10; M-3		P-4, 10
curled, webbed	leafrollers	Berries & Tree Fruits	leaves rolled and closed		P-4, 8; M-1, 4	M-2	
FRUITS holes	lygus bugs	Beans	match-head size hole in pods		P-2, 4		P-2, 4
	cucumber beetle	Tree Fruits	greenish bug with black spots				P-1, 2, 3, 4, 6; M-1, 2
deformed	redberry mite	caneberries	fruit hard, red, small	P-11 P-13	P-5, 11, 13		P-5, 11, 13
	thrip	Berries	fruit underdeveloped		P-1, 2, 6		P-1, 2, 6

*CONTROL: *P (pesticide)*

P-1	diazinon	P-5	kelthane	P-9	baits
P-2	malathion	P-6	rotenone	P-10	thiodan
P-3	methoxyclor	P-7	pyrethrum	P-11	dormant
P-4	sevin	P-8	bacillus thuringiensis		lime sulfur

INSECT DAMAGE KEY

Plant Part Symptom	Possible Insect	Food Crop Affected	Watch For:	egg	Insect Stage/*Control larvae/nymph	pupae	adult
FRUITS, cont'd. worms	corn earworm	corn	silks and kernels eaten		P-2, 4, 8; M-1	M-2	
	cherry fruit fly	cherry	one or two white worms		M-2		P-1, 2, 3, 4
	walnut husk fly	walnut	many worms		P-2		P-2
	apple maggot	apple	brown tunnels		M-2		P-1
	codling moth	apple, pear	tunnel into core	P-13	P-1, 3	M-2	P-1, 3
EDIBLE ROOTS holes	flea beetle	potato	tunnels just under skin of potato		P-3, 4, 6, 10		P-3, 4, 6, 10
	wireworm	Vegetables	tan, wiry, segmented worm		P-1		
	carrot rust fly	carrot, celery, parsley, parsnip	tiny holes in roots, soft rot likely		P-1; B-2		P-1
	radish maggot	radish, turnip	small, fat white worms		P-1; M-5		P-1
TOP SIGNS that tell of something working on the roots — plants weak or stunted	symphylans	Veg. & Berries	pull and check for stubby roots		P-1, 12		P-1, 12
	nematodes	- All -	knobby and dead roots		P-12; B-2		P-12; B-2
	cabbage maggot	Vegetables	holes chewed in main roots		P-1; M-5		P-1
	root aphids	Tree Fruits	gray, wooly clusters near roots		P-1, 10; M-2		P-1, 10; M-2
	cucumber beetles	Vegetables	holes chewed in main roots (similar to cabbage maggot damage)		M-1, 2		P-1, 2, 3, 4, 6
new plants die	cutworms	Vegetables	curled worms in soil surface		P-3, 4; M-1, 2, 5	M-2	
	cabbage maggot	Vegetables	small curled worms near dead stems		P-1; M-5		
	millipedes	Vegs. & Berries	roots eaten		P-1, 4, 9		P-1, 4, 9
	symphylans	Vegs. & Berries	roots stubbed		P-1, 12		P-1, 12
	borers	Tree Fruits	sawdust from holes in crown area		P-1, 4, 10; M-2, 4	M-2	
old plants die	crown borer	Caneberries	dying canes		P-1; M-4	M-2	
	prune root borer	Tree Fruits	sawdust and gum from holes in crown		P-10; M-2	M-2	
	cane borer	Caneberries	upper parts of canes die		M-4	M-2	
	root weevil	Berries	crown eaten away		P-2		P-2
	shothole borer	Tree Fruits	many small round holes drilled in trunk				P-10
seeds don't come up	seed corn maggot	Vegetables	hollowed seed shells		P-1		
	symphylans	Vegetables	hollowed seed shells		P-1, 12		P-1, 12
	millipedes	Vegetables	seeds hollow & rotten		P-1, 4, 9		P-1, 4, 9

P-12 vapam fumigation	*M (manual)*	M-5 collars
P-13 dormant oil spray	M-1 smashing	
	M-2 removing	*B (biological)*
	M-3 washing off	B-1 predatory insects
	M-4 pruning out	B-2 soil rotation

Watch for ladybug or lacewing egg clusters as welcome additions to your garden insect populations. Ladybug eggs are orange and laid in upright clusters. Lacewing eggs are on slender filaments. Both beneficials produce several generations per year; egg clusters can be found on leaves and stems.

Every garden has a few natural predators that help much more than you realize. They should be encouraged. However, ladybugs and other beneficial sorts will not stay around if their food source is destroyed. Therefore, dependence on purely biological methods demands that you accept the continuing presence of the bad sorts that serve as food for the good guys.

Praying mantids do not survive in our climate, so purchased egg masses will hatch long before their natural prey emerge from winter hibernation. Don't waste your money on this predator. Know that biological methods are under investigation, but know also that there are shortcomings involved when one depends wholly on natural predation. Until much more is known about biological controls, you may have to use insecticides from time to time.

Insecticides are formulated from plants that are deadly to certain insects or are chemically synthesized to affect a certain type or group of insects. Not just any insecticide will control or affect every pest, so you need to first identify that you have an insect problem and then identify the insect which is troubling your plants before selecting an insecticide. If you cannot identify the insect from the symptoms listed above, take it intact to your nearest garden shop or to your local Extension office or Experiment station. If an insecticide is called for, look through those available to home gardeners to learn if your particular pest is included on one of the labels. Also check if the chemical is okay to use on the crop you're trying to protect. If everything matches, read the label further to see how it can be safely and effectively used.

Some of the commonly used botanical insecticides include rotenone, Pyrethrum, and Bacillus thuringiensis. Each of them are rather specific for the types of insects which they will control.

The common chemical types include diazinon, malathion, Sevin, methoxyclor, Kelthane, and Thiodan. Each serves a different function, has a different period of effectiveness, and residual effect or toxicity. Sevin is a powerful weapon against invading hordes of worms, beetles and other assorted pests. However, because of its residual and somewhat slow acting qualities, Sevin is also deadly to bees. Avoid using Sevin when and where bees are active. Kelthane is actually a miticide, specific against mites. Since mites have fast population turnover they may develop a resistance to other

INSECTICIDES GENERAL SUMMARY

Name	Source1	Action2	Vegetables*	Small Fruits	Tree Fruits
Bacillus thuringiensis	A	I	caterpillars, imported cabbageworm, leaf miners, loopers, tomato hornworm.	leafrollers, loopers, root weevils, tent caterpillar.	fall webworm, filbert leaf-roller, tent caterpillar
diazinon	C	C & I	aphids, armyworms, cabbage flea beetle, corn earworm, cucumber beetles, cutworms, garden symphylan (ltd), onion & cabbage maggot, thrips, wireworms.	aphids, crown-borer, leafrollers, strawberry crown moth, thrips, Western raspberry fruitworm.	aphids, catfacing insects, codling moth, grape mealybug, leaf-rollers, peach twig borer, pear slug, scale insects, Western cherry fruit fly.
Kelthane	C	C & I	spider mites.	cyclamen mite, dryberry mite, redberry mite, spider mite, twospotted spider mite.	rust mite.
malathion	C	C & I	aphids, armyworms, asparagus beetle, cabbage maggot, corn earworm, cucumber beetles, grasshoppers, flea beetles, imported cabbageworm, leaf hoppers, loopers, spider mites, thrips.	aphids, cherry fruitworm, grape leafhopper & mealybug, imported currant worm, leafrollers, obscure root weevil, thrips, twospotted spider mite.	aphids, apple mealybug, fruit-tree leafroller, lecanium and San Jose scales, walnut husk fly.
methoxyclor	C	C & I	armyworms, asparagus beetle, corn earworm, cucumber beetles, cutworms, flea beetles, pea weevil.	currant fruit fly, leafrollers, Meadow spittlebug, tent caterpillar.	tent cater-pillar, Western cherry fruit fly.
Pyrethrum	B	C	aphids, beetles, cabbage loopers, caterpillars, corn earworm, leafhoppers.	grapes: leafhoppers and thrips.	lygus bugs on peach.
rotenone	B	I	asparagus beetle, cabbage worm & looper, Colorado potato beetle, cucumber beetle, flea beetles, pea weevil.	Western raspberry fruitworm	
Sevin (carbaryl)	C	C & I	aphids, armyworms, asparagus beetle, corn earworm, cucumber beetles, cutworms, Colorado potato beetle, flea beetles, grasshoppers, imported cabbage worm, loopers, lygus bugs, squash bug, tomato hornworm, tuber flea beetle.	grasshoppers, leafrollers, spittlebug, straw-berry aphid.	alfalfa looper, codling moth, filbertworm, leafrollers, oriental fruit moth, peach twig borer, blister & rust mites of pear, tent caterpillars, Western spotted cucumber beetle.
Thiodan	C	C & I	aphids, caterpillars, Colorado potato beetle, cucumber beetle, cutworms, imported cabbageworm, squash bug, tomato hornworm, tuber flea beetle, whiteflies.	cyclamen mite, spittlebug, straw-berry aphid, symphylans (pre-dip for straw-berry plants).	aphids, borers, catfacing insects (incl. lygus & stink bugs), cut-worms, filbert aphid & bud mite, leafhoppers, leaf rollers, peach twig borer, pear leaf blister mite, pear psylla, rust mites.

1Source: A — bacterial
        B — botanical
        C — chemical

2Works through:
    C — contact
    I — ingestion

*cantaloupes, muskmelons, and watermelons may be injured by insecticides. To reduce this possibility apply insecticides when foliage is dry.

This chart gives general recommendations for the use of insecticides; information derived from "Pacific Northwest Insect Handbook," Extension services of OSU, WSU, and University of Idaho, February, 1981. For specific application be sure to read and follow label directions.

insecticides. If mites are a problem, alternate Kelthane with your regular insecticide treatment.

Successful insect management is primarily dependent on preventing excesses, and prevention is a direct result of the timing and use of effective control measures. Experience in dealing with bugs that like Northwest gardens will allow you to develop a balance between all methods of insect prevention and cure — biological, manual, chemical, and cultural. This balance you develop is integrated pest management.

Diseases

The Northwest's plentiful rain, abundant and diverse plant life, and moderate temperatures provide ideal conditions for the development of numerous plant diseases. A disease is defined as an infection by parasitic fungi, bacteria, or virus that interferes with the plant's ability to develop normally. Severity and final effect of infection is directly related to climatic conditions. A warm, humid spring increases the chances of blights ravaging the vegetable row or wiping out a treeful of blooms. Plants growing in poorly drained soil, stagnant air, or shady spots in the microclimate provide the places where disease most often strikes. Disease spreads rapidly during wet, warm, and still air periods but slowly during dry and hot spells.

Most diseases are not actually controlled. Instead we try to prevent them from starting, but if unsuccessful, prevent them from spreading. In the food crop chapters we suggest using plant varieties sold as "resistant" to certain diseases. For plants easily affected by virus we support buying berries and fruit trees certified as "virus-free." Preventing verticillium wilt, fusarium wilt or some of the more serious virus diseases is dependent upon buying clean plants to start with. Prevention of bacterial or fungus disorders is largely a matter of providing the right environmental conditions and maintaining sound gardening practices.

Sanitation is basic to a disease prevention program. Keeping the garden free of infected, dead and dying vegetation reduces both the likelihood and subsequent spread of disease. Good practice dictates burning or otherwise destroying infected plant parts. Do not compost this material. Compost piles seldom heat up enough to destroy fungus spores or bacteria particles. If you spread compost made from diseased plants you'll probably also be spreading disease.

Pruning is a major part of a sanitation program. Pruning to remove infected plant parts or improve air circulation will prevent disease organisms from infecting healthy plants. Certain bacterial diseases of stone fruit trees must be surgically removed by cutting out infections in the trunks or main limbs.

Rotation planting short-circuits buildup of soil pathogens that attack the roots of some vegetables and fruits. A basic element of a disease control program involves a multi-year plan for the vegetable garden so that the same plants are not located in the same soil year after year. Rotation is mostly for annual vegetable crops but it also should be considered when replacing fruit trees or planting berry crops.

Fungus Diseases:

The most common plant diseases in the Northwest stem from fungi that attack and infect new leaves and shoots, fruits, trunks, and roots. Fungi are parasitic plants that reproduce by *sporulation* or the production of spores. Spores are reproductive, usually single-celled, bodies. The entire process of sporulation is analogous to seed production in plants. A crop of spores can be identified as black, brown, white, yellow or red masses of mold on dying plant tissues. Spores are carried by wind, by water splashing from one leaf to another, on bugs or other animals. When the spore arrives at a receptive site, it germinates and grows inside its plant host robbing the plant of nutrients. This is the point at which symptoms begin showing. Leaves become spotted, new shoots wilt, fruit softens and rots, or roots turn from white to brown and show widespread patches of dead cells. Sporulation and spread of infection will continue as long as climatic conditions are favorable, unless the gardener intercedes.

Sanitation and rotation seldom are completely successful in keeping plants free of fungus diseases. Another tool to be used along with these efforts is a class of chemicals called fungicides. Fungicides are used as dusts or sprays to keep spores from infecting new plant tissues. Integrated into a sanitation and rotation program, the proper use of fungicides can be a final line of defense against fungus diseases. No chemical will eradicate a fungal infection yet it will prevent continuing infections.

Fungicides establish a protective barrier between arriving spores and the plant's surface. The powdery mildew infection of grape leaves, for example, cannot be reversed but dusting sulfur will help protect new, unblemished leaves and berries. The club root fungus in affected cabbage roots cannot be eradicated but fungicide applied to the planting row will help protect the roots of newly planted cabbages or related vegetables.

The key in using fungicides to control disease in the garden is to apply the protective barrier before the disease has invaded the plant's tissues. This means that the fungicide must be used regularly during times when climatic conditions (temperature, moisture) are right for the disease to infect. It would be nice to apply a fungicide in early spring and have full season control, but too many things work against this fantasy. No fungicide remains effective more than several weeks once it is sprayed or dusted onto a plant even if not diluted or washed away by rain or irrigation. Furthermore plants grow, consequently new tissue not protected by the last fungicide application is exposed.

The best way to deal with fungus disease is to treat disease susceptible plants on a regular basis. Begin when new plant tissues are developing and

STAGES OF LEAF GROWTH

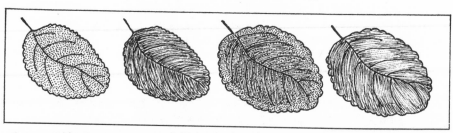

when mild temperatures and high humidity favor the diseases that like the particular plant you are trying to grow. Continue treatments until hot, dry weather. Spray schedules for all of the tree fruits and berry crops grown in the Northwest are available from Extension offices. Chapter five has specific suggestions for protecting vegetables.

There are two fungus diseases which attack nearly every plant if environmental conditions are right. To help you identify them watch for:

BOTRYTIS (gray mold)

*Symptoms: new leaves and shoots die, sometimes turn black; dead tissue is covered with gray mold.
*Mostly On: new, tender shoots and ripening berries.
*When: periods of mild temperature and high humidity.
*What to Do: cut away or pick off affected parts, provide better air circulation, use fungicide.

POWDERY MILDEW

*Symptoms: white, powdery spots on shoots, or leaves coated white; new shoots deformed, twisted; fruits cracked and dry (grapes).
*Mostly On: fruit trees, grapes, squash, berries.
*When: periods of warm temperatures and high humidity.
*What to Do: prune away infected pats, increase air circulation, use sulfur dusts or sprays.

The timing of fungicide applications is generally more significant than the particular chemical that is used, but some fungicides have been developed which are particularly effective in specific situations. We list here some currently available to home gardeners:

1. Terraclor and captan — soil fungicides. Terraclor worked into the soil before planting will help ward off soil diseases that destroy roots of potatoes, tomatoes, and peppers. Potato seed pieces dusted with captan are protected against decay. Seed decay protection can also be given corn and bean seeds by dusting with captan just prior to planting.

2. Vapam and formaldehyde — soil fumigants. Vapam is used primarily to reduce soil insect populations (see discussion in *Soil*) but it is also useful in controlling diseases. Formaldehyde is used to disinfect small quantities of soil for starting seedlings. To make your own drench, mix one cup of

commercial formaldehyde (formalin) with three gallons of water. Place a 4" layer of soil in a box or pan and sprinkle one gallon of this mixture per square foot of soil. Cover for 48 hours. Remove the cover and allow to air for several days. Do not plant seeds in the treated soil until all traces of odor are gone.

3. Captan, benomyl, ferbam, Zineb, maneb and copper — foliage sprays. Captan, copper, and ferbam are preferred for use on fruit trees and berries. Zineb, maneb, and benomyl are generally used for vegetable protection. All are used to control many of the blights, molds, and leaf spots. Fungicides for home garden use are accompanied by label instructions; follow them carefully for control in your specific situation. 4. Liquid lime

4. Liquid lime sulfur, fixed copper and Bordeaux mixes — dormant sprays. During dormancy fruit trees and berry plants can be sprayed with high concentrations of any of these fungicides without damage to the plants. High concentrations give longer lasting protection to the buds and twigs, help control some overwintering bugs, and keeps moss or lichens from taking over. One caution, do not use lime sulfur on apricot trees. Dormant sprays should be applied to cover all buds, twigs and limbs. Spray when at least three hours of dry weather will follow application.

5. Sulfur and Karathane — specifically effective in controlling powdery mildew. Either should be used as needed to prevent loss of plants or fruits to powdery mildew.

BORDEAUX

Bordeaux (bore-dough) is one of the oldest chemical mixtures used to control fungus and bacterial diseases. It is made by combining copper sulfate (bluestone or blue vitriol) and hydrated lime in water.

Bordeaux formulas are given by three hyphenated numbers, e.g. 8-8-100 or 6-12-100. The first number refers to pounds of copper sulfate. The second number refers to pounds of hydrated lime and the last number refers to gallons of water.

The formula of this mixture varies and is the result of research on a disease of a specific crop. For example:

6-3-100	is recommended for filbert bacterial blight;
6-6-100	is recommended for strawberry leaf spot;
6-12-100	is recommended for pepper leaf spot;
8-8-100	is recommended for peach coryneum blight;
12-12-100	is recommended for cherry bacterial canker.

Freshly mixed Bordeaux is one of the best disease prevention materials available, but because of the inconvenience of mixing, most gardeners prefer to use commercially available fungicides. If you want to try this compound, we recommend making your own. To mix small amounts for example, using powdered copper sulfate and good quality hydrated lime (calcium hydroxide), a 1-1-100 formula converts to 1/3 tablespoon copper sulfate, 1 tablespoon hydrated lime, and 1 gallon of water. An 8-8-100 formula converts to two and 2/3 tablespoons copper, 8 tablespoons hydrated lime, and 1 gallon of water, etc.

For a one gallon mix, stir the copper sulfate in ½ gallon water. Stir the hydrated lime in a separate ½ gallon of water. When the copper sulfate is dissolved, and while the lime is still in suspension, pour the two together, stir thoroughly, and use immediately.

FUNGICIDES GENERAL SUMMARY

Name	Available In:	Veg.	Small Fruit	Tree Fruit	Comments:
benomyl	50% wettable powder, emulsion concentrate	X	X	X	foliage spray; in vegetables it reduces incidence of some molds, powdery mildew, fusarium wilt, root rot; may control cane canker in blueberries; used to control scab and brown rot in tree fruits.
captan	wettable powders, dusts, liquid		X	X	foliage spray; reduces leaf and cane spots, cankers and blights.
		X	X	X	soil or seed treatment; reduces fungus.
ferbam	76% & 95% wettable powder, dusts		X	X	foliage spray; controls several rusts and blights.
formaldehyde	liquid	X	X	X	soil treatment; decreases weeds, soil insects, and incidence of soil diseases; primary use — potting soil.
Fixed Copper	insoluble; water suspensions and dusts	X	X	X	foliage spray; controls some vegetable blights; part of control on cane rust and several canker disorders on fruit plants.
Karathane	wettable powder, emulsion concentrate	X	X	X	foliage spray; controls powdery mildew.
lime sulfur	liquid		X	(X)	dormant spray; reduces leaf and cane spot, powdery mildew, rust, scab. Not for use on apricot trees.
maneb	wettable powder, dust, liquid	X			foliage spray; controls bean rust, some blights, downy mildew on brassicas.
sulfur	dust, wettable powder	X	X	X	foliage spray; reduces incidence of powdery mildew; rust on beans; blossom blight on cherries.
Terraclor	wettable powder, dust, emulsion	X	X	X	soil treatment; decreases incidence of fungus such as club root.
Vapam	liquid	X	X	X	soil treatment; primarily used to reduce soil insect populations; also reduces soil fungus incidence and weeds.
Zineb	wettable powder, dusts	X			foliage spray; reduces downy mildew incidence, leaf spot and blight.

This chart gives general fungicide uses; information derived from ''Pacific Northwest Plant Disease Control Handbook,'' Extension Services of OSU, WSU, and University of Idaho, March, 1981. For specific application be sure to read and follow label directions and spray schedules.

Bacterial Disease

Bacterial diseases are the second most common type of disease in Northwest gardens. They are usually introduced to gardens by bringing in infected plants or plant parts. The original infection spreads to other plants by splashing water or it can be carried on gardening tools.

Bacterium enters a plant's system through natural openings in the plant's system (such as stoma) or through wounds (caused by insects, pruning, cat scratches, etc.). Once inside, the bacteria multiplies by simple division and causes soft, rotting areas in the plant's tissues. As the bacterial population grows, pressure forces some of the bacteria out of the plant and gives the characteristic oozing symptom of a bacterial infection.

Vegetables that are subject to bacterial infection include beans, cabbage, corn, lettuce, potato, and rhubarb. Other types of vegetables may also succumb to bacterial infection and in all cases, should you discover an oozing infection, pull and destroy the vegetable plants. On woody plants such as caneberries and tree fruits, prune away infected plant parts and burn the prunings. It is also critical to disinfect gardening or pruning tools that have contacted the bacteria. Avoid transferring the disease to other plants by using denatured alcohol to disinfect tools.

Chemical controls for bacterial disease must follow the same rules as for fungus diseases. Bactericides are only useful in preventing infection and are of no value in curing the problem. A preventative copper spray for stone fruit trees and blackberries should be made in the fall to prevent infection from several bacterial diseases.

The most effective way to prevent the introduction of bacterial diseases to your garden is to buy healthy plants from reputable dealers. When buying woody plants try to find specimens that are certified disease-free. Certification comes from state or federal inspection services to safeguard production of fruit and berry plants.

Virus Diseases:

The third type of disease that can seriously affect food crops grown in the Northwest is caused by viruses. Viruses are tiny bits of ribonucleoprotein, which means that they exist somewhere between a living cell (fungus) and non-living organic molecule (sugar). A virus infection spreads rather quickly throughout the entire plant as it is carried in the plant's own vascular system.

Viruses do not cause dead tissues like fungi, nor oozing spots like bacteria. Virus can cause plants to become deformed (e.g. peas with Enation Mosaic), discolored (e.g. squash with Aster Yellows), stunted (e.g. corn with Maize Dwarf Mosaic), or may prevent fruit formation (e.g. cherry with Sour Cherry Yellows). These are only a few of the abnormalities caused by the more than fifty different virus strains that affect food crops in our area.

Prevention is the only sure control against virus infection. Here are several gardening practices to assist in prevention. First of all, buy fruit trees and berry plants that are certified virus free whenever possible. Avoid bringing obviously abnormal plants to your garden.

Second, if virus symptoms are found on plants in your vegetable or fruit planting, get rid of the infected plants immediately. An infected plant serves as a source for virus particles that can then be spread to other plants by sucking insects, such as aphids and leafhoppers, or inadvertently by you.

Finally control the pests that carry the virus. Many viruses of vegetable plants reside in the weeds that grow nearby. Pigweed, Lamb's Quarters, and clover are all capable of harboring a virus while not displaying problems in growth. This is one reason we continually advocate weed control in the garden. The main insect carriers of virus particles are aphids and leafhoppers. Control them by chemical or biological means.

Most plant diseases can be checked by cultural practices alone; thinning, pruning, raking and burning diseased leaves, regulating fertilizer and water, and by rotating planting areas. Some diseases though can only be restrained by use of chemical tools.

Plant diseases are difficult to organize for easy identification. Symptoms of infection may be nearly identical to stress caused by other factors such as weather, insects, or chemical damage. As a general guide to help you wend your way through the possible fungus, bacterial or virus intruders to your garden, the following "Plant Disease Key" will give you a place to start.

PLANT DISEASE KEY

Plant Part/Effect	Name	Plants	Cause	*Control	Comments
SEEDLINGS					
seeds do not sprout	seed decay	vegetables	fungus	1, 2	can be caused by wet soil
seedlings sprout and topple over	damping off	vegetables	fungus	2	warm, damp conditions favor development
ROOTS					
roots brown, soft & rotten	root rot	all	fungus	3	poor drainage promotes
crowns decay	soft rot	rhubarb	bacteria	4	first signs are yellowing leaves and collapsed stems
roots with brown core, outer parts soft	red stele	strawberry	fungus	3, 4	infected plants appear undernourished, anemic
FOLIAGE					
dead spots	leaf spot	all	fungus	6	spots may be brown, yellow, red
smokey and puckered spots	scab	apple, pear	fungus	6a-b-c, 6f	begin spraying when new leaves first appear in spring
leaves & shoots wither, moldy	botrytis	all	fungus	5, 6a, 6f	common in spring on new growth
white, powdery coating on leaves	powdery mildew	all	fungus	6b, 6f, 8, 9	air circulation is needed

Plant Part/Effect	Name	Plants	Cause	*Control	Comments
yellow, powdery growth	rust	all	fungus	7, 8	mostly on blackberries
leaves streaked, discolored	virus	all	virus	4	spread by insects & people
leaves fleshy, deformed, colorful	leaf curl	peach	fungus	7, 5	dormant sprays are the key to control
FLOWERS blossoms brown, appear watersoaked	botrytis	blueberry	fungus	6a, 6f, 9	continue sprays if wet weather prevails
blossom clusters killed, covered with mold	brown rot	stone fruits	fungus	6a, 6c, 6f, 8, 9	in severe cases, entire twigs may be killed
FRUIT brown, corky, dark margined spots on skin	scab	apple, pear	fungus	6a-b-c, 6f	badly scabbed fruit will crack
corky, rough spots	scab	potato	fungus	1, 4	russet varieties have some resistance
depressed spots with brownish tissue below	bitter pit	apple	physio-logic	10	problem results from calcium deficiency in fruit
numerous, slightly sunken reddish spots	coryneum blight	peach, apricot	fungus,	6a, 6c, 6e	disease survives on infected twigs
round, sunken spots, turning black	anthracnose	pepper, eggplant	fungus	6c-d	fungus survives in crop debris
black, slimy spots, may affect entire fruit	walnut blight	walnut	bacteria	6e	sprays must begin before blossoming & continue until dry weather
STEMS & BRANCHES dry, sore, cracked areas, may encircle entire limb	canker	tree fruits	fungus	5, 7	prune and burn infected limbs
wet, sore, cracked areas, gum exuding	bacterial canker	stone fruits	bacteria	5, 6e, 7	prevalent on cherry trees
small, round, tan to purple slightly sunken spots	coryneum blight	peach, apricot	fungus	6a, 6c, 6e	infection occurs quickly during wetter than normal spring weather
brown, dead spots develop on canes	cane blight	caneberries	fungus	5, 7	frost injury may also cause this symptom
buds shrivel and die, surrounding tissue turns brown and dies	spur blight	caneberries	fungus	6a, 7	Willamette red raspberry is most susceptible
warty growths on or around stems	cane gall	caneberries	bacteria	4, 5	bacteria can be transferred from plant to plant on pruning tools

*Control:
1. dust seeds with Captan fungicide.
2. dry the environment, replant with treated seed.
3. provide better drainage.
4. replant with healthy or certified plants.
5. surgically remove diseased parts.

6. spray new foliage (any unless specified**)
   a. Captan
   b. Wettable Sulfur
   c. Ziram
   d. Zineb
   e. Copper
   f. Benomyl

7. dormant spray with lime sulfur or copper.
8. dust with sulfur.
9. provide better air circulation.
10. not controllable with fungicides, see information in Chapter 7.

**Always check the labels of pesticides to make sure the plant you plan to treat and the problem you are trying to control are listed for that product. Follow all safety precautions.

Weeds

Insects wander into the garden, diseases may waft in, but weeds will always be there. Weeds are the native plants of Northwest gardens and are doing their best to reestablish their territory. Weeds are a never ending problem — sprouting where they are least wanted and resisting every control effort with the kind of tenacity you would like to see in the food crops you are growing.

Weeds compete for light, air, water and space with our tender plants and if all this is not enough they also harbor insect pests, fungi, and viruses. If not controlled, they use much of the water and fertilizer destined for the food crops. They furnish a haven for aphids, mites and other insects that feed on them until something more interesting comes along, like your vegetables. Many weeds found around the garden are hosts for virus diseases that are then spread by sucking insects moving from weeds to your fruits or vegetables.

Weeds are categorized by their life cycle as annuals, biennials or perennials. Most garden weeds are summer annuals, germinating along with the radishes and lettuce in the spring, living through summer, and going to seed and dying in the fall. This is the easiest type to control but even annuals require constant attention. Use a hoe, a mulch, or some of the herbicides that are safe in the garden to get rid of them. The hoe is best. Annual weed seeds may remain in the soil for years waiting for the right moisture, temperature, and light conditions to sprout. This is why you can find a new crop of annual weeds a day or two after you have completely cleaned the garden by hoe or pulling. A weekly effort will keep most of the annual weed threats down.

Mulches are effective in smothering young annual weed seedlings. They can be organic (lawn clippings, barkdust, sawdust, etc.) or sheets of newspaper or black polyethylene plastic sheeting. The black plastic will also work to smother some perennial weeds. Whichever material fits your situation will work if you get the mulch on early.

Herbicides are available to home gardeners but make sure you have checked them out completely to avoid damaging your planted crops. Those available to home gardeners are the pre-emergent types which means they must be applied before the weeds come up. Generally they cannot safely be used in vegetable rows until the planted crop is up and growing.

In perennial food crops such as berries and tree fruits, the hoe and mulch are still the safest control measures. However, there are several stronger herbicides that can assist your fight against annual weeds. Simazine and Dacthal can be used around most perennial fruit crops. Casoron can be used around woody vine crops and tree fruits except apricots. Always check the label instructions before purchasing to make sure the material can safely be used on or near your crops.

Annual weeds come in two types in the Northwest, summer annuals and winter annuals. Winter annuals sprout in the fall and fill the dormant

COMMON ANNUAL WEEDS — REPRODUCE BY SEED

Annual Bluegrass, *Poa annua*. Appears in cool, moist weather, any open area. 2" height.

Bittercress, *Cardamine oligosperma*. Appears in late winter in shady, moist places. 6" height.

Chickweed, *Stellaria media*. Appears in cool, moist weather, any open area. Useful as winter mulch mat, leaves useful as salad (rich in iron). 18" stem length.

Clover, Small Hop, *Trifolium dubium*. Appears in early summer and fall, any open area. 2–10" height.

Lamb's Quarters, *Chenopodium album*. Appears in early summer, garden areas. Leaves edible source of vitamins C and A. 1–4' height.

Mustard, Yellow, *Brassica campestris*. Appears in late winter, garden areas. Ancestor of the rutabaga. 6" to 6' height.

Pigweed, *Amaranthus retroflexus*. Appears in early summer, any open area. Leaves and stems can be cooked like spinach. 18" height.

Purslane, *Portulaca oleracea*. Appears in hot, dry weather, any open area. Leaves and stems can be used in salad. 10" stem length.

garden or compete for nutrients with your winter garden. Winter annuals are not entirely offensive for they may serve useful purposes. Chickweed and annual bluegrass are the two main winter annuals; as a soil cover they help prevent erosion and compaction from winter rains. Chickweed can also be used as a winter cover crop and turned under in late winter to supply additional organic matter. This complacent approach must also recognize that these permissable winter annuals also leave their seeds for germination with the next cool, moist season.

Our next category is the biennial weeds. These grow one year into a small plant and store reserves in fleshy roots. The following year they bloom and set seed. The false dandelion is an example, as are tansy ragwort and wild carrot. To eradicate these plants you must pull them out at the roots as they resprout so quickly when you pull or hoe off the tops that your efforts may be cancelled in a day or two. Biennials are treated as perennials when chemical controls are used.

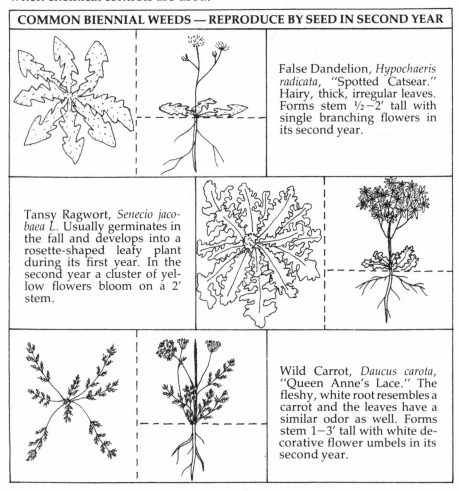

COMMON BIENNIAL WEEDS — REPRODUCE BY SEED IN SECOND YEAR

False Dandelion, *Hypochaeris radicata*, "Spotted Catsear." Hairy, thick, irregular leaves. Forms stem ½–2' tall with single branching flowers in its second year.

Tansy Ragwort, *Senecio jacobaea L.* Usually germinates in the fall and develops into a rosette-shaped leafy plant during its first year. In the second year a cluster of yellow flowers bloom on a 2' stem.

Wild Carrot, *Daucus carota*, "Queen Anne's Lace." The fleshy, white root resembles a carrot and the leaves have a similar odor as well. Forms stem 1–3' tall with white decorative flower umbels in its second year.

PERENNIAL INVASIVE WEEDS

Bindweed, *Convolvulus arvensis* ("wild morning glory"). Appears in summer, gardens and orchards. Roots may penetrate 20' deep, seeds remain viable for 30 years or more. Reproduces by seed and creeping root system. Stems 1'–4' long.

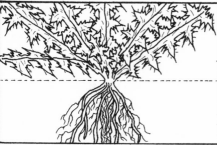

Canada Thistle, *Cirsium arvense.* Appears in early spring, gardens, berry plantings, and orchards. Spreads by rhizomes, roots, and seeds. 2'–5' height.

Dandelion, *Taraxacum officinale.* Appears in any open area. Leaves useful for spring salads, flowers and roots also edible. Spreads by seeds, sprouts and root parts. 3–8" height.

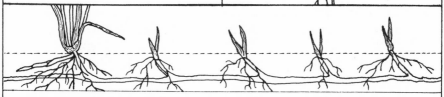

Quackgrass, *Agropyron repens.* Appears year 'round in areas with more than 12" rainfall, or creek bottoms. Spreads by rootstock and seed. 1½'–3' tall.

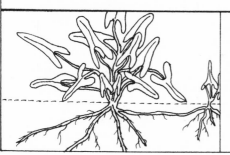

Sheep Sorrel, *Rumex acetosella.* Appears year 'round, especially in berry plantings. Leaves can be eaten raw or cooked. Spreads by rootstock and seed. 4" height.

Perennial weeds are by far the toughest to handle in the garden. They have long, invasive roots that are capable of sprouting at any point. Hoeing doesn't dissuade them and seems to stimulate the roots to grow another though larger stalk and leaves. Pulling is only partially effective because it is difficult if not impossible to remove all of the root parts. Often the effect of pulling is the same as hoeing — two regrow where one was pulled. Pulling and hoeing, if done frequently, may eventually weaken the weed to the point that it isn't a serious competitor, but the strategy will seldom annihilate a tenacious perennial.

Perennials should be dealt with before the garden is planted. Quackgrass, thistles and wild morning glory are the most common perennial weeds infesting Northwest gardens. If you can afford a season of summer fallowing devoted to perpetual plowing or rototilling, most of the perennial roots will be killed. However, even such a concentrated summer fallow regimen will see a few perennials survive and return.

Several foliar absorbent systemic herbicides are effective in controlling perennial weeds because they kill the root system. The leaves are able to absorb this type of chemical and pass it directly to the roots. The roots die and the plant is eradicated. Systemic herbicides are not selective, so great care must be taken to apply them only to the weed, carefully avoiding the foliage, stems or roots of desirable plants. One of the best herbicides of this type is glyphosate. Glyphosate is designed to be applied to the leaves of mature perennial plants. A single application properly carried out will result in dead morning glory, quackgrass or thistles in about two weeks. Glyphosate can be applied by directed sprays or rubbed on weed leaves with a rag or sponge. As with all pesticides, keep the chemical off of yourself.

Brushy weeds are common in Northwest gardens. The main offender is the wild blackberry that invades whenever it gets a chance. Roots extend into the garden from nearby wild patches or birds and other animals carry in seeds. However the plant starts, the young seedling quickly grows into a multistemmed monster that can take over the area. Chop them out, pull out the roots, and watch for regrowth. One way to fight an established patch is to cut the canes back to the ground and paint the cut stubs with a hormone weed or brush killer such as 2,4-D. Watch for new shoots and treat the same way. Glyphosate is also effective on wild blackberries. To get your money's worth and to insure a high degree of success, don't apply glyphosate to the foliage until the plant has matured in late summer. At that time everything in the plant is being carried down for winter storage in the roots and your glyphosate moves downward with ease. Give the plant a couple of weeks to die. Leave the foliage and stems intact until you see the effect of your treatment. Blackberries are tough; you may have to do a repeat performance.

Each type of food crop demands its own particular solution to weed problems. Recommendations for chemicals must be general, because plants vary so much in their tolerance to specific herbicides. For example, the treatment for perennial weeds around fruit trees will wipe out most of the vegetables in your garden. Here are some tips for weed control in various situations:

1. **In the vegetable garden —**
   a. for annual weeds; hoe, use mulches, pull. Herbicides useful in special situations include Dacthal, chloramben (Amiben), and Treflan.
   b. for biennial and perennial weeds; pull, hoe, cover with plastic film mulch. Spot treat individual weeds with foliar absorbed herbicides such as glyphosate that leave little or no residues in the soil.
   c. for brush; pull, cut, dig out the roots.

2. **In the strawberry row —**
   a. for annual weeds; pull to clean out the weed invaders then treat with simazine or Dacthal to keep new seedlings from returning.
   b. for biennial and perennial weeds; these are the tough ones in strawberry plantings and for the most part you must rely on pulling because there are no perennial weed killers that won't also damage your strawberry plants. If feasible and possible, rub glyphosate on the leaves of perennials, keeping it off of the leaves of the berries.

3. **In the caneberries and blueberries and around fruit trees —**
   a. for annual weeds — hoe, pull and use Casoron, simazine, or Dacthal after the weeds have been cleaned out. Mulches will be effective around blueberries and in the fruit tree planting. The suggested herbicides will provide control for several months. Casoron should not be used unless the berry plants or trees have been planted for three months or more.
   b. for biennial and perennial weeds; pull, dig out and/or use Casoron. Casoron will kill some established weeds but it works better if weeds are taken out first.
   c. for brush; pull or dig it out or spot treat with glyphosate.

Note: All of the soil applied herbicides mentioned above require moist soil. Several of them work better if they are lightly raked in. Casoron works best when it is covered with a mulch to hold some dampness at the surface. Glyphosate must be applied while the foliage is dry and should have several hours to dry on the leaves before the next rain arrives.

One caution about the use of herbicides in gardens or fruit plantings: any herbicide used at concentrations higher than label recommendations can become a soil sterilant. Soil sterilants have no place in areas where food plants are being grown. Sterilants are non-selective and applications made nearby may wash into the root zones of desirable plants. Likewise the hormone weed killer 2,4-D should never be used in or near the vegetable garden or near grapes. Fumes from this material can drift and cause vegetables and grapes to become deformed or die.

Weeds compete with garden plants for water, nutrients, light, and space and reduce the yield and quality of the crops you attempt to grow. Hand weeding is the safest and frequently the most effective way to control weeds in food crop gardens. However, some weeds defy all manual and cultural methods and so will require selected herbicides to do a proper job. Use the herbicides available as one of the tools at your disposal to protect your plants.

HERBICIDES GENERAL SUMMARY

Name	Physiological Action	Vegs.	USE Small Fruit	Tree Fruit	Comments
Casoron	not known at present; applied to soil		X	(X)	Not for use around apricot trees. May persist for several months in soil.
chloramben (Amiben)	regulates growth; applied to soil	X			Inactivated by soil microorganisms.
Dacthal	not known at present; applied to soil	X	X	X	Will co-distill with water vapor. Leaching limited under normal rainfall conditions. Diminished effectiveness in heavy, organic soils.
glyphosate	may inhibit plant use of some amino acids; applied to leaves	X	X	X	Quickly inactivated by soil/little or no residual effect. Non-selective, moves rapidly to roots.
simazine	inhibits photosynthesis; applied to soil		X	X	Long residual action.
Treflan	affects seed germination and associated growth processes; applied to soil	X			Moderate residual action. Requires soil incorporation to be effective. Broken down by soil microorganisms.
2, 4−D	affects plant enzymes, particularly relates to oxidation and electron transport capability; applied to leaves or plant parts	(X)	(X)	X	Drift injurious to grapes, vegetables. Broken down by soil microorganisms in 3−6 weeks, longer in dry or cold conditions. Do not apply spray during winds greater then 6 mph.

This chart gives general herbicide uses; information derived from "Oregon Weed Control Handbook," Extension Service, OSU, January, 1981. For specific application be sure to read and follow label directions.

Animals

Animal pests are the most visible but the hardest to deal with. In a few nights, rodents can destroy your garden. Gophers, moles, field mice, and deer are the principal diners in your garden. They seem to be persuaded that they enjoy your produce more than you.

Moles and gophers raise mounds as they excavate their elaborate network of tunnels. The mole mound looks like a volcano with soil being pushed up from below and has no obvious entry. The gopher mound is more or less teardrop shaped and has an open hole or a plugged entry hole at the narrow end of the pile. Both are nuisances in the garden by tunneling under plants and causing the roots to dry out. Here though the similarities end. Moles are there because they like your supply of worms, gophers because they like the plants you grow.

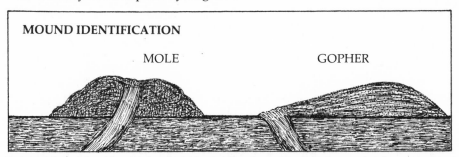

MOUND IDENTIFICATION

MOLE GOPHER

Being able to identify which animal is making the mounds is a prerequisite to catching them. Gophers cannot be caught by mole traps, moles cannot be caught by gopher traps but poison bait works on both. A gopher's mound is teardrop shaped because of his method of removing soil from his tunnel. He carries dirt up to the entrance between his front legs. When he arrives at the surface, the gopher flings the dirt out and ends up with a mound narrow at one end and wider at the other.

Additionally, the underground runways are used by field mice. Field mice will eat anything offered, especially if it is a plant root, an onion bulb, or the tender bark of a new tree root.

Moles are mostly carniverous and dine on worms, grubs, and other soil life. Moles do not usually eat plant parts. Should you suspect they have eaten your carrot crop, check the teeth marks — moles leave shredded tissues, field mice leave cleanly eaten holes.

Moles are social animals, so a number of them use the same tunnel network. In an urban setting, mole control almost needs to be a neighborhood affair because their tunnel system is so extensive. Trapping and baiting are the main means of mole control. Success with either depends on your perseverence.

Mole traps are designed to catch the mole as he moves a pile of dirt under the trip pan. There are several types but the double-scissors or "Out-of-Sight" is one of the better.

When trapping or baiting, the first step is to find a main, well used runway. These are usually a foot or more under the surface. The shallow, surface runs that you can see are hunting runs and are used at infrequent intervals. You can locate a main run with a probe. Use a metal rod 3/8" in diameter and about 4' long as a probe. Shove it into the ground a couple of feet away from a fresh mound in a circular pattern with the mound as a center. When the probe shoves through the soil and meets no resistance a foot or so below the surface you are into the tunnel. In baiting the tunnel, insert your probe carefully to locate the tunnel without poking into the floor. Drop bait into the hole and press the probe hole closed to keep out light.

To trap a mole, find the main runway, dig a hole large enough for the trap and as deep as the floor of the moles' tunnel. Place a couple of handfuls of soil on the tunnel floor below where the trap trigger will be. Open the trap and set it astride the tunnel passageway so a mole moving through the tunnel will encounter the dirt pile. (When he pushes the pile out of his way he trips the trap.) Sift loose soil around the trap and into the opened tunnel to shield out any light, or cover the trap hole with a box or cloth sack. Make sure to remove the safety catch on the trap, otherwise the mole can trip the trap but the safety catch will keep the jaws from grabbing the mole. Check the trap at least once a day. If you catch a mole, remove it and reset the trap. A properly set trap in a well used tunnel may catch a dozen or more moles.

Gophers come to the surface to forage but will also eat on underground plant bulbs, fleshy roots, and tubers.

Gopher traps are pincher types. They are designed to catch the animal in the tunnel as he's pushing a pile of dirt ahead of his body. This type of trap then catches him when the soil trips the trigger.

To set the gopher trap, slide the trap inside the tunnel through a hole. Fasten the trap to a stake driven outside the hole or the gopher may drag it into his burrow and you will lose it. Gophers are not social animals so you will seldom find more than a couple in the space of an average sized yard.

Field mice use the runs of both moles and gophers but they also make their own quarter-sized holes down to roots of tender plants. They do much of the damage for which the mole gets the blame. Field mice are especially numerous and damaging in gardens near vacant fields or during winters when snow covers much of their usual food supply of weed seeds, berries, and assorted other fruits. The presence of several holes an inch in diameter tells you field mice are dining nearby. They can be particularly damaging to the trunks and crowns of newly planted fruit trees. Trees are often girdled by field mice during the winter, especially if the trees are deeply mulched by snow or any other material.

Controlling field mice requires bait or stimulating the family cat to greater endeavors. Poison baits are mostly zinc-phosphide treated grains, sometimes called "black wheat." The dark color of the treated grain makes it unattractive to birds. The grain should be put into the holes and mole runways that are being used by the mice. Half a dozen grains to the hole, reapplied every several days for a week or two will usually take care of mice. Watch for signs of damage, like neatly chewed tree bark, particularly in winter. Bait early enough to get rid of the few that can start a population explosion.

Birds can be a problem at certain times of the year. Normally they are helpful in eating bugs, but when the blueberries are ripening or vegetables are coming up, you may find them a nuisance to your crop or new plantings.

The best way to keep birds out of the berry patch is with a net cover. Bird netting, of cloth or plastic and with about a one-inch mesh, can be spread over individual bushes or across a row of strawberries to insure that most of your crop will make it to your breakfast table or kitchen. With strawberries it helps to make a series of hoops to hold the netting above the row. Netting can be removed and stored away once the harvest season is passed. With blueberries, simply spread the net over the bush. A few berries will still be lost where birds can reach through to the uppermost fruits but at least most of the crop will be protected.

Pheasants enjoy eating the seeds of sweet corn after you have carefully sown and covered the row. They seem to have x-ray vision and can remove all the seeds while barely disturbing the soil. They also pull and eat the corn seedlings when the corn is about an inch or two tall. Constant vigilance together with several scarecrows will help to keep them from wiping out your new seedlings or rows of corn.

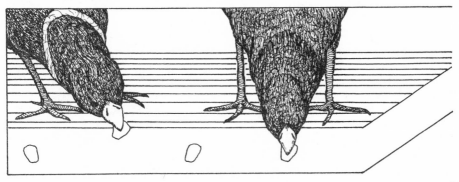

Deer, rabbits, raccoons, and opossums are some other creatures that may wander into the garden from the wilds and browse on goodies growing in your garden. Bags of blood meal hung in fruit trees or on posts will sometimes repel deer as will noisemakers of various sorts. Refreshen the blood meal frequently because its effect wears out quickly. Opossums and raccoons generally come into the garden to feed on ripening fruit. Rabbits are interested in the vegetable garden through the season. A tight, small mesh fence is the best way to keep small animals out.

Animals generally are casual visitors to the garden but they can be destructive nuisances in some areas. As with all pests, constant tending and watching of the garden environment is the surest way to keep them from ending your gardening efforts.

Chapter 5: Food Crops: VEGETABLES

Site Evaluation
Planning: Timing & Yield
Soil Preparation
Planting Methods
Managing Plant Growth
Taking & Giving

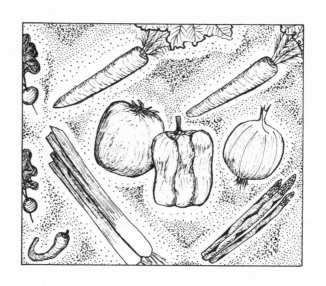

Site Evaluation

Nearly any soil will grow plants, but some soils do it so much better than others you quickly realize that there are a number of factors to be considered. One factor is the past history of the area you plan to plant to garden. What has been growing on the spot where you want to put the vegetable garden? Did a Laurel hedge run across the area? Was lawn growing there? Did a walnut tree dominate the scene? Almost everything a gardener does leaves it mark or causes a change in some way. The lawn may have been treated with herbicides to prevent weeds, which may affect your vegetables. The Laurel hedge is a heavy feeder, so new plants in the area may have difficulty in finding enough nutrients to make expected growth. Walnut trees are among several plants called *allelopathic*. These plants produce chemicals which prevent certain other plants from growing and this effect may remain in the soil for some time after the tree is removed.

Visual clues that all is not right, usually are: 1) the plants refuse to grow as expected or 2) they display one of the deficiency symptoms described later on in this chapter under "Managing Plant Growth." Soil chemicals (herbicides, sterilants) may cause leaf discoloration or death. Tree and/or shrub competition generally cause the nearby vegetable plants to become spindly and weak.

What to do depends upon your analysis of the factors described above. Sometimes a soil test (described fully in Chapter 3) will help determine some elements that are needed and also some that may be excessive. Later on in this chapter under "Soil Preparation," we'll talk specifically about how to make these corrections.

Many soil problems can be eased by working rich organic matter into the top six to eight inches, thereby diluting any toxicity and stimulating soil bacteria and fungi to act as scavengers to bring the soil back to a biological balance.

Soil, as mentioned in Chapter 3, is a biological entity, one that lives, thrives with good management and suffers when we are careless. If you have read Chapter 3, you know soils are complicated. Let's review some soil requirements for vegetable gardening.

How deep is the soil in the garden area? Most vegetables have an effective root depth of six to eight inches. This means you should have at least six inches of reasonably good soil. Some soils are shallow with only a few inches of topsoil above a clay layer or above a restricting layer of rock, compacted soil or something else.

Few gardeners are blessed with the ideal soil, but with a few amendments and sensible management, most soils can be made "right" for most vegetables. Generally, the deeper the combined clay, silt, sand and humus that constitutes topsoil, the easier it will be to grow vegetables. Obviously, a soil only an inch or two deep will allow only a few shallow rooted plants to grow. Topsoil needs to be added simply to obtain enough depth for plant growth.

SITE AND SOIL

HISTORY — PAST OR PRESENT

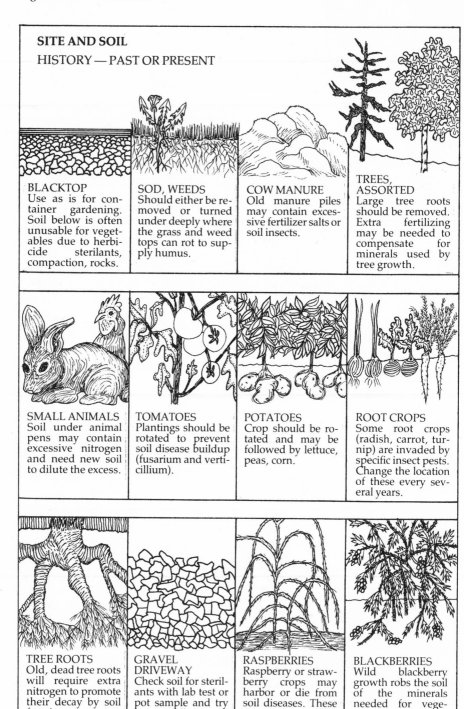

BLACKTOP
Use as is for container gardening. Soil below is often unusable for vegetables due to herbicide sterilants, compaction, rocks.

SOD, WEEDS
Should either be removed or turned under deeply where the grass and weed tops can rot to supply humus.

COW MANURE
Old manure piles may contain excessive fertilizer salts or soil insects.

TREES, ASSORTED
Large tree roots should be removed. Extra fertilizing may be needed to compensate for minerals used by tree growth.

SMALL ANIMALS
Soil under animal pens may contain excessive nitrogen and need new soil to dilute the excess.

TOMATOES
Plantings should be rotated to prevent soil disease buildup (fusarium and verticillium).

POTATOES
Crop should be rotated and may be followed by lettuce, peas, corn.

ROOT CROPS
Some root crops (radish, carrot, turnip) are invaded by specific insect pests. Change the location of these every several years.

TREE ROOTS
Old, dead tree roots will require extra nitrogen to promote their decay by soil fungi.

GRAVEL DRIVEWAY
Check soil for sterilants with lab test or pot sample and try some seedlings.

RASPBERRIES
Raspberry or strawberry crops may harbor or die from soil diseases. These can also affect growth of vegetable crops.

BLACKBERRIES
Wild blackberry growth robs the soil of the minerals needed for vegetable growth.

Topsoil purchasing is risky and unless you have the time and ability to look at and judge what is being sold as topsoil, you will be better off using whatever lies in the garden area. Most subsoil can be made to grow plants by following the suggestions in Chapter 3. Organic matter, basic nutrients, aeration and drainage are the important factors for making good soil. Often, by loading the soil with manure, some phosphorus for plant energy needs, some nitrogen for growth and perhaps some calcium to "sweeten" the soil, a good garden can be grown in subsoil.

Slope, or the way your land slants, can be good or bad depending on how much and which direction. Obviously a steep slope that drops five feet in ten feet of horizontal distance is too steep for anything but running goats. Unless you plan to do some terracing, better forget it for vegetable culture. Remember, a garden should be something you enjoy, not a tedious chore. Steep land may be more usable and more easily cared for as rock gardens or something less demanding of your energies than vegetables. A gradual slope to the south or west will be a warm site for early gardens and you will enjoy your vegetables a few weeks earlier than a gardener with a northerly slope. When gardening a slope, remember that erosion may occur. Plant rows or beds across the slope, rather than running the rows up and down the hill.

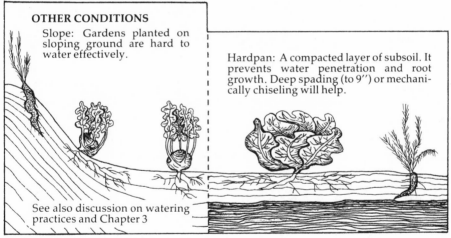

OTHER CONDITIONS

Slope: Gardens planted on sloping ground are hard to water effectively.

Hardpan: A compacted layer of subsoil. It prevents water penetration and root growth. Deep spading (to 9") or mechanically chiseling will help.

See also discussion on watering practices and Chapter 3

Drainage is vital to the roots of your vegetables. Few edible crops can grow in soil which remains wet and cold for weeks on end. Drainage is often thought of as surface water removal when in fact, the importance of drainage lies in the soil water, that which remains after irrigation or rainfall. In poorly drained soil, the water replaces air. Air is needed for the life of roots.

Soil drainage is related to percolation factors, or how the soil structure allows water to move downward and eventually out of the root zone. A way to test your site for percolation is to dig a hole one or two feet deep, fill it with water and see how long it takes for the water to disappear. If it is gone within several hours, your soil is reasonably well drained. If the water remains a day later, you have a problem.

Drainage can be handled in several ways. The best and most permanent method is to install drain tile or perforated pipe below the depth needed for plant roots. The system must be designed so the pipes collect the excess water and carry it off to a natural waterway, storm sewer, creek or dry well. This is an expensive operation but properly done it will last many years. Other methods of overcoming the drainage problem include the use of raised beds, berms or planters and containers to get the plant roots above the water problem area.

The color of your soil and its feel will give you some clues as to its goodness for growing vegetables. Soils rich in organic matter are usually dark. When wet soil containing lots of organic matter is rubbed between your finger and thumb, it will make little balls. Dark soils warm much faster in spring than do light colored soils. Soils predominantly clay are usually red or yellow or of a lighter color and when wet will have a slick feel. Silt will be sort of slick with a slight grittiness and sand will be even more gritty. Soils with a slick feel compact easily and will need lots of organic material to grow good crops.

Nearly all vegetable plants need at least six hours of direct sunlight daily and the more sunlight the plants receive, the better they will do. Sunlight filtering through the leaves of shade trees is not enough for most crops. Keep the garden out in the open where the sunlight can reach the plant leaves. If your options for placement of your garden are limited, put it where the afternoon sun shines. The afternoon sun is the hottest and brightest and longest, so take advantage of it.

Air circulation is necessary in the vegetable garden to keep foliage diseases to a minimum. Planting a mildew susceptible plant, like snap beans, in a confined corner where air stagnates is a loser. You might as well consign the seed to the garbage can. Either avoid tight enclosures surrounded by dense hedges and fences or plan to provide the necessary air movement needed to dry the foliage and keep diseases controlled. No pesticide can overcome lack of air circulation.

On the other hand, windy areas are tough on growing plants also. The force of continuous or gusty winds may be enough to discourage all but the hardiest crops. Corn plants not only blow over in the wind, but they also stop growing when the wind blows and may take several hours after the wind stops to start their systems again. Gardening is similar to many other things in life, and moderation in all things is preferred; avoid extremes.

Microclimates: Here is a mysterious and worldly word to use to dazzle your fellow gardeners. It is a convenient way to put a simple name on the multitude of influences that occur in your yard which affect plant growth. Almost every yard has a microclimate that differs in some way from its neighbor. Microclimate is the sum total of a garden's surroundings all of which must be accounted for by the successful gardener. When evaluating your site, consider all the surrounding plants, buildings, and natural forces such as wind and sun.

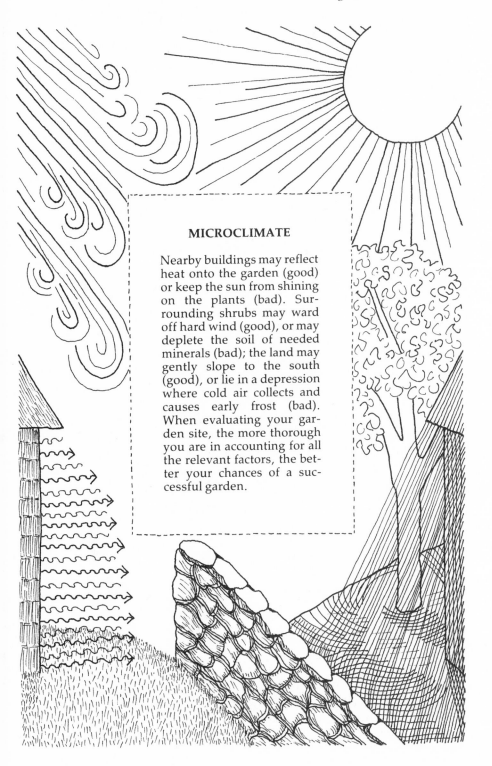

MICROCLIMATE

Nearby buildings may reflect heat onto the garden (good) or keep the sun from shining on the plants (bad). Surrounding shrubs may ward off hard wind (good), or may deplete the soil of needed minerals (bad); the land may gently slope to the south (good), or lie in a depression where cold air collects and causes early frost (bad). When evaluating your garden site, the more thorough you are in accounting for all the relevant factors, the better your chances of a successful garden.

While doing all this evaluation, consider also the best placement of certain vegetable crop plants. Perennial vegetables, those which remain in place and come back every year, should be placed where they can remain undisturbed for years.

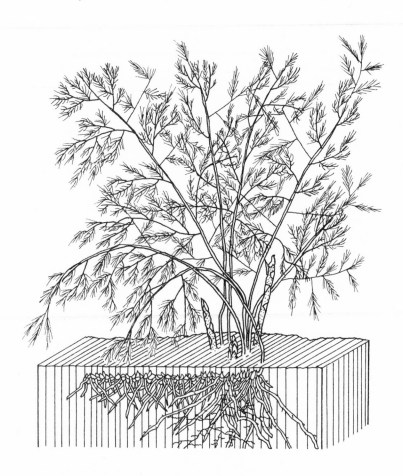

Asparagus is a good example of a perennial vegetable whose growth originates annually from a permanent root system. Plant parts of asparagus and rhubarb are planted in late February or early March.

Asparagus, artichokes, rhubarb will flourish for years in the same spot with only a little care. If planted in the regular vegetable garden, they get in the way of spading and tilling. Put them off to the side, where they can happily be by themselves. If space is limited, slip them into the landscape where they can be admired as double duty plants, yielding foliage interest and good eating.

Rhubarb is a permanent herbaceous perennial which, if space is limited in the vegetable garden, can be used to complement the summer landscape.

The placement of annual vegetables must be considered to make sure the shorter crops are not shaded by the taller ones and that surrounding buildings and vegetation do not shade them all out. Plan for the corn and sunflowers and pole beans toward the north or east side of the garden site so they won't shade the other vegetables.

Also, think of the space needs of vegetables while evaluating your site. Consider what can be planted to use the available space efficiently. Vegetable plants needs a certain amount of space for normal development. Crowding them usually means less growth and consequently a smaller crop. If your space is limited, forget the globe artichoke that needs nearly 2300 square inches of space and plant carrots that take only 4 inches each. In a 4' × 4' area, your can grow any one of the following:

4 tomatoes	24 beets	24 leaf lettuce	8 broccoli
6 pole beans	24 chard	96 carrots	1 zucchini
6 cabbage	72 turnips	1 pumpkin	12 mustard
144 radishes	48 spinach	72 onions	
8 potatoes	9 corn plants	32 bush beans	

Rotation in vegetable gardening simply means not planting the same vegetables (or members of the same vegetable family — see Appendix) in the same spot year after year. Many vegetables have specific diseases or insect parasites which may build up in the soil unless the particular crop is planted elsewhere every few years. Tomatoes, potatoes, turnips, carrots and beans are examples of crops which should be shifted every so often.

Finally, is the site convenient, both to the basic chores of gardening and to the kitchen. Gardens are likely to be cared for more conscientiously and harvested at the peak of perfection if they are handy to the house. This is especially true of herb gardens, but is just as important to the general run of vegetables. For care and harvesting, how handy is the site to water, tool storage and supplies? The nearer they are to the growing area, the more likely they will be used properly.

Planning: Timing & Yield

There are two major factors bearing on vegetable garden planning which we will explore here. One factor is timing and the other, yield.

Timing of certain garden preparation chores is necessary to prevent soil damage and to allow amendments the time needed to function. Avoid at all costs working the soil when it is wet. This means no spading, tilling, plowing or excessive foot traffic; also no planting when the soil is wet. This has been covered in *Soil*, but warrants mentioning here because of the importance of soil management. The soil in your garden is your most important resource. It needs careful tending. When the soil is passed onto the next generation of gardeners, it should be in better condition than when we started. Disturbing the soil when it is wet changes the soil structure, causing the soil particles to move closer together, and results in clods and compacted ground. The best way to avoid working wet soil in early spring is to prepare it the previous fall. Deep plowing and soil turning done in the fall allows freezing and thawing processes to mellow the soil. Some light, final preparation probably will be needed in the spring but if properly done, will not ruin the soil structure.

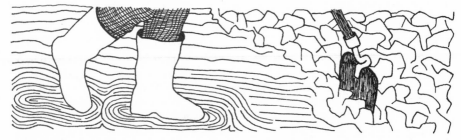

Cloddiness, compaction and consequent poor growth of vegetables can be the result of attempting to prepare soil while it is wet. ⎯⎯⎯⎯⎯⎯⎯⎯⎯⎯⎯⎯⎯⎯

Soil amendments need some time to act before plants can benefit from their use. Lime, used to correct acidic conditions and to add calcium to the soil, needs several months to react. Where needed, lime should be applied and worked into the soil in the fall. This gives the lime enough time to correct acidity before planting.

Organic matter takes some time to decompose and to stimulate soil microorganism growth for soil fertility. Applying and working manure or compost into the soil at planting time often means the nitrogen needed for plant growth will be used to decompose the organic material rather than supplying plant needs. Apply organic material in the fall. A layer of manure, compost, leaves or other organic matter, applied in the fall, will decay during the winter and build the soil for spring planting.

Organic fertilizers need some lead time to release their nutrients. Mineral nutrition from organic sources, manure for example, must come from the activity of soil bacteria and fungi. For these soil inhabitants to work, they need a soil temperature of around 45–50°F. If your soil remains wet and cold until mid-May, either plan to use fast acting non-organic fertilizers or apply the organics in the fall while the soil temperatures remain high enough for soil activity.

The effective length of Pacific Northwest summers for growing vegetables ranges from 1½ to 2 months in the higher and drier sections to 200–275 days in the lower, more moderate areas. Because the sun is so important for raising green crops, the successful gardener will carefully plan to prepare the ground and to plant seeds or transplants to take full advantage of the sunny days of the year and the frost-free time available. The key words here are "frost-free" days. How many days are available to you from the time of the last killing frost in the spring until the first cold snap in the fall?

Minimum temperatures are the ones important here. While the number of sunny days is greater east of the Cascade Range, the number of nights with temperatures above forty or fifty degrees F is limited. Seed packets often tell how many days are needed from planting until ready for harvest. This means days with an optimum day temperature, usually between 60 and 65 degrees. Plan carefully before you plant.

Perennials are plants which take two growing seasons to reach maturity. Once established, they live in the garden for many years, continuing to yield a harvest of good eating for as long as you care for them.

Annual vegetable plants (those that are planted and harvested the same year) yield a crop of table fresh edibles much sooner than perennial plants. Among the annuals, those which are eaten for their foliage or roots are quickest to mature. Those that must develop a fruit, such as tomato, corn, pepper, cucumber, will take longer. The most convenient spot for fast maturing types is near the kitchen where you can hustle out at a minute's notice and pick a mess of chard or pull an onion or two for the salad.

Annual vegetables are also classified as *cool season* or *warm season* plants, depending upon their ability to grow during the cooler temperatures of spring and fall. Cool season crops are those which will grow to maturity in the spring or can be planted in late summer to develop to maturity in the fall. They generally respond to hot weather by "bolting," i.e. going to seed. Cool season plants that have bolted are not much good for the table. Therefore, what we are talking about here is timing the planting of these cool season crops so that the plants do not approach maturity during hot weather.

Cool season vegetables can be planted as early in the year as you can get the soil ready. Here is where fall soil preparation is helpful. If the area can be spaded, tilled or plowed in late fall before it gets too wet, the soil will be mellow and more easily prepared for spring planting. Cold and wet soils are the bane of every gardener. While the soil is cold, even the cool season vegetable plants take a long time to start growing and the warm season plants do not grow at all. When cold is accompanied by excessive moisture, the seeds of warm season plants usually rot in the soil or the seedlings turn purple from the cold and refuse to grow even after the weather finally warms.

Warm season crops come from the tender, succulent plants which provide the "fruits" of the vegetable diet. Tomato, sweet corn, squash, melons, cucumbers, peppers and eggplant are typical warm season plants that simply will not tolerate cool temperatures. Wait to plant these until the soil warms and night air temperatures no longer dip below fifty degrees F. Your wait will be rewarded.

Here are some timing suggestions for both cool and warm season vegetables:

1. These can be planted in late winter if the soil is dry enough to prepare a seedbed:

chives	lettuce	peas	spinach
collards	onions	radishes	

2. These can be planted two weeks before the last predicted spring frost:

beets	carrots	chard	parsnips
broccoli	cauliflower	mustard	potatoes
cabbage	celery	parsley	New Zealand spinach

3. These should not be planted until the soil has warmed and frosts have ended:

lima beans	eggplant	pole beans	squash
bush beans	melons	pumpkins	sweet corn
cucumbers	peppers	salsify	tomatoes

4. These can be planted in midsummer to mature in the fall:

beets	carrots	kohlrabi	radish
broccoli	cauliflower	lettuce	rutabaga
Brussels sprouts	endive	peas (*virus*	spinach
cabbage	kale	*resistant*	turnip
		varieties)	

Growing times vary widely from one crop plant to the next. One of the speediest vegetables is radish which, in good soil, proper moisture and a mild temperature, can yield a batch of crisp edibles within 30 days. One of the slowest is pumpkin which takes around 110 days before you have anything to harvest. Here is a list of common vegetables with approximate days from planting to edible maturity.

GROWING TIMES FOR VEGETABLES

[1]CROP	EARLY VARIETY	LATE VARIETY	COMMON TYPE
Bean, broad — WS			120
Bean, bush — WS	56	72	
Bean, lima, bush — WS	65	78	
Bean, lima, pole — WS	80	95	
Beet — CS	50	80	
Broccoli — CS/t	70	150	
Brussels sprouts — CS/t	90	100	
Cabbage — CS/t	62	110	
Carrot — CS	60	85	
Cauliflower — snowball, CS/t	55	65	
Cauliflower — winter, CS/t	120	180	
Celery — CS/t	90	110	
Chard — CS	50	60	
Chinese Cabbage — CS/t	70	80	
Chives — CS			90
Collard — CS			75
Corn — WS	70	100	
Cress — CS			45
Cucumber — WS	60	70	
Eggplant — WS/t	70	85	
Endive — CS	80	100	
Kale — CS	60	90	
Kohlrabi — CS	55	65	
Leek — CS			150
Lettuce, cos — CS			70
Lettuce, head — CS	60	85	
Lettuce, leaf — CS	40	50	
Melon, casaba — WS			120
Melon, Honey Dew — WS			115
Melon, Persian — WS			115
Muskmelon — WS	83	90	
Mustard — CS	40	60	

(Crop)	(Early)	(Late)	(Common)
Okra — WS	50	60	
Onion — CS	85	120	
Parsley — CS	70	85	
Parsnip — CS	100	130	
Pea — CS	58	77	
Pepper, hot — WS/t	70	95	
Pepper, sweet — WS/t	60	80	
Potato — CS	90	120	
Pumpkin — WS	110	120	
Radish — CS	22	40	
Radish, winter — CS	50	60	
Rutabaga — CS			90
Salsify — WS			150
Spinach — CS	40	50	
Spinach, New Zealand — CS			70
*Squash, summer — WS	50	68	
Squash, winter — WS	80	120	
Sweet potato — WS/t	120	150	
Tomato — WS/t	65	100	
Turnip — CS	40	75	
Watermelon — WS	75	95	

1Crop: WS = warm season
        CS = cool season
          t = days from planting transplants.
*Squash — summer squash include zucchini, spaghetti, crookneck, and patty pan types; winter squash include acorn, hubbard, turban, and banana. They are called "winter" squash to indicate long-storage qualities.

The growing season can be stretched by starting young plants from seed indoors. These young plants are normally referred to as "transplants." By starting transplants indoors, you may gain several weeks on the time needed for the crop to mature. "Planting Methods," discussed later in this chapter, gives specific information about transplants and timing.

Not only is timing important in planning for the best use of the growing season, it is also needed to make sure the harvest will continue over a long time or come at a convenient time for use or preservation. Vegetable varieties usually mature within a short time range so the crop may be more than the average family can use within a reasonable period of time. Lettuces planted on a single day will, for example, mature within a few days of one another and who can use thirty heads of lettuce in a week? Stretch the harvest by successive seedings or plantings of the same variety, planting a small row to start, followed by another short row one or two weeks later. The same with radishes, plant a few now and some more later. In this way you can keep the kitchen supplied all season without too much at one time.

Another way to stretch the harvest season is by planting varieties of the same vegetable which take different lengths of time to mature. Sweet corn of the same variety, planted as mentioned above will nearly always mature at the same time no matter how hard you try to stagger the planting. This is because sweet corn grows quickly once the right soil and air temperatures are reached and will practically refuse to grow until then. To continue harvesting fresh sweet corn over a longer time, plant different varieties. Some will mature in 70 days, others may take 100 or more days to ripen.

To get the most out of the vegetable garden, plan to include cool season crops in the early growing season, followed by warm season plants and then if weather permits, follow into the fall with another round of cool season crops. For example, in a small garden area begin the season with lettuce, peas, cabbage, carrots and radishes. These will usually have matured by early summer when it is warm enough to seed sweet corn, green beans, squash or plant tomato and pepper transplants. The corn and beans will normally be finished by late summer, when it is time to plant turnips, carrots, parsnips, kale, cabbage and cauliflower. Here are some ideas for other succession crops:

1st crop	*followed by —*	*followed by —*
Spinach	Peppers	Beets
Lettuce	Sweet Corn	Carrots
Peas	Fall Cabbage	— — — —
Cabbage	Fall Cauliflower	— — — —
Onions	Tomatoes	Turnips
Beets	Cucumbers	Kale
Carrots	Snap Beans	Brussels Sprouts
Chard	Squash	Mustard Greens

Timing can be refined to help grow better quality plants. Bolting occurs when cool season crops are exposed to too much summer heat. Spinach and chard should be dense, leafy, succulent plants but with summer heat they "bolt" and suddenly grow a tall, coarse stem with small leaves. To avoid bolting, plant these vegetables to grow during cool weather, either in early spring or late summer:

broccoli	cauliflower	lettuce
Brussels sprouts	chard	radish
cabbage	kale	spinach

Garden peas should be planted early because they can tolerate cool weather, but there is a more important reason, i.e. to avoid insect pests. Peas are susceptible to many virus diseases which are carried into the garden by aphids and leafhoppers from surrounding weeds. The best way to grow healthy peas is to plant them early, long before the insect pests get busy.

Some root crops, turnips and parsnips for example, are planted in late summer so the fall frost can enhance their flavor and quality. While frost certainly does not enhance all vegetable crops it does seem to sweeten some of the root crops.

In areas where summer heat can be a problem, timing the maturity of certain vegetables to avoid the heat will produce better quality products. Cucumber bitterness, woodiness in radishes, pungency in green onions all are partly caused by excessive summer heat. Plan harvesting dates before the hot August weather arrives.

Vegetable gardening is a gamble at best. Take some of the gamble out by carefully planning the timing of gardening activities.

The new gardener usually plants everything imaginable, trying everything in quantity. This often results in deluging the family table and freezer with an oversupply. Take it easy, plant the vegetables that are reasonably easy to grow and in only enough quantity to be easily cared for and to furnish some basic needs. Then, as you gain gardening experience broaden your crop expertise by adding some new crops for testing and tasting. Too often the new gardener puts in so much that the care and use of the vegetables becomes a detested chore. A garden should be something you enjoy. However, one of the genuine pleasures of gardening is getting a humungous crop from a small spot.

Small garden areas intensively used can produce as much as larger conventional areas. The key word here is *intensive*. Intensive vegetable cropping means finding ways to get the most use out of your garden site. It requires discarding conventional methods of gardening and trying something different. Upper story/lower story, short row, wide row intensive, and scatter planting illustrate a few of the ways you can get more plants in the space available.

Double cropping involves planting two vegetable types in the same row. It works as long as several needs can be met. First, select for differences in growth rate, height or shade tolerance. Thus, you can plant low-growing vegetables which tolerate some shade in the same row as taller types. Cabbage, broccoli, leaf lettuce, chard, spinach and endive can endure sites where the sunlight may be only half of normal. Or, plant fast maturing crops along with slower varieties. This way, one is harvested before the slower variety needs more room. Radishes planted with carrots, for example, works well. Not only do the radishes come out long before the carrots, but also for the new gardener, the radishes sprout quickly and mark the row (carrots being rather hard to see when they first come up).

Second, make sure extra fertilizer and water are supplied. In intensive

PLANTING METHODS

Upper Story/Lower Story — maximizing space by mixing smaller, shade tolerant plants with tall types. This is one way of "double-cropping."

Short Row — For most moderately sized gardens, shorter rows are easier to manage and maintain for intensive vegetable production.

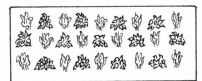

Wide Row Intensive — a method of utilizing all the garden space available for varieties suitable for close planting.

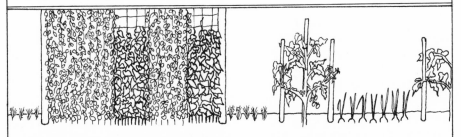

Scatter Planting — A balance between space, plant requirements and their susceptibilities; random planting of vegetable varieties to use the space more efficiently and to avoid concentrations of insect prone groups.

plantings, two or three plants use the space normally used for a single plant. With the extra plant or two, careful irrigation and fertilizing will be needed. Check the soil frequently and keep it damp. At planting time use the normal amount of fertilizer per square foot and make additional applications of nitrogen when the plants are about half grown. Watch for signs of hunger and replenish the soil minerals as a need is seen. Check for deficiency symptoms discussed in Chapter 3 and further on in this chapter.

Another way to increase the yield per area of certain vegetable crops is the wide row intensive method. With this system a gardener can grow many carrots, radishes, heads of lettuce, and other root or leafy crops in the space normally remaining between rows of conventionally planted vegetables. Instead of planting vegetables in rows, group them side by side in a bed conveniently wide to tend from the side. But remember one important point — even though the vegetables are being planted in a wide bed, space them as widely as recommended. All plants need room to develop, this is true whether in a row or massed in a group. With wide row planting, the same number of vegetables that could be grown in the conventional way can be produced in about one-fourth the area. A further advantage of wide row growing is that it is much easier to take care of a 2' × 4' bed of carrots than to maintain a 50' row of them.

Some easy-to-grow vegetables for wide row intensive planting include lettuce, carrots, radishes, onions (both green and bulb), beets, turnips and mustard greens. Basically any vegetable not requiring more than four to six square inches of space nor needing support for vining, will do well in wide row plantings.

Now, back to the conventional methods of planting vegetables in rows. It is much more economical and convenient to plant lots of short rows rather than several long rows. Four short rows of green beans for example, ten feet long, are easier to care for than a single long row. Of course, if space allows and the family is large, a big garden with long rows of produce give a gardener a feeling of being right with nature. More of us though have small garden sites and for these areas, row arrangement needs careful planning to fully utilize and reap all the benefits possible. Short rows seem to make weeding less of a chore than looking at the weeds that must be pulled from a fifty foot row of corn. With sweet corn, which must be pollinated by wind, several short rows side by side, give each young ear of corn a better chance of being pollinated. With a single long row, if the wind doesn't cooperate, you end up with a lot of nubby, unfilled ears.

While insect pests seem to have a way of searching out their preferred vegetable diets, it may be possible to increase the chances of a pest-free crop by scatter planting. Scatter planting simply means somewhat randomly scattering the plants of a crop such as peas or green beans or cabbage around the garden site to limit damaging populations from developing. A disadvantage is that the garden looks like a hodgepodge of plants without much semblance of order or convenience for maintenance and harvest. There are other methods which will be discussed later for control of garden pests.

Plant spacing suggestions can be found in the Appendix; for now, just a caution. When planting vegetables pay attention to the spacing recommendations listed in this book or on the seed packets. Every plant needs a certain amount of room to grow to maturity. Some, like carrots, do fine with four square inches of space, others like the winter squash need sixteen square feet. Either of these examples, if planted too closely, will produce weak, spindly plants with consequent poor yield. Get the most for your money and effort; plant them far enough apart to grow well and yield a good crop.

While there are plenty of mechanical methods of measuring, here are a few ideas for a quick way to space plants, using items that are always with you. Fingers, hands and feet work as well as yardsticks or measuring tapes and seldom are the latter handy when you need them. Knuckles on an adult forefinger are about an inch apart. If the recommendations call for green onions to be planted two inches apart, use two knuckles worth. The width of a hand is about right for spacing spinach. Measure your foot. If yours is nine inches long and rows of green beans should be 18" apart, place two feet between the row stakes and start planting.

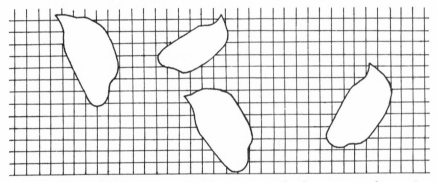

Certain planting terms may be confusing or misleading to a gardener. An example is a "hill of corn." A hill in vegetable gardening language means a spot where several seeds are planted, not a mound of earth. _____

While considering yield possibilities for vegetable planting, look at the places in the landscape where vegetable crops can be included. The cost of land is a major expense and it should be used effectively. Many vegetable plants are attractive enough to be included in the landscape for their ornamental value as well as for their produce. Here again, planning is important. Plan areas where summer annual vegetables can be used to enhance the yard, or places where perennial artichokes or asparagus can dress up a part of the landscape. How about leaf lettuce to edge the sidewalk or rhubarb chard for a splash of color and good eating? Here are some ideas for landscape vegetables:

— For tall background planting

sweet corn	pole beans	Jerusalem artichoke
dill	staked tomatoes	trellised cucumbers

— For "points of interest" plantings

asparagus	globe artichoke	rhubarb chard
bush acorn squash	chives	parsley
eggplant	kale	rhubarb
tomatoes	peppers	

— For foregound, edging, ground cover plantings

radish	green onions	lettuce
cucumber	bush beans	mustard greens
		New Zealand spinach

— For mass planting effect

zucchini squash	hubbard squash	melons

Limited space for vegetable gardening means more careful planning will be needed to get full use of the area. Many crops can be grown up into the air by staking or trellising rather than letting them scramble around on the ground. While keeping the new growth on the support requires some extra attention, more plants and, consequently, more produce can be grown on a small plot of land. Even cucumbers and melons can be grown upward on trellises or fencing in order to use less garden space. Tomatoes staked, tied and pruned for air circulation will often yield more than those allowed to spread over the ground. When staking vegetables, use materials that will last the season. Treated stakes are okay but avoid using wood stakes treated with pentachlorophenol, as fumes from this chemical may damage nearby plants. Trellises can be made of wood, netting, wire or

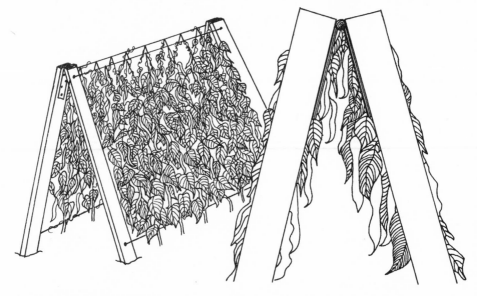

An A-frame trellis is useful for supporting beans, cucumbers or garden peas in small areas and is easily stored.

whatever is available to hold plants upright. Plants can be fastened to stakes or trellises with any soft, but strong material; just make sure the fastening doesn't cut into the stem of the plant.

Variety selection is another place where planning can increase the yield. The size of the area to be used needs to be coordinated with the mature and expected size of the plant. With unlimited space a wide range of vegetable varieties can be planted. Large plant varieties are enjoyable to watch grow and will yield an abundance of edibles. In limited space, consider using varieties which can be manipulated onto upright frames or trellises, or look for more compact bush forms of those that naturally spread halfway across the garden. Pole beans can be used in place of bush types, bush type squash can be used in place of the normal vining types.

Use your imagination to make the space available for vegetable gardening more productive. Seed catalogs are an enjoyable reminder of the good things that can be grown in the garden and there are always new types of plants to try. Pay a visit to a local community garden for some new ideas. People gardening together come up with some great ideas for growing vegetables. How about combining pole beans with sweet corn? The pole beans twine their way up the cornstalk for support and as a legume, the bean may actually supply the corn with some needed nitrogen. All legumes, in combinaton with certain bacteria, will increase nitrogen content in the soil.

EFFICIENCY IN THE USE OF GARDEN SPACE

EXCELLENT	GOOD	FAIR	POOR
Beans, snap	Beans, lima	Asparagus	Artichokes, globe
Beets	Broccoli	Chinese cabbage	Cantaloupes
Carrots	Brussels sprouts	Okra	Sweet Corn
Leaf Lettuce	Cabbage	Sweet Potato	Cucumbers
Onions	Cauliflower		Eggplant
Radish	Celery		Kale
Spinach	Chard		Pumpkins
	Endive		Rhubarb
	Garlic		Winter squash
	Kohlrabi		Watermelon
	Leek		
	Head Lettuce		
	Parsley		
	Parsnip		
	Peas		
	Peppers		
	White Potato		
	Rutabaga		
	Summer Squash		
	Tomato		
	Turnips		

To get a running start on vegetable production, certain plants can be purchased or grown indoors for transplanting. Tomatoes are nearly always purchased as young plants simply because it takes too long in the average Northwest garden to grow an edible tomato fruit from seed outdoors. Others generally planted in the home garden as young plants include: broccoli, cabbage, celery, chives, eggplant, globe artichoke, kale, lettuce, melons, and peppers.

Some vegetables are purchased as plant parts from which a new plant grows, these include: asparagus, garlic, Jerusalem artichoke, onion sets, potato, rhubarb, and sweet potato.

Most annuals are fast developers in the garden so are grown directly from seed planted in outdoor soil. Among them are: beans, beets, carrots, chard, sweet corn, cucumbers, dill, endive, kohlrabi, leek, mustard, parsnips, peas, pumpkins, radish, rutabagas, spinach, squash, sunflowers, and turnips.

When selecting vegetables for the highest yield look for those having some resistance to local problems. Verticillium wilt is a fungus disease found in many soils and is deadly to tomatoes. Fusarium wilt is another strange sounding fungus which kills tomatoes also. To make sure these two problems do not destroy the tomato crop look for varieties marked "VF" after the name. This symbol tells you the variety is resistant to those two destructive diseases. Tomato varieties known to be resistant in the Pacific Northwest include: *Betterboy, Big Set, Heinz 1350, Jetstar, Red Pak, Small Fry, Spring Giant, Spring Set, Supersonic,* and *Wonderboy.*

In selecting the highest yielding vegetable varieties look for pest resistance, hardiness to the local climate and speed of growth. Some vegetables never seem to be affected by insect and disease pests, while others suffer from anything that comes along. Though it is hard to plant an entire garden that will totally resist insects, here are some that are rarely invaded by pests: parsnips, summer and winter squash, beets, celery, sweet corn, parsley, garlic, pumpkins, and rhubarb. Diseases can be kept to a minimum by careful variety selection, but the best way to prevent diseases on vegetables is to provide sufficient sunlight and air circulation.

Hardiness means the vegetable variety should be able to grow to maturity in a normal time without suffering from weather extremes or climatic aberrations. Speed of growth must be considered with hardiness. If a plant's rate of growth is longer than the number of frost-free days available, hardiness is no longer a reliable indicator. Hardiness applies to more than temperature extremes. It relates also to wind, drought, cold soils and heat. For the best yield chances, stick with locally adapted and known hardy varieties for the area.

Days to maturity as listed on seed packets is an indication of the amount of time needed for a vegetable variety to grow from seed to a mature or edible crop. This time factor relates to optimum temperatures for growing the variety. Most warm season vegetables have an optimum temperature range of 60–65°F. If the summer squash seed packet says it will take 80 days to mature, it means 80 days when the temperature averages 60−65°F or above. Optimum temperatures for cool season crops generally range from 50−60°F, so when radishes are listed at 28 days it means 28 days of optimum growing temperature. Obviously, the faster growing varieties will give a faster yield and will usually be the first to the dinner table.

Where do you buy your garden seeds and plants? Spring mail brings many colorful catalogs and flashy advertisements for all sorts of new plants. Some are good and worth the money, others may be of questionable value for growing in Pacific Northwest conditions. Seeds are the least of your gardening expenses but are one of the most important, so buy from reputable dealers who handle varieties adapted to your climate.

Gardening should not be a chore which requires all of one's spare time. Some vegetables seem to need attention from the time they are seeded until eaten, while others can almost be tossed on the ground and forgotten until time for harvset. If gardening time is limited, plant some of these: zucchini squash, winter squash, sweet corn, lettuce, carrots, onions, chard. Some vegetables require more time controlling pests than others (green beans, potatoes, tomato, radishes). Others need special care in pruning, thinning, and training (sweet corn, tomato, trellised vine crops).

The new gardener should plant the tried and true vegetables that are the mainstay of home vegetable gardens. Vegetables such as radish, carrot, sweet corn and summer squash are easy to grow and can stand some neophyte neglect without dying. Basic needs for the diet can be met with these minimal care vegetables and will at the same time give a newcomer confidence to try other vegetable crops. Try something new every year for variety, for fun, and to learn more about the world of edible plants. There are dozens of vegetable crops which can be grown. Here are a few unusual ones to test on a small scale: salsify, winter radish, cardoon, spaghetti squash, edible pod peas, sweet potato, peanuts, kohlrabi, garlic, okra and Chinese cabbage. Some others are also listed in the Appendix.

The vegetable garden can also be a place to experiment to find substitutes for some of the old time types, again for fun or perhaps for something easier to grow. Jerusalem artichoke is an interesting vegetable but one which may eventually be a problem to get rid of. It can substitute for potato, has a texture similar to water chestnut and, planted in the landscape, can serve as a tall background annual. Some energy advocates feel Jerusalem artichokes may be useful in producing alcohol, due to the mass of fleshy roots they produce.

Other substitutes one might consider include growing kohlrabi instead of turnips. They taste about the same but the turnip crop grows underground where it is susceptible to root maggot infestation. Kohlrabi produces its edible part on the surface, above any root infesting pests. Spinach can be a nuisance given its tendency to bolt with the first hot weather. Try chard as a substitute. Chard produces more edible foliage per unit of area and is not as apt to bolt as spinach.

Soil Preparation

Obtaining a soil analysis of the first-time garden is a good investment and not a bad idea for older gardens. A soil test will reveal any excess amounts of minerals, for example, boron, potassium or calcium. Boron, necessary for walnut orchard production may still be present in high enough amounts to damage some vegetable plants years after the orchard was removed. Potassium and calcium may accumulate in soils where wood ashes have been used extensively. An analysis will also show deficiency problems and which minerals are needed for best growth.

Laboratory analysis will vary from one testing institution to another and prices will differ accordingly. Generally a "complete" soil test will tell the pH level (whether the soil is acidic or alkaline in reaction and to what degree), and the phosphorus, potassium, calcium and magnesium levels. Some labs will also test for minor elements, such as boron, zinc, sulfur, iron, manganese, etc. Some will also test for organic matter content, nitrogen level and for the gardener who wants to become really involved, a CEC reading. CEC or cation exchange capacity is a measure of the holding capacity of the clay particles for cations, such as Ca, K, Mg and NH_4, etc.

For most gardens, a simple analysis for phosphorus, potassium, calcium and magnesium plus pH is sufficient to guide a fertilizing program.

Small soil test kits are generally of limited value unless they are used often enough to calibrate the readings with the vigor and growth of plants in the tested soil. The small test kit which is used once a year and sits on a garage shelf the rest of the year will seldom retain enough accuracy to be dependable.

To get a better idea of the particle content of garden soil, try the jar test method on page 131. This is a simple method of determining the approximate percentage of clay, silt, sand, and organic material in soil. Fill a jar about half full of soil from the garden, add water until the jar is 3/4 full, close the lid and shake hard for about three minutes or until particles are separated from each other. Set the jar aside several hours. By then the layers of sand on the bottom, silt in the middle, clay on top and organic matter floating will be easy to see.

A review of a few soil terms might be helpful at this point. Words like loam, friability, texture, compaction, soil particles all seem to become part of a gardener's vocabulary, especially after a year of trying to manage some of the wet Northwest soils.

Loam is a term often used in a vague manner to describe a certain desirable soil type. It is seldom found in the average garden. More commonly, the Northwest garden is in a yardful of silty clay. The silty, clay soil is not all bad and, with a few amendments and careful planning, a garden can be grown successfully with relative ease. Given time, lots of careful building and loads of organic matter, it might even approach loam.

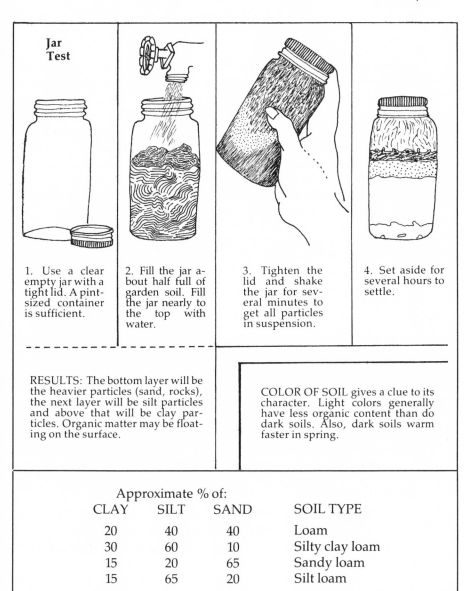

Jar Test

1. Use a clear empty jar with a tight lid. A pint-sized container is sufficient.

2. Fill the jar a-bout half full of garden soil. Fill the jar nearly to the top with water.

3. Tighten the lid and shake the jar for several minutes to get all particles in suspension.

4. Set aside for several hours to settle.

RESULTS: The bottom layer will be the heavier particles (sand, rocks), the next layer will be silt particles and above that will be clay particles. Organic matter may be floating on the surface.

COLOR OF SOIL gives a clue to its character. Light colors generally have less organic content than do dark soils. Also, dark soils warm faster in spring.

	Approximate % of:		
CLAY	SILT	SAND	SOIL TYPE
20	40	40	Loam
30	60	10	Silty clay loam
15	20	65	Sandy loam
15	65	20	Silt loam

Friability refers to the crumbliness of the soil, or the ease with which it can be pulverized when reasonably dry. A friable soil will loosen easily in the spring after it has dried and will remain airy and fluffy for some time. A desirable characteristic of soils, it can be achieved by incorporating organic matter and gypsum. The organic matter promotes growth of soil organisms. Gypsum causes chemical changes leading to eventual breakage of clay soils. Tilth goes along with friability. The tilth of a soil relates to its ease of preparation and its ability to support plant growth. Compaction comes about when the soil is disturbed during wet periods. With water and outside pressure, the soil particles are squeezed together, thus destroying friability and affecting tilth.

Rocks and debris have no function in a vegetable garden unless the rocks are being used for pathways or retaining walls. Large rocks, old roots and debris of various sorts should be raked out of the garden area before soil preparation for planting begins. Rocks get in the way of root crops, often stay warmer than surrounding soil and may cause localized dry spots in the garden. They can interfere with cultivation. In rocky areas, it may seem a new crop of rocks appears every year for they gradually work up into the top layer of soil. Debris gets in the way of cultivating tools, looks untidy and is generally a nuisance. Spend some time cleaning out the garden before the season begins.

The jar test mentioned previously is a method of determining the soil consistency, whether mostly clay, silt or sand. Topsoil usually will contain organic material in variable quantities; subsoil will seldom have enough to show. Both soil layers, top and sub, can be made to grow vegetable crops. If amendments are added and drainage conditions corrected, subsoil taken from the basement excavation will do nicely as a growing medium for most vegetables. In fact, correcting the few problems of subsoil is often better than buying topsoil. Topsoil brought from another area may be of completely different texture and may introduce another variable into the garden soil, that of layering differences. Work with what is available in the garden where possible.

While clay particles are often called the seat of chemical activity in soils, organic matter particles may be called the sites and sources of soil microorganism life. Microorganisms include the soil fungi and bacteria which complement other forms of life in a healthy soil. These are the catalysts which convert nitrogen fertilizers to forms usable by plants. In fact, most fertilizing materials must be attacked and converted by bacteria or fungi before becoming usable by plant life. Few fertilizers can be directly injected into plants; most must be channeled through microorganisms in the soil. Organic materials in the proper amounts are the stimulus for soil life.

Common sources of organic matter for home gardeners include compost, animal manures, deciduous tree leaves, old hay and peat moss. Others are sawdust, barkdust, straw, wood chips, leaf mold and shredded paper. All function to make air pockets in clay soil; act as water sponges in sandy soil; and to provide sites for soil microorganism life. In clay soils, the addition of organic matter helps separate the tight clay particles and in sandy soils organic matter gives the soil the capacity to hold water and minerals against leaching by irrigation water. Some organic materials such as animal manures or properly prepared compost, contain a variable amount of mineral nutrition. The nutrient content of manures will vary according to animal source, length of storage, type of bedding included and type of feed consumed by the animals. The next chart gives you a general idea of amount of nutrients involved. Try to apply enough manure during soil preparation to supply 1—2 pounds actual nitrogen per 1000 square feet. This means poultry manures might be needed at 200 lbs/1000 sq. ft. and strawy, old weathered manures at 1500 lbs./1000 sq. ft.

MAJOR MINERAL NUTRIENTS IN FRESH ANIMAL MANURES
(% of fresh weight)

Animal	Water	Nitrogen	Phosphorus	Potassium
Beef	80	0.7	0.45	0.55
Dairy	84	0.6	0.25	0.6
Horses	60	0.6	0.25	0.45
Sheep	65	1.05	0.35	0.95
Laying Hens	75	1.0	1.25	0.5
Broilers	30	2.8	2.30	1.8
Turkeys	30	1.3	0.75	0.5
Other Organic Sources:				
Digested sludge	—	2.0	2.0	0.5
Activated sludge	—	6.0	4.0	0.5

Purchased manures sometimes include the acquisition of problems. One of the most common problems bought with manure is the garden symphylan. This tiny pest feeds on tender root systems of many plants including vegetables. If possible, inspect the manure first. Dig a shovelful from the pile, look for tiny (¼″ or less) white insects which move quickly to avoid the light. Most frequently they will be found on older piles. If symphylans are present, use something else for the organic matter supply.

All organic matter sources require a certain amount of nitrogen to assist in the decomposition process. Some manures, especially those with large quantities of straw, wood chips or other carbonaceous material, do not contain enough nitrogen for their own breakdown and will rob soils of nitrogen for a time. This is why garden soil amended with sawdust needs extra nitrogen for 2—3 years. The nitrogen feeds the bacteria which decompose the organic matter particles which eventually supply nutrients to the garden crop— it all becomes rather an involved process, invisible to the gardener but as important to vegetable growth as sunlight.

The minerals needed for vegetable gardening include those discussed in Chapter 3. For most gardening soils the main needs are N-P-K-Ca-Mg. A soil analysis is needed for exact determination but a few general rules will be helpful.

In new soil (that which has been in pasture, weeds, lawns or used for other than vegetable crops) additional nitrogen will usually be needed at about 2 lbs. actual nitrogen per 1000 square feet. To supply this amount of N, add one of the following:

Ammonium nitrate (33-0-0)	—	6½ lbs.
Ammonium sulfate (21-0-0)	—	9 lbs.
Calcium nitrate (15-0-0)	—	14 lbs.
Blood meal (11% N)	—	18 lbs.
Chicken Manure (1-2.8% N)	—	100 lbs.

After a year of gardening and evaluating your results, nitrogen rates may be adjusted up or down depending on plant growth results, soil amendments and cover crops.

Phosphorus will be needed for plant energy when new seedlings emerge or transplants are set out. Phosphorus does not move readily thru the soil with water as N does and must be placed where plant roots can find it easily. In preparing garden soil, a base amount should be spaded or tilled into the top six inch layer of soil. One pound actual P/1000 sq. ft. is enough for most soils. To supply this amount of P, add one:

Single super phosphate (0-20-0)	—	5 lbs.
Treble super phosphate (0-45-0)	—	2 lbs.
*Ammonium phosphate (16-20-0)	—	5 lbs.
Rock phosphate (3% P)	—	33 lbs.
Bone Meal (15-20% P)	—	5 lbs.

*note that we begin listing fertilizer mixtures which supply more than a single element.

Potassium is needed for vegetable plant hardiness, pest resistance and root development. About the same amount of K (potassium) is needed as nitrogen i.e., 2 lbs. actual potassium per 1000 sq. ft. To supply this amount of K, add one:

Muriate of K (0-0-52)	—	4 lbs.
KNO_3 (potassium nitrate) (13-0-44)	—	4 lbs.
Wood ashes	—	10 lbs.

WOOD ASHES can be a valuable source of mineral elements, but some care needs to be used in their application. Wood ashes contain calcium, magnesium, phosphorus and potassium but the amounts vary depending on the type of wood, how it has been stored and what else has been burned along with the wood. Oak for example, contains about six times as much potassium as does Douglas fir. Ashes stored outside in the rain for some time will have been leached and will have lost much of their mineral content.

The amount of ash that can be safely used also depends on the type of plant to be grown. Acid loving plants for example will not tolerate the high amounts of calcium contained in wood ashes. Most garden vegetables can tolerate about five pounds of wood ash per hundred square feet per year, and benefit from the minerals contained in the ash but it is easy to build up high amounts of calcium and potassium at this rate. Beware of using ash containing byproducts left from burning cardboard boxes and bags. Sometimes the glue used in paper products contains boron. Boron is an element needed in only very minute quantities and it may be easily overdone with indiscriminate use of fireplace, wood stove or burn-barrel ash.

Calcium is usually supplied as ground limestone, dolomite limetone or wood ashes. In gardens west of the Cascades, an application every several years is needed to keep everything working right. An application of 50-80 lbs./1,000 sq. ft. is generally sufficient. In parts of the country where soils are naturally alkaline, i.e. the eastern parts of Oregon and Washington, and Idaho, gypsum is used to supply Ca and sulfur and to avoid sending the soil pH higher than normal. Gypsum also "loosens" clay soils through flocculation, a process of granulation of particles of clay. This is a very slow process and one with which most gardeners become disenchanted after seeing no effect for three or four years. A quicker method to loosen clay soil is to add organic matter to the soil.

Magnesium is sometimes deficient in garden soils and may show its effect as a lighter than normal green color in foliage. Generally a local application of magnesium sulfate (epsom salts work well) of ½ cupful per ten feet of row will correct this problem.

Drainage is vital to the growth of vegetable roots. Drainage refers to the permeability of soil which allows excess water to move downward and to allow the entry of oxygen. Poorly drained soil remains wet long after a rain or following irrigation, and may take on a sour smell through the action of bacteria which can live in the absence of oxygen. Sometimes a poorly drained soil remains wet enough to allow moss to grow on its surface. Often the soil becomes puddled or compacted as traffic, foot or equipment, presses the wet soil particles together. Altogether, drainage in Northwest soils is often the limiting factor for the growth of vegetables. Refer to Chapter 3 and the first section of this chapter for suggestions on dealing with drainage problems.

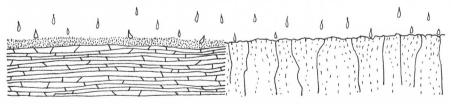

Moss grows on poorly drained soil because of continual saturation. Well drained soil allows excess water to pass and be replaced with air. _____

To prepare the garden area for planting, spade, plow or rototill the top six to eight inches of soil to loosen the ground for root growth; to get some air into the soil; and to mix the materials previously described in this chapter into the plant root area. Be sure to include organic material. Do not try working the soil while it is wet. Hold a handful of soil, press it into a ball, drop it onto a hard surface — if the ball crumbles when it hits, the soil may safely be worked; if the ball of soil lands with a sodden thud and holds together, forget it for another day or two.

Do not work the soil any more than necessary to mix amendments, to break up clumps and clods and to generally loosen the soil. Too much tilling may damage soil structure. Rake out rocks, remaining clods and debris. The seedbeds and transplant beds should be smooth, loose, free of weeds and slightly damp when you plant.

Planting Methods

There are nearly as many methods of growing vegetables as there are vegetable types. Whichever method is used, a gardener must understand that living plants require warmth, moisture, oxygen, sunlight, nutrients, and physical support.

Most methods of planting and growing vegetables involve sowing seed or transplanting seedlings (transplants) into the soil in a standard, open garden area and/or raised beds, and/or containers. Within these most common types of accommodations, one may plant in the traditional, single row furrow method or the wide row intensive method, being as structured or as casual as your character dictates.

If you have followed the suggestions in the previous section, *Soil Preparation*, your standard, open garden area is now ready to plant. If you want to try raised beds, here are some additional ideas.

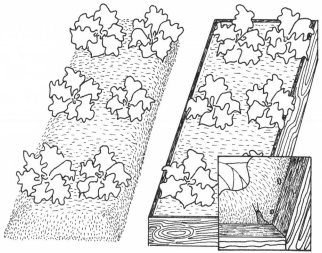

Raised beds may be prepared with or without retaining sideboards. Retaining walls may serve as hiding places for insect pests.

Raised beds are easy to prepare and function well in providing drainage for vegetable crops. The beds should be planned to supply around eight inches of depth for root growth. Raised beds may be enclosed with boards to stabilize the soil but they seem to work better if made with sloping sides without boards; not so steep that they will erode but with enough slant to reach the height needed without wasting space. During the dormant season, after gardening is done for the year, raised beds should be enriched with organic mulches for the next season's use.

PREPARING RAISED BEDS

Here is one of the easier, more effective ways to prepare a raised bed. Start by tilling or spading a level garden area. This will loosen the ground and make it easier to add needed organic material. Organic matter is the secret ingredient for most successful gardens and is almost essential for raised bed soil. Several inches of manure, ground bark, sawdust, leaf mold, compost, clean straw, mushroom compost or whatever is handy, should be worked into the top six inches of loosened soil. While you are at it, add the extra nitrogen needed to decompose them. Sprinkle ¼ pound of urea or ½ pound of ammonium sulfate per hundred square feet for each inch depth of organic matter, plus a cupful or two of ground limestone. Mix these ingredients into the top six inches of soil. Now you are ready to make the raised bed.

Shovel a walkway about 18" wide and place the excavated soil, which has previously been mixed with all the goodies mentioned above, on top of a 4' wide bed. (Or any width desired. Make it convenient to work from either side.) Shovel out enough to lower the walkway about 5–6", which will put several inches on top of the bed. Now rake and flatten the bed, angling the sides as steeply as possible short of caving in. Keep your feet off the raised bed. Walking on it compacts the soil and you lose the advantage of the raised bed. Now, to finish off the job and make things neater, cover the walk with sawdust, bark or other organic matter which will start decomposing for use next year.

Single Row Furrow Method of Planting:

Mark the row ends with stakes. Stretch a string between the stakes to make straight rows. With the edge of a hoe blade or end of a broomstick, make a furrow from one end of the row to the other. Furrows should not be more than two inches deep, but for small seeds, such as carrots, radishes, spinach and beets, the planting furrow only needs to be an inch deep.

After depositing seeds, rake a thin layer of soil into the furrow and lightly tamp with a rake or hoe to firm the soil around the seeds. If yours is a soil which tends to form a crust after a rain or irrigation, cover the seed with something besides soil. Sand, vermiculite or sawdust will supply protection for the seed yet not form a hard, impermeable crust and will also mark the row. If crusts should form, watch for seedlings lifting parts of the soil. Then with the tines of a rake carefully break the crust to allow seedlings to emerge easily. Crusted soil may be so impermeable that seedlings die before they are able to push through, or are so damaged by the effort they never recover.

FURROW PLANTINGS

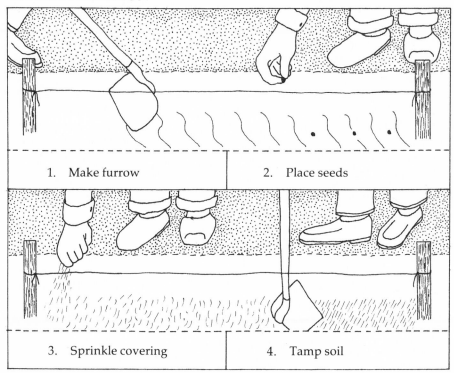

| 1. Make furrow | 2. Place seeds |
| 3. Sprinkle covering | 4. Tamp soil |

Wide Row Intensive Method of Planting:

First of all mark the boundaries of the prepared garden area to be planted. A handy size for each bed is 1½' × 4', but the size can be whatever is most convenient. The same dimensions can be used to plant raised beds. Scatter seeds over the bed or wide row surface. Try to space the seeds the proper distance apart. After seeding, press the seeds into the soil with the flat side of a hoe or a board. Then rake a little soil in from the side to give a light covering.

BANDING FERTILIZER: ROW PLANTINGS & TRANSPLANTS

An efficient way to fertilize vegetable plants, if fertilizer has not already been tilled in during soil preparation, is to apply a band of fertilizer at planting time just below and to the side of the planting row. In effect, the fertilizer is placed where the roots can find it easily. The most convenient way to band fertilizer is to put it in just before planting the row. The band of fertilizer should be about 2" below and 2" to the side the seed. Make a trench 3–4" deep, place the recommended fertilizer in the bottom, then plant the vegetable seeds at their correct depth in a second shallow trench above and to the side of the fertilizer band. Fertilizer can be of organic or chemical types. A general recommendation is about ½ cup per 10 feet of row with a chemical fertilizer such as 5-10-10 or 6-20-20. Transplants should have about 1/8 cup placed a few inches to the side and below the root systems. Rotted manure, compost or other organic materials may be used but larger quantities will be needed.

It is most important to avoid burying seeds too deeply. Seeds include an embryo, which will grow a stem upward and a root downward, and a place where the seedlings' energy reserves are stored. A seed carries enough energy to break through the soil covering so the seedling can reach the sunlight and begin manufacturing its own food. If it must grow several inches before it reaches the light, the seedling may become too weak to make it. On the other hand, if the seed is too shallowly placed in the soil it may be blown away or washed out before it can grow. A rule of thumb is to plant seeds no deeper than twice their diameter. Common sense, though, tells us to plant strong growers such as sweet corn deep enough to support and anchor the vigorous stems they soon grow. In most cases, the directions on seed packets should be followed. If the garden soil is fine-textured and apt to pack or crust, plant shallowly; if it is deep, easily loosened and loamy, plant deeper.

When planting seeds, follow the suggestions in the appendix for spacing. Seedlings grow into large plants which need room to develop properly. Spacing farther apart than necessary simply wastes space. Remember, if seeds are planted too closely you will need a very hard-hearted approach when it comes time to thin the seedlings. The idea that planting lots of seeds so the bugs can have some and leave you the remainder doesn't really work. If the bugs find a tasty crop, they usually can muster up plenty of friends to infest the entire planting.

Sowing methods are not particularly important as long as the seeds are placed in a reasonably uniform manner and pressed into the soil. Large seeds are easy to place and easy to reset if the spacing doesn't come out just right for the variety and amount of seed. Small seeds are sometimes difficult to plant evenly because they are so hard to see and hold. Some gardeners mix small seeds with sand in a salt shaker to give them better distribution.

A NOTE about planting radish seeds and controlling radish or cabbage maggot . . . This insect is the larvae form of a fly. The adult lays eggs on or near the stem of young radish plants. The maggot hatches and burrows into the fleshy part of the radish root, ruining a fine, tasty crop. This is the same pest which destroys or seriously affects the growth of cabbage and related plants. For cabbage family transplants, some control may be obtained by collars placed around the stems, but radishes would be nigh impossible to collar individually. One method which has worked reasonably well is to use diazinon granules applied in the row at planting time. Diazinon lasts about three weeks in the soil and if all goes well the radish crop will mature in four weeks, thus giving control for three weeks. Depend on prayer for the fourth. ———————————————————————

The first thing needed after seeding is moisture. Spring gardeners know they can depend on spring rains to water their seeds in and to furnish moisture for germination, but beds seeded in summer or early fall need help. Moisten the soil an inch or so downward to provide the dampness seeds need for germinating. Do this first watering with a gentle sprinkler head or soaker hose. A hard, forceful jet of water will either wash the seeds away or cover them with eroded soil. To conserve moisture, place a ¼" mulch of sawdust or bark dust over the surface of the row. Mulch is especially valuable during dry weather and can prevent the rapid loss of water by evaporation. During dry weather, water the seeded area often enough to maintain damp soil one to two inches downward. In sandy soils this may mean once per day. Clay soils may only need re-wetting every four or five days.

Finally, after the planted crop has sprouted and is growing, the gardener must be hard-hearted and thin the planting to give the remaining plants space to grow. In spite of trying to space the seeds at recommended distances, a gardener will usually plant seeds too closely. Once they are up and on their way to making healthy plants, pull out enough to give the remainder room for growth. If the plants remain crowded, they will never amount to anything. Crowded sweet corn will not develop ears, radishes will not make size, and closely planted squash will likely starve before they get large enough to bloom. Thinning should be done while the plants are young. Most should be thinned by the time the first or second *true leaf* has formed. Sweet corn should be thinned before it reaches five inches in height.

Transplants, or young plants grown indoors, are important for growing warm season crops which need many days of warmth to mature. Transplants are also used for some of the cool season crops and present a way to use the garden for double cropping, i.e. filling a harvested and vacated row with partially grown plants for the next crop. Transplants can be grown in various types of containers but transplant more easily and suffer less shock during planting if grown in individual pots.

Do not move transplants to the garden until their growing temperature needs have been reached. Tomatoes, peppers, eggplants, squash, cucumber and melons should not be planted in the garden until all danger of frost is passed, unless some means of protection is provided. Lightweight covers can be used, but they are unhandy and, the one night a gardener forgets to cover the peppers, will be the night of the heaviest spring frost. Be patient, wait until the soil warms and night temperatures are no longer nippy before planting these tender varieties.

Cole crops, i.e. cabbage, broccoli, cauliflower, Brussels sprouts, plus lettuce and celery can be transplanted to the garden whenever the soil is ready. Generally an early planting in March or April will be harvested by midsummer followed by another set of transplants put in by August for fall harvest.

Most gardeners tend to start their transplants too early and consequently end up with leggy, tough little plants that are best consigned to the compost pile. Most seedlings only need three to four weeks to develop a healthy root and top for moving oudoors. A longer period simply means the seedlings stretch for the light, become hungry and either become so tall and spindly that they collapse or so deficient in minerals that they are too starved when moved outdoors.

Several steps are involved in growing transplants including germinating lots of seeds in a seed flat or pot, transplanting to individual pots, using clean growing medium or soil, furnishing light, moisture and heat. The steps are the same whether using a windowsill, greenhouse, coldframe or hotbed.

PASTEURIZING SOIL

An easy way to make sure soil used in seedling production is free of harmful organisms is to pasteurize it in the kitchen oven. All you need is a reasonably large flat pan and an oven thermometer or soil or dairy thermometer. Place a 2−3″ layer of slightly moistened soil in a baking pan, set the oven at its lowest setting (usually 200°F). Stick the thermometer an inch or so into the soil. When the soil temperature reaches 180°, begin timing. Maintain 180° for thirty minutes and soil diseases, weed seeds and bugs are controlled. Let the soil cool and it is ready for planting. Pasteurize a large enough batch so some can be stored in a clean container or plastic bag for later use.

SEEDLING DEVELOPMENT

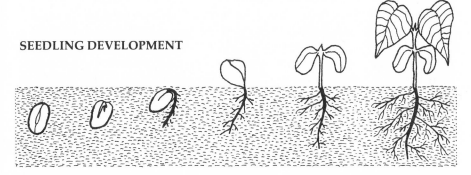

A bean plant begins growth by starting its root system, then it pushes the cotyledon leaves above the surface, followed by the first set of *true leaves*. Do not transplant seedlings until the first set of true leaves has developed.

Shown from left to right: bean with seed coat (testa), testa shedding, first root developing, seedling emerging and breaking ground, growth to first set of true leaves.

Plant the seeds so they are barely covered. Most seeds do best when they are covered with only a light dusting of peat moss. Water carefully, but thoroughly and let the excess drain away. Now cover the container with a sheet of newspaper or a glass pane. This covering will maintain high humidity around the seeds and protect the tender young shoots as they emerge. Keep the seed container in a spot where the temperature is between 60 and 70°F. When most of the seeds have sprouted, gradually remove the cover and allow air to circulate across the seedlings. When they have grown their first set of true leaves, they are ready to move into individual containers. Most seedlings, except those like onions and corn, sprout with a set of cotyledon leaves which were the storage organs for the seed embryo. After the plant has formed a few roots and is ready to turn on its food manufacturing process, it shoots up a true leaf or two which contain the chlorophyll for photosynthesis. At this point the seedling can be transplanted most easily and with the greatest chance of success.

Containers for the initial transplant can be peat pots, small flower pots, styrofoam cups, egg cartons, or any other small clean container. Make sure the containers have a hole from which excess water can drain. In this initial transplant operation we need to use a good potting soil so the seedlings can do their best. Use some of your pasteurized soil mixed with 1/3 part fresh peat moss. Fill the containers with the potting mix then poke a hole in the soil to receive the seedling.

When transplanting young seedlings, do it carefully; they are very tender and can be easily damaged. Using a small stick such as a pot label or popsicle stick, carefully loosen the soil around the seedling. Then, prying with the stick and gently lifting, bring the individual seedling out of the soil with its roots intact. Place the roots in the planting hole and softly press soil around the roots. The seedling should be set at the same depth as it grew in the seed flat. Now water the soil, let it drain and put the new plant in a place with lots of light, temperature of 60–70°F and where air can circulate to keep diseases to a minimum. Water whenever the soil feels dry.

Here are a few things to watch for —

1. Weak and spindly growth means light is not strong enough and/or temperatures are too high.

2. Toppling over and dying is a sign of damping-off disease, accelerated by lack of air circulation and often caused by soil organisms in unpasteurized soil.

3. Leaves pale green means the plants are hungry and need a light feeding with a soluble, quick acting fertilizer. Be careful though, overfeeding can be harmful.

If you are intent on growing your own transplants and if indoor space is limited, see discussion on coldframes and hotbeds in Chapter 2.

"HARDENING OFF"

Hardening off is a term used to describe a toughening up process in young growing plants. When the young vegetable seedlings are being grown indoors with just the right amount of heat, light, moisture and nutrition, they are succulent, crisp and tender, usually too tender to move directly into the garden. To acclimatize them for outdoor conditions, the transplants should be hardened off for a week or so before planting by gradually exposing them to more sunlight and cooler temperatures. This toughening process reduces the shock which would result from a sudden move from cozy indoor conditions to the cold cruel world.

All transplants will get off to a better start if some special care is provided. First of all, don't take a tender transplant directly from a warm, cozy greenhouse or kitchen window and move it to a cold, windy garden. Give it a few days in an outdoor protected spot to get used to the temperature. This is a part of the hardening off process and the only one necessary in Northwest gardens. In other parts of the country the hardening off process includes withholding water and fertilizer, but for Northwest gardens we need vegetable plants which will "land running and keep growing," so keep them watered and fed while they get accustomed to the cooler temperatures.

Transplant during the cool part of the day. Evening is best, as the plant can recover from any wilting during the night and be ready to greet the sun the next morning. Do not transplant during the hottest part of day. No matter how carefully a transplant is handled it will invariably lose some roots during the planting process. Root loss means less uptake of soil water and more wilting. Wilted plants exposed to hot sunlight die quickly. Give the transplants a chance, plant early morning or evening, not mid-sunny day.

Check the spacing needs of the vegetable being set into the garden. Since the transplant is obviously healthy enough to grow give it the room needed to mature.

Prepare the soil beforehand as suggested under *Soil Preparation* so the young plants can get off to a good start. Dig a hole large and deep enough to hold the root ball attached to the young plant. Loose soil will settle when it is watered so set the transplant about an inch lower than its level in the pot or flat. In other words, set it deep enough that an inch of soil can be placed over its root system. Tomatoes are the exception to this rule. Tomatoes have the ability to grow roots from the stem above the root ball. Tall, gangly tomato plants can be buried almost to the bottom set of leaves yet grow vigorously, whereas other vegetables so planted would probably die of root smothering.

Now water the plant so the soil particles are brought into intimate contact with the root system. In new garden soils, or soils where some difficulty in establishing the new plant might be expected, water with a soluble fertilizer to give the young plant a boost. A tablespoon of 20-20-20 per gallon of water or a cup of manure tea per gallon of water makes a good solution which can be used at a cup per plant as a booster.

To give the transplant some additional mineral nutrition, (if the soil has not been previously fertilized) several inches to one side of the plant dig a hole a few inches deeper than the one dug for the plant. Place two rounded tablespoons of complete fertilizer, such as 5-10-10 or 6-12-12 in the bottom or, using organics, place four tablespoons of tankage, fish meal or blood meal in the hole and cover.

One last item before leaving the transplant to do its thing. Irrigation sometimes becomes a problem once the plant grows to its mature size and sprawls several feet across the garden. One way of making sure the root system is watered is to bury a tall juice can several inches to the side of the transplant. First punch a number of holes in the bottom of the can sides. Then bury so the bottom of the can is about five inches below the soil surface. When watering the row of transplants simply fill the can planted alongside each plant. When additional fertilizer is needed, place it in the can and irrigate it into the root system. This system will also help hold down summer weeds by restricting water and fertilizer to the area used by the vegetable plant.

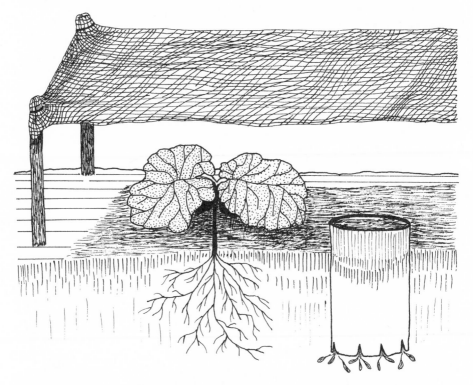

Insure the growth of new transplants by providing water to its roots (illustrated here using the "juice can" method). In hot areas provide a little shade until the plant is accustomed to the location. _____

In situations where transplants must go into hot sunny sites, shade the row temporarily with frames of lath, covers of cheesecloth, or whatever is handy to screen off some of the sunlight.

In windy areas protect the transplant from continual wind with a wind shield. A board, shingle, shake or sheet of cardboard should be placed to screen the plant until it is established and growing.

Now, another word about mulching. Mulches do a great deal of good in Northwest gardens. They help control weeds, decrease the loss of soil moisture to evaporation, and affect soil temperatures. Black and clear polyethylene mulch will warm the soil beneath them. Clear poly sheeting will, however, allow weeds to grow beneath the plastic. Organic mulches act as insulation and should not be put on the garden until the soil warms in early summer. For example, if a barkdust mulch is placed over the garden in early April, it may be late June before the soil warms enough for sweet corn to grow.

Transplants are admirably suited for mulching. A row of plants is easily seen and can be mulched without worry, whereas seeded rows may be smothered by the mulch.

While most plants are easily grown from seeding directly in the soil and are not commonly transplanted, an excellent scheduled cropping system can be managed by starting a few seeds, in a pot indoors, moving them into the garden when they attain transplanting size and planting the entire clump. For example, fill a four-inch pot with potting soil and plant 18 radish seeds, or 12 carrots. Set this pot indoors where it will stay warm and well lighted and can be watered. In a week or ten days when the plants are up, take the pot to the garden. Remove the soil ball and plant it. Now start another potful indoors. When the first plants are ready for harvest, pull them all for a mess of radishes or a dozen carrots. Next week pull another. The kitchen can be kept supplied from early spring through fall using this scheduled cropping system.

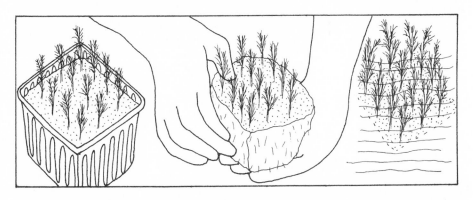

Garlic, onions, asparagus and rhubarb are planted as plant parts. Garlic and onions are bulbs, asparagus is planted as a "crown" and rhubarb as a part of a fleshy crown with at least one bud to grow. To plant these parts, prepare the soil as suggested for transplants. Several inches below the base of the garlic or onion, work a couple tablespoons of 5-10-10 complete fertilizer, bone meal, or fish meal into the soil if you have not previously added fertilizer when preparing the soil. Set the bulb so the top is about an inch below the soil surface. Asparagus and rhubarb are perennial plants which will remain in the same spot for many years. Prepare their planting area by burying several spadesful of manure or compost 6-8" below their roots. A good way to get a bed of rhubarb or asparagus started is to dig a trench 1½ feet deep in a well drained site. Fill the trench about a foot deep with manure or compost then top off with 4-5" of soil before setting the crowns. Set the crowns of either with about an inch or two of soil over the top of the bud.

For the what, when, and how much to plant see Appendix I.

Managing Plant Growth

Weeding: One of the most time consuming chores in managing a garden is weed control. In the mild climate west of the Cascades weeds thrive through the entire year. Summer weeds sprout with the seeded vegetables and continue to come up through the growing season. Then in the fall a winter group of weeds invades the garden, keeping it green and weedy all winter and will still be present when spring planting time comes. Weeds can be tedious pests, or with some planned management ideas may not be so bad after all. Planting methods aimed at maximizing productive space, irrigation methods that insure water is directed toward the prized crop, and using mulches to hinder weed growth, all reduce time spent getting rid of weeds. Chemical controls that may be effective in the vegetable garden are discussed in Chapter 4.

Weeds are competitors. In fact they are the Olympic winners in Nature's continuing competition for survival of the fittest. They have made it through countless years of evolution and climate changes. And weeds have successfully withstood the onslaught of insect and animal predators. Their only competitors are their relatives. Even when crowded in parched, poor soil they are able to grow, bloom and set a crop of hundreds of seeds. Consequently, those non-competitive, tender little vegetable plants, so lovingly placed in neat rows and beds, stand about as much chance of making it on their own against weeds as the proverbial snowball in a hot place.

A gardener may wonder how it is possible to completely clean out a miniature forest of weeds one day, only to return several days later and find a new stand of the pests. Weed seeds remain in the soil for years, ready to sprout whenever conditions are right. Every time the garden is cultivated, new seeds are brought to the surface and are ready to sprout. Pigweed seeds which have been buried for fifty years still retain their viability, sprouting as soon as moisture, proper temperatures, and light are available.

For the small home garden the best advice is to hoe and hand-pull the offenders — and keep at it. Weeds use the moisture and minerals needed for vegetable growth. Start early and pull or hoe young weeds before they completely discourage the desired vegetable plants. Young weed seedlings can be pulled and spaded or tilled under to add organic matter to the soil. Old weeds with seed crops attached should be removed from the garden and burned. Composting old weeds in the hope of killing weed seeds is seldom successful. Generally the seeds remain viable and when the compost is spread over the garden a new crop of weeds is sown.

Weeds can be controlled by mulching. A layer of bark or sawdust an inch or so deep will discourage some seedlings. A layer of newspaper, roofing paper or plastic sheeting will smother most. Black polyethylene is very effective and will warm the soil slightly as an added benefit. Clear plastic sheeting will act as a greenhouse so weeds will flourish unless the heat becomes sufficiently intense to kill the tops. For seeded crops, a deep mulch must wait until the seedlings are up, else they may be smothered along with the weeds. For transplants, a mulch applied at planting time eases the need for continuous weeding chores. When using plastic, cover the row to be planted, burying the edges to prevent wind from blowing it away. Cut an opening for each plant just large enough for the planting operation and weight down the cut flaps with a clod. When the plants need to be irrigated, simply water through the planting hole.

Several herbicides which can be used on certain vegetable crops safely and effectively are available from your nearest garden store. However, none can be used in all situations for all vegetable varieties, nor be expected to control all weed species. Be careful with herbicides in the garden. It is much safer and less costly to take care of weeds in other ways.

A new gardener, yet unsure about whether a plant is a weed or a desirable vegetable can prepare for this confusion by planting several seeds of each variety in a pot indoors. Use a clean, weed-free potting soil so you know the plant emerging is one of your vegetables. Then, when the young seedlings emerge, take the potted plants to the garden to identify the vegetables. Here are some other ideas:

1. Remember where the vegetable seeds were planted. Watch for seedlings in rows or some pattern indicating they were hand planted and not scattered randomly as weeds are.

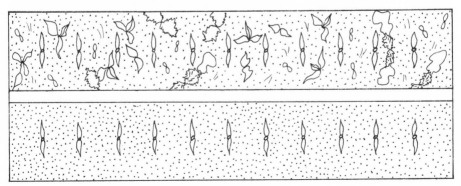

2. Look at the unplanted areas of the garden and match the suspected weeds with those coming up via Nature's planting.
3. Those growing the most vigorously are probably weeds.
4. A last resort — pull everything up, those that grow back will be weeds.

The garden should be weeded often enough to prevent competition between weeds and vegetables. Usually, once a week is sufficient unless you live or garden in particularly weedy and fertile soil. Every time the garden is visited though, any weeds which have regained a foothold should be pulled. These efforts will pay off in better vegetables.

For the optimistic gardener who likes to see some good in everything, take heart, weeds are not always bad. Many are edible, some do well as cover crops, others prevent erosion, and young weeds can add to the value of a compost.

Chickweed, a winter annual, grows lush in the bare garden area and can be plowed under in spring as a cover crop. While not as effective as legumes or coarser stemmed cover crop plants, it still adds some organic materials from its succulent stems and foliage.

Annual bluegrass, chickweed, clover and many other low-growing weeds serve well in preventing soil erosion. With their strong roots and tangled mat foliage, rainfall and runoff water is intercepted and kept from rushing off with the valuable topsoil.

Some weeds pose a menace to the garden because they are so invasive and hard to get rid of. Bindweed and morning glory, quackgrass, thistles and sorrel are the five most offensive and noxious. The first two are vining perennials with attractive flowers but they strangle and climb on and over any plant, fence or structure they come near. Pull, pull and pull and when you despair of ever winning the battle, check the local garden stores for a leaf-absorbed systemic herbicide which can be used to help control these invaders. Quackgrass and sorrel, and to a lesser extent thistles, move into the garden via invasive and vigorous root systems. Pulling them is good exercise but nearly every root left behind in the soil will produce a new plant. Heavy, black plastic mulches are fairly effective in smothering their growth. If all else fails, look for spot application herbicides as mentioned above. If perennial weeds take over completely, soil fumigation will be needed. Metham, generally sold as *Vapam*, is effective but one must plan to fumigate at a time when soil moisture and temperature are right for the fumigant to work. The area cannot be planted for two to three weeks following fumigation.

Watering: With all the rain received by the Northwest during our winters, one would expect we could coast through the summers without worrying about soil moisture. However, as soon as the rains stop, the soil dries; luckily for us, since if it didn't drain away quickly, our gardening would be hydroponic.

New seedlings and transplants should be watered often enough to keep the soil damp an inch below the surface. To maintain this level of moisture may require daily watering for midsummer plantings but only weekly during the cool and humid spring. Once the plants are up and growing well, decrease the frequency to about once a week but increase the amount applied so the soil is dampened four to six inches downward.

Apply water only to the planted row or wide bed, not to the space between rows where vegetable roots cannot reach the moisture and where you will only stimulate weeds. Minimize water loss by using soaker hoses or drip irrigation systems. These supply water in the row where needed. If sprinklers must be used, adjust them to cover the garden only, and not the surrounding area.

The amount of water needed to dampen six inches of garden soil varies by the type of soil. On sandy soil an inch of water will do the job, while clay loam soils will require 1½″. These recommended amounts are particularly important if you are using overhead sprinklers. If overheads are used, set an empty can somewhere in the sprinkler pattern and check it from time to time during irrigation to see how much you are delivering to the soil. The length of time required to supply an inch of water through a sprinkler may surprise you. Whether using soakers or sprinklers, take the time to dig into the watered row a day later to see how far the moisture has soaked. If it is still dry at the six inch level, better add some time to the irrigation schedule.

Older, leafy plants in dry summer heat will need water more frequently than will young plants in the cool spring. The closer a vegetable plant approaches maturity, the more water it will need to develop a high quality crop.

Obviously the garden will need more water during dry, windy and hot periods.

Wilting of foliage is the first sign most gardeners see when the plants lack water. But, before wilting occurs, the observant gardener will see a subtle change in color. Other effects from water shortages may include dropping of bean blossoms before they can be pollinated, shriveling of pea pods and death of young squash fruits. Some plants draw moisture from developing fruits to stay alive, leading to blossom-end-rot on tomato and peppers. When these signs appear, replenish the soil water quickly and deeply, as the plant is in severe stress.

There are several ways to supply water to the vegetable garden. Select the method best suited to your soil type (see Chapter 3) and which will most economically provide water to your style of planting.

Sandy soils absorb water quickly and pass it out of the root zone almost as fast. Sandy soils must be watered more often than other types to support plant growth. Clay soils absorb water much slower and hang onto it longer. A clay soil may be able to supply sufficient moisture for several weeks following irrigation.

A slow application of small water droplets is best for most soils. A soaker hose or a drip system laid alongside the row of vegetables are two of the better means of economically putting water where it is needed.

The buried juice can mentioned previously is a way to supply moisture to the root systems of bushy, spreading vegetable plants. This method insures that the water reaches the lower roots without furnishing water for weeds growing nearby.

Once the garden is past the seedling stage, plan to water the garden soil deeply about once a week. Deep infrequent watering is more effective than daily light applications. Light and frequent applications simply keep the surface inch or two damp and stimulates the growth of shallow surface roots. Deep watering encourages the roots to follow the water into the soil, which results in a stronger, far-reaching system of roots which can maintain the plant during dry periods.

A major problem encountered by gardeners experimenting with raised beds is keeping the bed watered. Raised beds tend to dry much faster than level ground and once dry completely are difficult to moisten. During a dry summer, a raised bed may need daily watering to maintain plant growth. To meet this problem leave a soaker hose on the bed through the summer.

The best time for watering is early morning. If your water service is a city system, the pressure is usually highest in early morning. By watering before the sun gets too high and heats the environment, less water will be lost to evaporation. Early watering helps control foliar diseases as the foliage will have a chance to dry off before evening.

Water is a major component of vegetables. It is used internally in plant tissues to transport minerals and plant foods and is evaporated to control the plant's temperature. A steady level of water must be maintained by the plant. A carefully planned and managed irrigation program whose objective is a relatively constant water level in the soil is critical to good gardening.

Excessive moisture, alternating with dry periods can not only kill or stunt plants but also alter the edible parts of vegetables which diminishes their food value. Tomatoes may develop cracked skins, carrots may split, and radishes crack. Potatoes stop growing in dry soil. When moisture is restored, the tubers make a fast expansion which results in knobby potatoes. So make every effort to avoid extremes of wetness or dryness.

Feeding: Keep in mind the basic facts discussed in Chapter 3 regarding types of minerals and their use in growing plants. Of the major plant nutrients, phosphorus is needed for energy use by young plants, nitrogen is needed for foliage growth and potassium for hardiness. Of these phosphorus is the least mobile and once banded alongside the row or tilled into the bed, will probably last the entire year. Potassium generally stays around and will seldom be needed more than once per year. Nitrogen is mobile, soluble, and quickly used. As a result, N may need to be re-supplied a month or so after the plants begin growth.

Remember that all plants need a basic supply of the major nutrients nitrogen (N), phosphorus (P), and potassium (K) but that each plant has a differing ratio of needs. Vegetables grown for their foliage, such as spinach, chard, lettuce, mustard greens and celery need more nitrogen than phosphorus and potassium. Fertilizers which encourage foliage have a ratio of 2-1-1 (10-5-5, 6-3-3) or a combination of equal parts calcium nitrate (15-0-0) and a complete fertilizer such as 5-10-10. Nitrogen alone can be supplied using ammonium sulfate (½ cup), ammonium nitrate (⅓ cup), calcium nitrate (¾ cup) or urea (¼ cup) per twenty square feet. If organics are preferred, sidedress with rotted manure, compost or other organic material in larger quantities. Manure tea or fish emulsion can be used to supply nitrogen in liquid form.

Plants grown for their fruits, seeds or flowers produce better with a fertilizer supply ratio of 1-2-1 (5-10-5, 10-20-10) or a combination of superphosphate (0-20-0) and 5-10-10. Tomatoes, peppers, cucumbers, squash, pumpkins, artichokes, root crops, peas, beans and sweet corn are plants needing more phosphorus than nitrogen.

Top quality vegetables come from management of water, soil, fertilizer and pest control resources. To insure the best use of fertilizers, all summer applications of fertilizer must be followed by a good deep watering to dissolve and move the nutrients into the root zones.

Vegetables may be "sidedressed" with fertilizer by making a trench several inches deep and three or four inches to the side of the row or it can be broadcast evenly alongside the row and watered in. For wide rows and beds, broadcast the fertilizer evenly across the beds keeping the chemical fertilizers off the leaves. After applying, irrigate to dissolve the fertilizer and move it into the root system.

TIMING SUPPLEMENTAL FERTILIZER

Additional fertilizer in early summer will stimulate growth. The timing is important lest the stimulus prevents the setting of fruits or promotes excessive leafiness in crops grown for root or fruit production. Here is a guide to timing for those vegetables normally benefiting from an added feeding:

Crop	Time of Application
Beans	After heavy bloom and as pods are forming
Broccoli	Three weeks after transplanting
Brussels sprouts	Three weeks after transplanting
Cabbage	Three weeks after transplanting
Cauliflower	Three weeks after transplanting
Chard	When plants are 4" high
Cucumber	About a week after blooming begins
Eggplant	After first fruit set
Kale	About a month after planting
Lettuce	2-3 weeks after transplanting
Melon	1-2 weeks after bloom begins
Onions	When bulbs begin to swell
Peppers	After first fruit set
Potatoes	After blossoms begin
Tomatoes	After first fruits are nearly ripe

Deficiency symptoms vary from one species to the next, so we will not attempt to describe every mineral deficiency sign for every vegetable. In the Pacific Northwest, on moderately fertile soils sustained by an annual application of fertilizer, only three or four mineral deficiencies and their symptoms occur in the typical garden. Most Northwest garden soil analyses show high amounts of phosphorus and potassium in soils which have been fertilized annually with complete fertilizer, manure or wood ashes. The four elements in which our soils are likely to be deficient are nitrogen, magnesium, iron and occasionally, phosphorus.

A shortage of nitrogen causes stunted plants and lighter than normal foliage color. The same symptom will be seen in all plants in the area and will affect all of the foliage on every plant. Magnesium shortage affects the older leaves making them a pale green with deeper green veins. Iron deficiency causes chlorosis (lacking green color) and can be detected by a yellow-green cast on the newer leaves. Phosphorus deficiency which occasionally occurs in cold soils or during cold spring periods, induces a general purpling of the foliage. Mineral deficiencies will not be seen in the garden of the informed gardener who has learned to read the plants and respond to their needs. Refer to Chapter 3 for specific advice on correcting mineral deficiencies.

Several vegetables have specific requirements for specific elements. Tomatoes and peppers need calcium to prevent blossom-end-rot, a blackening of the bottom end of the tomato or pepper fruit. Remember though, that blossom-end-rot can also result from insufficient water during fruit development. See Chapter 3 for recommendations on amending soil for calcium. A note of caution: avoid using lime or ashes in ground to be planted to potatoes. Scab, a fungus disease affecting the skin of potato tubers, is usually worse in limed soils.

Boron may be deficient in some soils, but be extra careful with this element. A little is fine for most crops but too much is deadly. Boron should be supplied only on the basis of a soil analysis. Some indications of boron shortage are: scabby beet roots, split celery stems, hollow stems in cabbage and cauliflower, and dark spots in the flesh of radishes. If a soil test shows less than 0.5 ppm, boron may be added in the form of a 10% material such as agricultural borox or 20 Mule Team borax at the rate of ½ lb. per 1000 square feet. With so small a quantity it is easier to mix it with water and apply as a spray.

Sulfur is needed by cabbage, cauliflower, broccoli and cole crops. If you don't believe these plants use sulfur, drive past a rotted cabbage field in late winter and breathe deeply. Sulfur can most easily be applied, along with the necessary nitrogen, as ammonium sulfate.

Insect and Disease Control: Insect pests and plant diseases in the garden may cause direct injury or abnormal growth, or both. The cause may be obvious or obscure. There may be easy remedies or none at all. One of the gardener's most important objectives should be learning to evaluate the effects of visiting bugs, the onslaught of plant diseases and how to minimize damage.

An old farming concept, presently called Integrated Pest Management (IPM) has become popular nationwide. It is an idea that makes a lot of sense in the home vegetable garden. In simple terms, to grow healthy and productive vegetables, IPM advocates integrating natural predators with rational plant growing techniques and careful use of chemicals. It recognizes and emphasizes the importance of naturally occurring pest predators that can help prevent insect damage and suggests that a natural balance may or may not exist between the bad bugs and the good. It also urges the careful use of pesticides when destructive pests outnumber the beneficial.

Few problems, insect or disease, affect all types of vegetables. Most affect only certain types of plants so the watchful gardener will often find them affecting only one or two plants in a row. Treat these individual plants rather than saturating the entire garden for one colony of plant lice on a bush bean plant.

In the Pacific Northwest, almost any time a radish or cabbage crop is planted, the root maggot can be expected to appear. The maggot may kill young cabbage plants by chewing into the lower stem of the plant, or leave a radish looking like Swiss cheese. Mildew is equally certain, if we have not provided adequate air circulation. Prevention is the best means of controlling both root maggots and mildew: prevention by pre-treatment of the radish row for the maggot, and of mildew by planning the layout of the garden to promote air movement.

There are any number of ways to protect vegetables against pest problems. Washing the foliage periodically will remove some insects and mites. Freeing the leaves of sweet corn or bush beans of dust will help keep spider mites under control. Wash (with a high pressure water nozzle) the foliage in the early morning so water on the foliage during a warm, still night doesn't lead to other more serious fungal disease problems.

Watering practices have an important effect on the incidence of plant disease. Keep foliage dry, especially during warm and humid days and nights. Plant diseases are encouraged by warm, moist conditions when the air is still. In general, irrigate by applying the water to the soil at the crown of the plant rather than over their tops. Soaker hoses and drip systems are preferable to sprinklers.

Here are further suggestions to prevent disease and insect problems:

1. Prune for air circulation. Ventilation and air movement prevent plant diseases from obtaining a foothold. Blights will invariably attack the dense tangled growth of unstaked tomato plants or the foliage of snap beans planted too closely for air to circulate. Keep the pruner handy and remove the extra foliage from dense plantings.

2. Sanitation. One of the keys to successful gardening is keeping it clean. Garden refuse should be removed to the compost or spaded under. Diseased plants should be removed and burned. Weeds should be pulled, not only because they compete with vegetable plants for nutrients and water, but because they harbor insect pests. Some weeds, clover for example, carry virus diseases which can seriously affect peas and other vegetables.

3. Barriers. Insects frequently deposit eggs near their favorite plant food, so when the larva hatches it readily finds its way to the plant. Cabbage maggot is an example. Paper collars around the stem at or just below the soil level prevent this worm from reaching the plant. This strategy can be used successfully to deal with cutworms, flea beetles and cucumber beetle larvae.

Cabbage maggot larva may be kept away by using collar barriers.

Insect pests in the vegetable garden are to be expected. By expecting them, the gardener can watch for the first to emerge and take care of them before the population becomes damaging. There are volumes written about garden pests, but the typical gardener will usually have to deal with only a few. So here we list the inevitable, three of the probable and a couple occasional pests you may encounter.

Inevitable —

APHIDS. Small, soft-bodied, colored from pale green to black insects which suck the juices of plants. They usually cause sticky and curled foliage. They often spread virus diseases in the garden. They are eaten by ladybugs, aphid lions and several other predators. If predators seem to be working, wait to see if they can control the problem. If the aphid population enlarges, resort to the use of one of the insecticides, botanical or chemical, specifically formulated to control aphids.

CABBAGE MAGGOT (also called RADISH MAGGOT). The maggot, a white, legless worm, ¼" or less in length, chews its way into young cole crop stems, causing them to topple and die, or into the fleshy part of radishes, making them inedible. Collars may protect cole crops but prevention with the proper insecticide at planting time will provide more total control.

SLUGS. Voracious feeders on any new foliage, look like a shell-less snail and are, undoubtedly, the worst garden pests in the Pacific Northwest.

While they can be briefly controlled by various traditional means ranging from sprinkling salt on them to beer in a saucer, no single practice other than poison baiting works for long. Eliminating their hiding places (under rocks, odd bits of lumber and other debris) is the single best cultural measure you can take.

SPIDER MITES. A certain resident on almost any vegetable during the dry, and dusty part of the summer. Tiny, sucking spiders, their presence is usually shown by loss of leaf color, a dusty appearance and tiny webs. Washing the foliage will help. If predators are being overwhelmed, use a pesticide labelled for mites several times at weekly intervals.

Probable —

CUTWORMS. Gray, brown or black, usually curled, worms about an inch long. Several types affect gardens, feeding on young plant stems during late spring and later coming to the tops of plant as foliage feeders. Handpick or control with insecticide.

FLEA BEETLES. Little, fast moving beetles that chew roundish holes in leaves of potatoes, beans and tomatoes. Larvae of the flea beetle burrow under the skin of potato tubers. Difficult to control in the soil. Apply insecticide labelled for beetles to foliage if damage is seen.

SYMPHYLAN. This is one the gardener may never see. It lives in the soil, is seldom more than ¼" long, fast moving, white, many legged, and avoids light. Often brought into the garden in manure, it feeds on the small feeder roots of almost anything. Frequent cultivation or tilling to break up its pathways will sometimes help. Any one of several insecticides labelled for soil drenching near vegetables will help. When the population grows to the point that areas of the garden refuse to grow anything, resort to soil fumigation.

Occasional —

WESTERN SPOTTED CUCUMBER BEETLE. This pest looks like a ladybug with a green paint job, light green with black spots. It chews holes in foliage, eats blossoms and pods of beans and other crops. Dust or spray if large numbers are present.

CABBAGE MOTHS and WORMS. The white butterfly dancing over the garden is the adult of the worm which chews large holes in the head of a cabbage or leaves of any of the cole crops. Botanical or chemical controls can be used if handpicking becomes tiresome. See the next page for a chart of common pests.

COMMON PESTS OF VEGETABLES

CUTWORM. 1–2″, grayish or brown, plump, smooth-skinned. Usually found curled at base of plants, particularly seedlings and transplants. Nips off plants at or below soil surface.

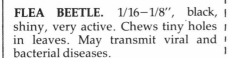

FLEA BEETLE. 1/16–1/8″, black, shiny, very active. Chews tiny holes in leaves. May transmit viral and bacterial diseases.

CABBAGE MAGGOT. 1/4–1/3″, yellowish-white. Feeds on roots and stems just below soil surface; particularly damaging to seedlings and transplants. May introduce fungus diseases.

APHID. 1/8–1/5″, green to black, soft-bodied, winged or wingless. Sucks plant juices. Colonies usually found on new growth and underside of leaves. May spread virus.

SLUG. Up to about 6″, yellow, gray to black or brown. Eats large holes in foliage; mostly feeds at night. Egg masses resemble translucent tapioca.

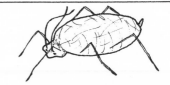

WESTERN SPOTTED CUCUMBER BEETLE. ¼″, greenish-yellow, 12 black spots. Eats holes in leaves, attacks seedlings. May carry bacterial wilt.

LEAFHOPPER. 1/8″, light greenish yellow, very active. Sucks plant juices. May spread virus.

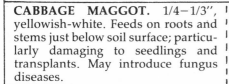

Certain diseases may be expected at specific times in the growing season. Disease control is mostly a matter of prevention. Here are a few diseases to watch for:

DAMPING OFF. A complex of several fungi which attack seedlings, causing the stem to die. Provide air circulation and let the seedlings dry slightly between waterings to minimize opportunities for these fungi to develop. A dusting of garden fungicide will help. Once the seedlings have grown a few true leaves, this problem disappears.

POWDERY MILDEW. A white, powdery fungus found on the foliage of beans, squash and other vine crops. It limits the ability of leaves to photosynthesize plant foods. Air circulation, sunlight and reduced humidity will keep this problem to a minimum but a fungicide may be needed. Affected foliage should be pruned away.

VIRUSES. Many viruses attack vegetables. Symptoms include deformed leaves, discoloration, stunted plants or abnormal growth. These same symptoms are readily confused with those resulting from insect and nutritional problems. If you have prepared your soil correctly and can find no evidence of an insect invasion the symptoms are caused by a virus. Viruses produce systemic diseases rather than local infections, and once in the plant system, are there to stay. Viruses are spread by moving plant juices from diseased plants to healthy ones. Usually the juices are transported by aphids or other sucking insects. Viruses more commonly infect garden peas, squash and beans than other vegetables. To control viral disease, pull and burn diseased plants, get rid of weeds which act as hosts for viruses and control insects which spread the disease from plant to plant (aphids, leafhoppers, etc.).

TOMATO BLIGHTS. A family of diseases which usually show up in midsummer during warm, humid weather. First showing as black spots on the lower foliage, it eventually progresses into the fruit, causing discolored areas and making the fruit unusable. Prevention through providing ample room between plants for good ventilation and pruning away superfluous growth so sunlight can penetrate the plant are the best measures to take. Watch for the disease and treat with fungicides if these cultural practices fail.

General Management Tips:

While the vegetables are growing, your management skills will be called on to keep everything coming along on schedule. Pruning, staking, cultivating and otherwise directing the growth of plants will pay off in greater yields.

Tomatoes and vine crops (squash, melons and cucumber) can be pruned and trained to occupy minimal space. The small side branches of a tomato plant can be nipped off to permit entry of air and sunlight. Rather than allowing squash or pumpkins to ramble all over the garden, cut the vine off at the second or third node or leaf beyond the last flower to yield bigger and better fruit, less greenery and less occupied space.

To keep tomatoes off the ground, tie them to stakes. Start training the young plant by clipping the growing tip after the plant has grown four or five sets of leaves. The pruning will force several new shoots to grow from buds at the base of the top leaves. As the new shoots develop tie them to several stakes driven into the ground surrounding the young plant. Whenever the shoots make six or eight inches of growth, tie to the closest stake. If staking is too tedious for your taste, wrap the young plant with a cylinder of wide mesh wire to provide not only support but containment.

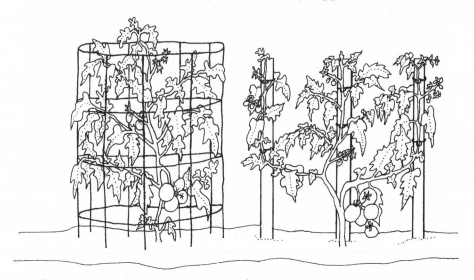

Staking or caging tomatoes gets them up in the air away from crawling pests, keeps the fruit clean and provides better air circulation for disease prevention.

As the crop is growing, do some early harvesting as you tend to other garden needs. The early pods of garden peas or snap beans should be picked as they develop rather than waiting for the entire vine to mature. Pick early to stimulate the growth of more. Begin harvesting as soon as there is something to eat. Larger vegetables are not better. On the contrary, the younger, less mature vegetables are tastier. Plants grow with only one objective, that of propagating a new generation by bearing fruit. So vegetable production can be increased simply by early harvesting and thus stimulating the plants to produce more. Beans, peas, summer squash and cucumber fruit should never be allowed to mature unless you are tired of eating them.

New potatoes can be harvested when the first blooms appear on the vines. Simply dig down carefully and rob a few spuds from beneath each plant. When thinning densely seeded vegetables, save the young carrots, lettuce and other leafy crops pulled to use in salads.

When broccoli develops a large central head, harvest and eat it. Removing the center part will stimulate more heads to sprout and so increase the yield from this vegetable.

ROBBING SPUDS

Cauliflower and celery will be of better quality if blanched while they are growing. Unblanched cauliflower may sunburn or develop an off-white color. To circumvent this problem, bring the large outer leaves together above the head when it is about the size of a teacup and bind with a rubber band. While taking a minute or two, you will be rewarded with a snow white head of cauliflower. Celery grows well in Northwest soils and early planting will yield long stalks by midsummer. It should be blanched while growing by mounding mulching material or loose soil around the lower half of the plant. The stalks which result will be light colored and of better quality.

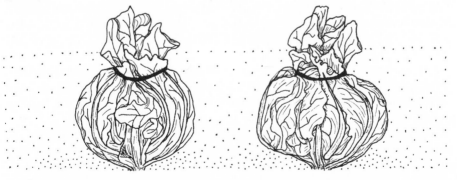

Lettuce may tend to become bitter and tough in direct hot sunlight. A little shading with lath frames, cheesecloth or netting will give a better quality harvest.

Taking & Giving

Home grown is not synonymous with good quality. The care and attention given to growing the vegetable plant will be vain, if the harvest is incorrectly timed — either too early or too late. Fresh vegetables are at the peak of perfection when the edible portion is just short of maturity, full of juices and succulent. Here is a guide to help you pick the best:

Asparagus: break tips in early spring before branching begins.

Artichoke, globe: cut the bud, just before its outer scales loosen.

Beans, snap: start harvesting when the seeds have just begun to form, but before the pods reach the diameter of a pencil.

Beans, lima: pick when the pods are fat and bulging. For tender, baby limas pick while the pods are immature. For "meaty" limas let the pods mature and begin to dry before picking.

Beets: begin harvest when beets are one inch in diameter. Tender tops make excellent greens. Main harvest comes when beets are 2–3" in diameter. Larger beets are tough but sweeter.

Broccoli: pick when stalks are firm, the flower buds green and compact and before any yellow color develops. Cut with 2" of stem attached. Smaller side heads will develop.

Brussels sprouts: remove and use the sprouts (small heads) when they are firm, beginning at the bottom of the plant.

Cabbage: start when first head is the size of a softball and before splitting occurs, harvest as needed. If you leave several of the lower leaves on the plant and give the plant some nitrogen fertilizer (about 2 tablespoonfuls) a second growth consisting of several small heads will follow.

Cantaloupe: pick when the stem slips easily from the fruit and the aroma of the melon is easily detected.

Carrots: small ones are tender, large ones are sweeter. Always pull the largest carrot first, they will have the darkest tops. Use thinnings in salads.

Cauliflower: heads will usually be ready 2–3 weeks after tying the outer leaves for blanching.

Celery: when stalks are 8–10" long, pick outer stalks or harvest entire plant.

Chard: as soon as outer leaves are large enough to eat and until they are a foot or more long. Merely break off the outer leaves. New leaves will develop from the center of the plant as you harvest.

Collard, Kale, Mustard, Spinach: harvest the leaves and leaf stems as soon as they are large enough to eat. Either harvest the entire plant or pick the outer, larger leaves to promote the growth of more leaves as with chard.

Corn: pick when the silks turn dark and begin to dry. Peel back the husk on a few ears and look at the kernels — they should be bright, plump and milky.

Cucumber: best when medium sized (5–7"), green and firm with spines beginning to soften. Too ripe if large, puffy and turning yellow.

Eggplant: pick when fruits are about 4″ in diameter and color is still bright and glossy.

Endive: harvest entire plant for greens when leaves are large enough to eat and up to 15″ in diameter.

Kohlrabi: harvest when the swollen stems are 2−3″ in diameter.

Lettuce: pick leaf lettuce as soon as the outer leaves are large enough to eat. Leave the smaller ones behind for the next picking. The first head lettuce can be picked when the size of a softball and thereafter as needed right down the row.

Melons: pick after the stem turns brown and shrivels. Watch for a change in color on the spot when the melon rests on the ground. When this spot changes from greenish yellow to creamy white the melon is ready.

Okra: pick pods when 2−4″ long. If permitted to grow longer they become fibrous and woody.

Onions: pull green onions when they are ¼−½″ in diameter. Bulbs are mature when tops fall over and the neck shrivels. If bulbs are of the size you want and tops remain green, break tops over to stop growth so they can be lifted later and dried for storage.

Parsley: whenever the outer leaves are large enough to eat.

Parsnips: best flavor achieved after several moderate freezes and when of moderate size. Can remain in ground all winter.

Peas: pick when pods are bright green and about ¾ full. Edible pod peas can be picked whenever the pods are large enough to eat. Yellowish, hard pods are over mature.

Peppers: pick when fruits are firm and full size. If red fruits are desired, leave on the plant another several weeks.

Potatoes: pick "new" potatoes whenever the plants have reached full size and begin to flower. Harvest for storage when tops have turned yellow or died.

Pumpkins: for storage, harvest before frost when color is even and dark and the skin hard. Remove the fruit with part of the stem attached.

Radishes: pull as soon as large enough to eat.

Rhubarb: harvest leaf stalks when ½−1″ in diameter. Do not use the leaves, they are poisonous. Do not pick more than ⅓ of the stalks in a season.

Rutabaga: dig when 2″ diameter or larger.

Squash: pick summer squash while the skin is tender enough to be penetrated by a fingernail. Zucchini is best when 6−9″ long, patty pan types when 6−8″ in diameter. Winter squash should be harvested before the first severe fall frost and after the rind has hardened. Remove from vine with a portion of stem attached, cure for 10 days at 80°F before storing.

Tomato: vine ripened are the best, pick when uniformly red and firm. If frost comes before final harvest, pick the fruits which have changed from grassy green to whitish color and ripen indoors at room temperature.

Turnips: start pulling and using when they reach 1″ in diameter. Best quality when moderate size, firm and fairly heavy. Large roots will be tough and woody.

Vegetables grown for their fruits or individual leaves will be kept vigorous and productive by continually harvesting. The plant is programmed to grow and make a flower and go to seed. If you prevent this from happening, by keeping the edible parts picked off, the plant continues yielding.

Very few vegetable crops in the Pacific Northwest are grown by home gardeners for dried use. Dry beans, dry peas, dry corn, can be produced by simply leaving the crop on the plant to final maturity. This also means the plant makes a single crop and dies, thus defeating the possibility of continual yields.

Several crops can be stored in the ground during winter, notably turnips, parsnips, carrots and rutabaga. These keep well in most garden soils through normal winters. To protect "garden stored" vegetables from slugs, animals and severe freezes, mulch the row with three or four inches of sawdust.

Saving Seed:

If you want to save your own seed from vegetable plants here are some tips: First, allow the seeds to mature before picking from the plant. Since many vegetable seeds are grown in fruits, allow the fruits to mature completely before taking the seeds. For those seeds borne on seedstalks, watch closely and collect the seeds as they are ready to fall from the stalk.

Do not waste time saving seeds of vegetables labeled F_1 hybrids. Seeds of any hybrids tend to revert back to original parents so you end up with an odd mixture of plants, most of which will be inferior to the ones you started with.

Some seeds are easily saved and will come true to type when planted. Tomatoes (except for hybrids), peppers, eggplant, beans, peas and lettuce are some from which the seeds can be easily collected and saved. Vine crops, such as cucumbers, squash, pumpkin and melons tend to cross with each other and sometimes cross with other types. Seeds saved from vine crops will grow some of the strangest plants and fruits, usually of inferior quality. Seed of vegetables which take more than one year to mature (biennials) is hard to save because of the work involved in growing the plants through two seasons. These include carrots, beets and cabbage.

Next, after collecting the ripe fruits of those vegetables you plan to save, separate the seeds from the fruit. In the case of beans and peas, shell the dry seeds from the dry, shriveled pod. For tomato, from a fully ripe fruit squeeze the seeds onto a paper towel or wire screen to dry.

Seeds must be dry for storing. Dry them on screen racks in sunlight for several days or place them in moving air at 110°F. Small seeds can be dried in an hour at this temperature, large seeds may take three hours.

Store seeds in a cool and dry place. Temperatures around 40—50°F are acceptable. Seeds may be kept dry by placing them in labeled envelopes inside a glass jar. Wrap a couple of tablespoonfuls of dried milk in a tissue and place in the bottom of the jar to absorb remaining moisture. Cap the lid tightly. Check every several months for moisture uptake by the milk and replace milk as needed. Dried silica gel may be substituted for dry milk as an absorptive.

If seeds are mature when collected, properly dried and stored, they will generally be viable for 1–5 years depending on the variety. Here is a table for estimating storage life:

Seeds good for —

1–2 years	Corn, onion, parsley, parsnip, salsify
3–4 years	Asparagus, bean, beet, carrot, chard, leek, mustard, pea, pepper, pumpkin, tomato
5 years	Broccoli, cabbage, cauliflower, Brussels sprouts, celery, collards, cucumber, eggplant, kale, kohlrabi, lettuce, radish, rutabaga, spinach, squash, turnip.

Post Harvest Considerations:

The harvest season is the time to make plans for next year. It is the time to consider rotation, cover cropping, erosion control and soil amendments.

Rotation means moving the vegetable plantings around in the garden so any one crop is not planted year after year in the same spot. Rotation minimizes the likelihood of developing serious soil disease or insect problems. Also, by moving the plantings, crops which take large amounts of nutrients from the soil can be followed by legumes or others which help build the soil.

Tomatoes for example should be moved every year to avoid heavy buildup of root-destroying diseases. Radish and cabbage plantings should be changed to reduce soil insect populations.

Here are some suggestions for rotation sequences:

Cabbage followed by Mustard
Carrots followed by Brussels sprouts
Chard followed by Kohlrabi
Corn followed by Beans
Lettuce followed by Carrots or Rutabaga
Onions followed by Turnips
Peas followed by Cabbage or Broccoli
Spinach followed by Beets
Squash followed by Peas

Cover crops are used by farmers to protect and build soil during fall and winter. Planted in early fall, while soil temperatures remain high enough for germination, they grow slowly through the winter and are plowed under in the spring. Cover crops, also called "green manure" crops, are beneficial in several ways:

1. They reduce erosion from wind and water.
2. Deep rooting crops loosen heavy textured soils.
3. Legumes (clover, vetch, peas) add nitrogen to the soil.
4. When plowed under, they add organic matter to the soil.

Cover crops can be planted in the garden as soon as the warm season crops are harvested. Usually, cool season types of vegetables will still be growing, but plant the cover crops between the growing rows and in the rows of harvested crops. Here are some suggestions for fall cover crops:

TYPE	LBS. SEED/1000 sq. ft.	BEST SOIL TYPE
Alfalfa	1	Loam
Crimson Clover	1	Loam
Sweet Clover	½	Loam (will grow better with lime)
Vetch	1½	Loam to heavy
Buckwheat	1½	Loam to heavy
Oats	2½	Loam to heavy
Annual Rye	2	Sandy to heavy
Garden Peas	2	Sandy to loam

Unfortunately, cover crops present some problems. Most of them grow so tall that garden tillers cannot turn them under. A good lawn mowing before spring tilling will solve this problem. Some of them, particularly the clover and vetch, come back as weeds since some of the seeds lay dormant during the winter. All in all, it would be well to consider other methods of soil building such as manures, composts and mulches.

Garden residue remaining after harvest makes a valuable addition to the soil. Spade under the old bean plants and dying squash vines. Chop the corn stalks into short sections and turn them under. Leave the soil surface rough and exposed to the elements through the winter. Rotting vegetation in the soil, plus the action of freezing and thawing leaves the soil in a mellow, easily worked condition by spring.

Manure mulches are of great benefit to garden soils. Get them on by early winter. Winter rains will wash nutrients from the manure into the soil. Earthworms will be encouraged by the organic layer and will pull bits and pieces into the ground as they feed. Let the manure prevent erosion through the winter, then spade it under as soon as the soil is dry enough to work in the spring. The manure mulch also will prevent soil compaction caused by pounding raindrops. If manure is not available, use leaves, chopped pruning debris or compost for mulching.

Winter weeds are a particular problem in Pacific Northwest gardens. West of the Cascades, weeds will grow all year. Some are strictly summer weeds, others show up during the winter and some, like the annual bluegrass, stay all year. While winter weeds could be considered beneficial, i.e. erosion control, root activity and organic matter when plowed under, still they do add more seeds to the soil and make it tougher to keep a summer garden weed free. Annual weeds can be controlled, in part by mulches three or four inches deep. However, perennial weeds, quackgrass for example, will pop right through. Plastic sheeting will keep both types down, but has the disadvantage of allowing compaction beneath the plastic and besides it doesn't look very nice in the yard. Unless weeds are a serious menace to the yard, let the annuals grow as a winter cover crop and plan to fight them harder during the summer. Do not use herbicides on winter weeds — residues could remain in the soil the following spring and kill the planted vegetables.

Several amendments should be placed in Northwest garden soils in the fall. Lime and gypsum, manures and composted materials need time to be decomposed by soil organisms to basic elements before they can help next year's vegetables. See the chapter on soils for more guidance.

Chapter 6: Food Crops: SMALL FRUITS

Introductory Overview

Our moderate climate makes the plants classed as "Small Fruits" naturals for Northwest gardens. The wild berries growing along roadsides and filling vacant lots are overwhelming proof that berry crops are well adapted to Pacific Northwest conditions. Indeed, it may seem ludicrous to plant and tend a berry patch since they grow so well without care. However, through breeding, domestic types have been developed which produce both a better quality berry and larger yield.

Berry crops round out the diet and add some luscious flavors from the home garden. Home grown fruit is superior to anything found at the local supermarket or stand. Small fruit crops are very perishable and easily bruise once they are ripe. They do not reach their peak of perfection however, until they are fully ripe on the vine. In the home planting you can fully appreciate the flavor, sweetness and texture of completely ripe small fruits.

To understand some of the management differences between the small fruit types you need to know what sort of a plant is involved. Some are soft plants, others woody vines and others are bushes. Perhaps this listing will help:

BERRY	TYPE AND GROWTH HABIT
Strawberry	Herbaceous perennial; a soft, low-growing plant, regrowing from a central crown each year.
Blackberry Boysenberry Loganberry Grapes	Woody, trailing vine; need trellising to direct growth upward and to keep fruit off the ground.
Red Raspberry	Woody cane; upright growing stems, self-supporting shoots; usually trellised to control spacing.
Black Raspberry Blueberries Currants Elderberry Gooseberry	Bushes; woody plants with many stems rising from the crown or center point.

For each of these small fruit crops, many varieties have been developed and new selections appear every year. Varieties differ in flavor, size, shape, vigor, yield and resistance to disease. The ambrosial qualities of small fruits may vary due to differences in climate or microclimate, and management methods, yet each variety is unique in some quality which makes it valuable in a certain place. To learn which varieties best fit your own conditions check with the local experiment station, Extension office, nurseries or experienced gardeners.

The small fruit garden should be planned as a long-term planting. If growing conditions are right for berry plants and if diseases, insects and pruning are managed properly, a strawberry planting can last twenty years. Grapes might last your lifetime and blueberries will remain productive for as long as blueberries taste good to you. But, things do go wrong — plantings are allowed to become weedy, plants are not pruned properly, pests are not controlled when necessary. So, plantings usually need to be redone every five or ten years. This chapter gives suggestions on how to maintain plantings longer by pointing up the needs of each type of berry.

Plan ahead to prepare the soil and to provide the necessary conditions for healthy growth. Nearly all berry plants are moved from nurseries to gardens during the dormant season. Thus, it is important that you plan far enough ahead to prepare the soil during the fall preceding berry planting. Soil drainage may need attention, minerals may have to be added, or the organic matter content of the soil increased. These preparations should be completed by late fall, while the soil is dry enough to till and in enough time that soil amendments can do their work. This is not to say that a berry garden could not be planted on short notice after a quick decision. What we want to point out is the importance of planning to insure a long, successful planting.

Once you have identified the varieties you wish to grow, find the best place in the yard to make your berry garden. All berry plants require sunlight and good soil drainage. Small fruits need at least six hours of sunlight and prefer full sun all day. Sunlight affects the type of growth the plants will make and will have an important effect on the nutrient composition of the fruit. Plants placed in areas receiving only a few hours of sunlight will become sparse, leggy as they stretch for the available light, and weak, so they are easily attacked by insects or diseases or crowded out by plants more tolerant of shade. Fruit produced in shaded growing areas will have less sugar, less Vitamin C, and generally will be smaller. To get the most from your berry garden, put it in an area open to full sunlight.

The next major need of all berries is good soil drainage. None of the berry crops can survive in soils which remain wet and soggy for most of the year. All berry plants need air in and around their root systems for respiration. If air is replaced by water, the roots die. Soil drainage was covered in Chapter 3, but its importance warrants some additional warning. Soil drainage problems are the main reason red raspberry plants fail. Poor drainage is responsible for conditions which allow the entry of root diseases into strawberry crowns. All in all, the ability of a soil to allow water to pass and be replaced by air pretty well determines the possibility of growing berries. Time spent detecting and correcting soil drainage problems is often the difference between success or failure with the berry garden.

Small fruit plants need air circulation around, over and between canes, stems and leaves to help resist disease. Powdery mildew on grapes, leaf spots on cane berries and botrytis on ripening strawberries are always worse in areas with little or no air movement. Moderate air movement is preferable to strong winds. Not only do plantings in windy areas have difficulty getting established, canes and vines are easily damaged by wind. Find a place in the yard where the movement of air is not blocked by hedges, fences or structures but at the same time the plants will be sheltered from strong prevailing winds.

Eradicate the hard-to-kill, noxious weeds before attempting a planting of berries. There is nothing as discouraging as watching quackgrass grow up through your favorite berry plants and crowd them out while you try vainly to kill it by pulling or hoeing. If quackgrass, morning glory, Canada thistle or sheep sorrel are the present occupants of the site, better spend a summer killing them out as suggested in Chapter 4.

Berry crops make their best growth in reasonably fertile garden soils. Incorporate organic matter such as manure or compost in the area before planting. Supplement with annual additions of manure, compost or leaf mold between planted rows. All of the berry crops do well in our natively acid soils. However, it is important to add lime to supply the plants with calcium. In the absence of a soil analysis, most berry plantings (except blueberries) will grow better if they receive 30–50 lbs. of ground limestone per 1000 sq. ft. every four years. This is a minimum application — any additional amounts should be based on a soil test.

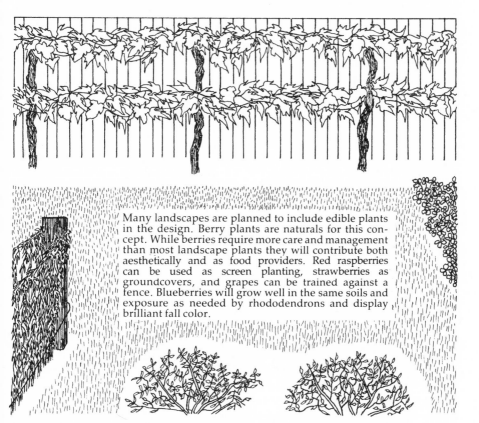

Many landscapes are planned to include edible plants in the design. Berry plants are naturals for this concept. While berries require more care and management than most landscape plants they will contribute both aesthetically and as food providers. Red raspberries can be used as screen planting, strawberries as groundcovers, and grapes can be trained against a fence. Blueberries will grow well in the same soils and exposure as needed by rhododendrons and display brilliant fall color.

The history of the planting site has a great deal to do with the success or failure of the small fruit planting. It also determines how much effort will be needed to correct inherited problems. Learn all you can from the old-timers in your area. Find out what small fruit crops and vegetable crops were grown before the land was developed for housing. How successful were they and what problems did they encounter? Check with local experts to learn if the berry crops were affected by problems which prevented successful cropping.

Don't plant small fruit in soil previously devoted to tomato, potato, eggplant or pepper crops. These plants may have infected the soil with verticillium wilt, a soil inhabiting fungus.

Also when evaluating a place to plant berries make sure you have enough space for unimpeded plant growth. Strawberries take up the least amount room so a family sized crop can be grown in an area ten feet by ten feet square. The other berries need considerably more room. Raspberries need at least ten square feet per plant while grapes need twice as much space. Blueberries are the largest of the bush berries and need twenty square feet for making their best growth. Select your berry plants to fit the space available and your family's taste.

There is nothing more disenchanting than a lovingly planted berry patch which is continually choked with weeds, eaten by insects or dying from lack of water. While planning the berry garden, consider how much time you have for necessary care and maintenance. Few plants can be put in the ground and left to develop, bear fruit and renew themselves without help. Berry plants demand a certain amount of management to help them develop. Weeds and insects will need to be controlled to allow the plants to grow and develop berries. All berry plants must be pruned, not only to prevent crowding and maintain good air circulation, but also to renew the fruit bearing parts of the plant. Raspberry plants, allowed to grow several years without pruning, will become thickets of weak, spindly and unproductive canes. Grapes and blackberries will take over the neighborhood if not kept in hand. Strawberries need to be clipped to stimulate new runner plants and remove old foliage which harbors insect parasites. Small fruit plants can provide more pounds of fruit per area than their tree counterparts but their demands on your time will also be greater. To get an idea of the maintenance needs of berry crops see *Management Calendar* in Appendix.

Also consider how much and when your berry garden can be expected to yield. Harvesting a large planting of blueberries is very demanding of your spare time. By planning for a few plants each of several small fruits the harvest can be extended over much of the summer with strawberries early, raspberries in midsummer followed by blueberries and blackberries. To help in planning the number of berry plants to grow, here are approximate yields one can expect from mature plants.

BERRY YIELD

Crop	[1]Pounds per Plant	[2]At What Age	When
Blackberries	12–20	3 years	late summer
Black Raspberries	2–3	4 years	midsummer
Blueberries	4–5	5 years	midsummer
Boysens	12–20	3 years	late summer
Currants	5–8	5 years	late midsummer
Gooseberries	8–10	5 years	late midsummer
Grapes	12–15	4 years	late summer
Elderberries	10–15	4 years	late summer
Logans	12–20	3 years	late summer
Red Raspberries	3–5	3 years	[3]mid to late summer
Strawberries	½	2 years	[3]early and late summer

[1]Yields will be affected by plant spacing, climatic differences, local weather conditions, and management practices. Follow the planting suggestions in this chapter to get the most from your plant.

[2]While berry plants take from three to five years to reach full bearing size, smaller harvests are possible after the first full growing year.

[3]Single crop varieties yield crops in early summer, everbearers give a partial crop through the summer with another major crop in late summer. Everbearing varieties generally require more pruning and management so are often grown as a second variety to supply some fruit after the single crop variety is finished.

Strawberries and most bush berries attract birds who will compete for your harvest. Plan to share, or provide some means to protect your crop. Protection can be provided by bird netting, scarecrows, imitation or real animal threats (cats, snakes, owls), or other scare tactics.

And finally, plan to try several varieties of whatever berry you prefer. Enjoy and discover the differences in flavor, sweetness and texture. New varieties are being developed every year. Some are excellent, others are outstanding. Visit local berry farms and sample these varieties. Experiment stations have a wealth of information, including the latest varieties and information about them. Keep in mind that berry varieties are quite localized, thus a variety that is a prize winner in Ohio may be a bust in the Northwest. To increase your chances for success use local varieties which have been bred for our climate and soils.

To give your berry planting the best chance possible, start with healthy plants. If your neighbor offers you some plants, take a look at his berry patch first, you may be accepting diseased gifts. Curly leaves, odd coloration or stunted growth are evidence of an unwelcome bonus. Viruses and root diseases can be brought into your garden by plants from infested areas.

Strawberry plants should be purchased as "certified." This means they have been grown under close observation to make sure virus diseases are not present. In some areas of the Northwest red raspberry plants are sold as virus free, however raspberry certification is not altogether a sure thing. To make certain you are putting the healthiest plants in your new planting buy from reputable, local growers or nurseries.

Strawberries

A STRAWBERRY PLANT

Fragaria chiloensis. A strawberry plant has a relatively shallow fibrous root system originating from a central crown. From the crown also grow the leaves, roots, flowering stalks, and runner plants. Plant new strawberry plants with the crown at the surface of the soil.

In a bowl, covered with cream or topping a shortcake, a strawberry may be the taste treat of the year. In the garden it is rather small plant with bright green three-part leaves. In the spring and early summer it has small white flowers which eventually become bright red fruits much to the delight of the gardener, all feathered friends and a few slugs. During the last half of summer the original plant sends out "runners" with all the facilities for making a complete new plant. Runner plants may be used to replace old plants, add more plants to the row or clipped and planted elsewhere.

A strawberry plant is an herbaceous perennial, which means it is a relatively tender, non-woody plant which sprouts anew each spring from its crown. Within four years the original plant will have died or been crowded out by the new runner plants, which then assume the job of bearing fruit and sending out their own progeny. While strawberry plantings are generally thought of as a permanent garden planting, they need careful tending to succeed year after year. Maintaining the original row or bed, preventing perennial weed invasion and replacing old plants with new runner plants are some of the key needs of this fruit.

Strawberry plants are not exacting as to space, sunlight or constant care. If left alone they are perfectly happy to scramble among other plants, lie among the weeds, and not give much of a yield. Their production and continued vigor is up to you. The more you can do to control and nurture their best growth, the more berries you can harvest.

PREVENTING BLACK-EYED SUSANS

"Black-Eyed Susans" is the name given strawberry blossoms nipped by frost. When the center of the strawberry flower turns black there will be no berry formed. Late spring frosts are one of the hazards of strawberry growing in the Northwest. While it is nearly impossible to avoid damage arising from widespread spring frosts, the gardener can at least avoid microclimates likely to have local frosts. Low lying areas are places where cold air collects, much like water collecting in pools. These pockets of cold air will produce black-eyed Susans.

Since strawberries do respond to any care the gardener gives, they can be used in many areas of the yard for landscape aesthetics. As a landscape plant they can be planted wherever they receive at least six hours of sunlight. As border plantings alongside the sidewalk they make a nice spring and summertime green leafy border with the blooms and berries as an added bonus. For a groundcover they may be planted in mass to cover a sunny bank or to dress up a bare part of the yard. Strawberries do not like competition from trees and shrubbery so give them their own space, an area not filled with roots from nearby woody plants.

Two important qualities should be considered when selecting a variety for your garden. First, choose a variety adapted to your own area. Strawberries are affected by hours of sunlight, light intensity and other environmental factors which differ from one part of the country to the next. The Northwest is fortunate in having local strawberry breeding programs conducted by universities and their experiment stations. These programs continually breed and test new varieties for our conditions. Buy locally to make sure you have a suitable, tasty and hardy variety for your garden.

The second matter of concern is that of virus diseases. Strawberries are affected by several virus diseases which are moved from plant to plant by aphids, leafhoppers, and other sucking type insects. Once a plant is infected the virus moves into all parts of the plant, including the young runners. To assure a healthy beginning start with certified plants. Certification means that the plants have been grown in isolated fields, inspected frequently for disease symptoms and are produced under the cleanest conditions possible. Accepting runner plants from your neighbor is not the best way to start a strawberry planting as you may be introducing unwanted diseases into your garden.

Strawberry varieties come in two habits, single crop and everbearing. The single crop varieties produce a single large crop in late spring or early summer, after which time they put their efforts into growing runner plants and getting ready for next spring. In an odd summer a few berries may develop later, although they will be borne at the expense of next year's crop. The single crop varieties usually have more, firmer, and larger-sized berries than do everbearing types. Single crop varieties generally bear fruit for about four years before they need to be replaced by runner plants.

Everbearers produce an early summer crop followed by a second crop in late summer. If your area is typified by late spring frosts which frequently kill spring blossoms, everbearers will supply strawberries from a second crop later in the summer. The parent plants of everbearers generally exhaust themselves after two years of production and must be replaced by young runner plants or newly purchased plants. Generally, the everbearing varieties are best used by eating fresh rather than preserving. The everbearing fruits are softer and smaller than those from single crop varieties. Their main virtue is the production of fresh, ripe strawberries over a long period of time.

Before placing a strawberry plant in the ground make sure the soil is right. Strawberries need well drained soil and they will do much better if the fertility is high. Soil structure and tilth must be made right before planting. Do not plant strawberries in areas where potatoes, tomatoes, eggplant or peppers were grown the previous year.

Red-stele is a soil borne fungus disease of strawberries, which may persist for years. It is usually worse in wet soils. The name comes from the discoloration in the core (stele) of the strawberry roots. Some strawberry varieties are less susceptible than others and sometimes it helps to plant on raised beds, but if the problem exists it is tough to overcome and supposedly resistant plants or raised beds may not be successful. If this disease has invaded your soil plant something else.

Do not expect strawberries to grow in places where the soil compacts easily nor in soils lacking organic matter. Work organic matter into the soil several months before planting. See the chapter on soil for advice on how to use organic matter in soil. While strawberries do not require extremely high levels of fertility to produce a good crop, it is important that they be fertilized adequately. Fertilizer should be supplied at planting time and annually thereafter. Calcium and magnesium, if deficient, should be tilled or spaded into the top six to eight inches prior to planting. Note that the only way to determine the need for these two minerals is through soil analysis.

Here are the important steps in preparing the soil for planting strawberries:

As far ahead of planting as possible —
1.   Eradicate noxious weeds. Quackgrass, wild blackberry, wild morning glory and thistle are the main weeds which must be completely eradicated before planting. See the weed section in Chapter 4 for details. If not controlled beforehand, they are impossible to control once the strawberries are planted.
2.   Provide drainage if excess water is present. Either install one of the drainage systems suggested in Chapter 3 or make raised beds.
3.   If soil analysis shows your soil to be moderately acid (with a pH of less than 5.0) or shows a calcium level below 3 meq., lime should be added to supply calcium and to raise the pH to a more acceptable level (5.5–6.5). Lime should be worked into the top 6–8" of soil.

At planting time —
1.   Loosen the soil by tilling, spading or plowing. When loosening the soil incorporate two pounds of 5-10-5 or similar complete fertilizer per 100 sq. ft. of area to be planted. Additional fertilizer should be applied after growth begins. This first application will get the young plants off to a good start.
2.   Rake out any clods, plant remnants, rocks or other debris which will interfere with plant roots. The prepared planting area should be smooth, loose, and of a fine texture to receive the new strawberry plants.

While strawberry plants are available year-round from nurseries which pot them, most new plants are purchased bare root while dormant. Buy your plants in early spring (March–April) and plant them as soon as possible. Spring planting gives a complete growing season to develop flower buds for a crop the following year. Plant as early as the ground can be prepared, to give the plant more time to establish itself.

Newly purchased plants do not look like the lush, green, densely foliaged plants you have seen growing in fields or gardens. They have a few dried leaves and a long set of roots, scarcely resembling anything that could produce a handful of juicy red berries. Have faith though, for in this small, dormant strawberry plant lives a crown made up of growth cells, buds, and new roots, programmed to grow roots, leaves, and fruits.

Keep the plants cool and wet until planted to prevent mold and drying out. Either wrap them in damp burlap or cover the plants with dampened peat moss. Certification of strawberry plants assures freedom from diseases but it does not give the plants any special protection from the hazards of drying or heating. If plants must be held for several days before being planted, immerse the roots in a pail of water and keep them in a shady, cool spot. They can be held for 3–4 days in this manner, if planting must be delayed.

Do not plant until the threat of heavy frost is passed as a sharp frost of 28°F or below will kill new plants.

Strawberries are usually planted in one of the following planting patterns. Single crop varieties are generally planted in a **matted row system**. With this planting system the plants are set in rows and are allowed to grow runner plants to fill the space between rows. Vigorous varieties such as *Shuksan* and *Northwest* are set 24″ apart in rows 42″ apart. Those varieties which grow fewer runner plants (*Olympus*) are set 18″ apart in rows 36″ apart.

By midsummer a matted row will be at least 18″ wide. Usually four of the larger runners per plant are allowed to grow and the rest are cut off. Space the runners evenly around the plant or move them as needed to fill gaps. New plants will grow at intervals along the runner and can be helped to root by pegging the runner down with a rock or stick. As the matted row fills with plants, you must hand weed, as it is impossible to cultivate between plants. The matted row system is self-renewing and is kept vigorous from one year to the next by removing the older and weaker plants. The row is cut back to a 6–10″ width immediately following harvest and the remaining plants are allowed to set new runners.

The **hill system** of planting uses a single row method. Runner plants are removed to maintain the original plant. This system is well suited to everbearing types. Generally the plants are set 15″ apart in rows 15″ apart. Every third or fourth row is left blank to provide a footpath. Runners are cut several times during the summer to maintain the original plant spacing. This system can be modified to use fewer original plants by spacing plants at

MATTED ROW SYSTEM OF PLANTING STRAWBERRIES

New plants are placed 18—24" apart with rows usually 3—4' apart to allow room for runner plants to fill the space between.

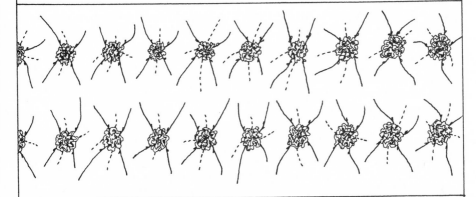

Runner plants are trained to fill the spaces. Generally only four runner plants are allowed to remain from each plant.

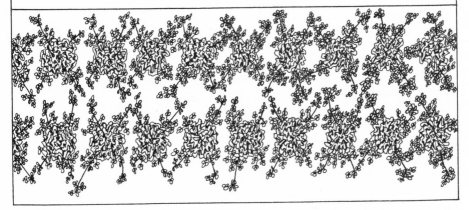

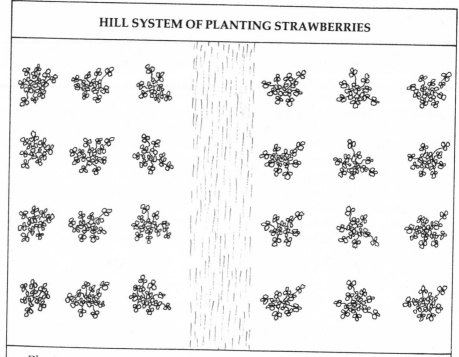

HILL SYSTEM OF PLANTING STRAWBERRIES

Plants are maintained at their original spacing by removing runner plants. Footpaths between every three rows allow access for necessary maintenance and harvest.

30 inches in the row and allowing runners to develop to fill the gaps. The hill system is a more orderly planting than the matted row.

The new, dormant strawberry plants you purchase from the garden store will have roots 8–10″ long. To make planting easier, trim the roots back to 5–6 inches. The plant must be placed with the crown at the soil line. The crown is the meeting point between the roots and the leaves. If set too deeply the soil over the crown will suffocate the plant. If set too high, so the tops of the roots are exposed, the plant will dehydrate. The roots should be spread in all directions, pointing downward and with soil firmly packed around them. The following method of planting is recommended:

1.   Keep the plants in a pail of water until ready to plant.

2.   Stake and string the row so the plants will be in a straight line if planting in rows. If planting for informal landscape use, plants may be placed in random patterns but allow 15–18″ spacing.

3.   Place the plants at the spacing desired (15″, 18″, 24″, etc.). Use a trowel to dig a hole in prepared soil, insert the plant, adjust its height and tamp dirt firmly around the plant.

4.   The new plants should be watered unless rain is expected within a day.

In soils of questionable fertility, the new plants may be given a boost with a "starter solution." Starter solutions can be made with a complete, soluble, high phosphorus fertilizer such as 12-53-0 (one tablespoon per gallon of water). Apply one cupful of solution to each newly-set plant.

Until the newly planted strawberry bed or row begins growing, annual weeds must be pulled and the soil must be kept damp. A mulch of barkdust, sawdust or clean straw can be used to conserve soil moisture and to discourage annual weed growth. The mulch should not be more than one inch deep. When runner plants are being established the mulch will have to be removed from the runner track. When the top inch or two of soil dries out irrigate to soak three or four inches deep. Summer irrigation on a weekly basis will keep the new berry planting vigorous.

When the plants have grown a cluster of new leaves and appear to be established give each plant a half-tablespoon of 5-10-5 fertilizer. Place the fertilizer in a ring around the plant, three or four inches away from the crown. Now the new plant has all the elements needed to make growth and build its reserves for making fruit.

New plants will sometimes bloom and try to bear a crop of fruit their first year in the ground. Don't let them overdo it. Give the new plants the opportunity to establish themselves by picking off the blooms, at least until midsummer. New blooms should be picked off just as they open, usually from late April until mid-June. It is tempting to have fruit the first year but the plants expend much of their energy on fruit growth so the new plant takes much longer to reach maturity. A few late summer flowers can be left on the plants to develop a fruit or two to give you an idea of what will come in quantity next year.

In mid-August give the new strawberry planting another application of fertilizer. This is the time of year when strawberry blossom buds are starting to develop inside the crown for next summer's crop. An all-purpose fertilizer such as 5-10-10, 5-10-5 or 6-12-12 can be used at three cups of dry fertilizer per 100 square feet of area. The fertilizer can be broadcast across the top of the row or it can be applied alongside the row or around the individual plants. Brush fertilizer particles off the leaves with a broom or by hand and water the fertilizer into the soil.

Your first year's maintenance should be directed toward developing a strong, vigorous strawberry planting. If the strawberry crop is to be in a matted row system, the earlier the new runner plants can be rooted the more flower buds they will have next spring. If the planting is to be a hill system, the larger and healthier these crowns are, the more fruit they will form. Keep the plants vigorous with adequate water, weed control and fertilizer to encourage their growth.

Disappointments in strawberry growing are most often the result of:

1.   weak or unhealthy planting stock — best to purchase certified disease-free plants;

2.   planting in poorly prepared soil — test soil, work organic matter, phosphorus and calcium in ahead of time;

3.   planting at incorrect depth — place the plant crown level with the soil surface;

4.   lack of soil moisture — critical time to irrigate new plantings is late spring and early summer;

5.   weather at blooming time — frosts kill the flower and prevent fruit set or cold temperatures slow activity of bees and other pollinizers.

Strawberries were given their name because they were mulched with straw in the fall to protect their crowns from severe winters. In the Northwest this sort of winter protection is seldom necessary, especially if varieties adapted to our climate are planted in the first place. In matted row systems the plant's own canopy of leaves will protect them in all but the most exposed sites. On windy, cold, exposed areas, cover the row with fir boughs. A mulch of sawdust or barkdust can be used to protect hill system plants in areas exposed to abnormal cold.

Control weeds in the new planting until the plants cover the ground. Once the bed is covered with strawberry foliage the annual weeds will tend to disappear since they too must have sunlight to grow. Perennial weeds are a continual threat since they may invade by runners or underground shoots from nearby parents. Quackgrass and sheep sorrel are the two worst offenders and must be pulled as you find them. In serious invasions spot treatment with a directed systemic herbicide is recommended.

Fertilizer should be applied annually once the planting is established. Since strawberries develop most of their flower buds in the fall, the most effective time for fertilizing is sometime between mid-August and early September. Strawberries thrive in fertile soils and will respond well to moderate levels of fertilizer. A 5-10-10 fertilizer, at 2 lbs. per 100 sq. ft., will adequately supply the major minerals needed. In a matted row system, apply the fertilizer over the tops of the plants during a dry day, then knock the fertilizer particles off the foliage with a broom. Water the fertilizer into the soil with a heavy irrigation. For plants in the hill system, apply the fertilizer in a trench 4" from the side of the row and three inches deep.

Irrigation is important during the first year to establish roots and promote growth of runner plants. In following years irrigation of single crop varieties before and during harvest is necessary to develop the berries. With everbearing types regular irrigation will maintain a continual yield. With both types, irrigation is needed in late summer when flower buds are forming for the next year. Almost any method of irrigation can be used so long as it applies water slowly enough to allow soil penetration without puddling or causing erosion. Avoid watering the bed or row during bright sunny weather when water droplets on leaves could cause some foliage spot injury. Early morning watering is best. Less evaporation loss will be encountered and the plant leaves can dry before evening. Several diseases may develop on damp foliage and fruit. One is botrytis, which causes berry rotting. The other is powdery mildew. Both can be minimized by decreasing humidity and increasing air circulation.

Pruning is used to increase the vigor of the plants and to keep diseases and insect pests to a minimum. Single crop varieties can be mowed or trimmed right after the early summer harvest is completed. Mowing cuts off diseased foliage and dead leaves and stems, eliminates hiding places for insect pests and gives you a chance to see what needs to be replaced. At this time old and weak plants can be removed, new runner plants shifted to fill any gaps and the row reduced to its original width by pulling or hoeing out some of the outlying runner plants.

With the hill system constant pruning will be needed to clip off unneeded runner plants in order to maintain the original row. Healthy runner plants can be dug for use in another part of the row or to start a new planting area. The hill system is well suited to everbearing varieties. The everbearers produce their best crops the first and second year. To continue the planting one must allow several runner plants to grow and root for replacement in the second or third year. After the second summer the original plant is pulled. Now the new runner plants are allowed to send out several replacements. Everbearers require more attention to replacement and rotation than do the single crop types.

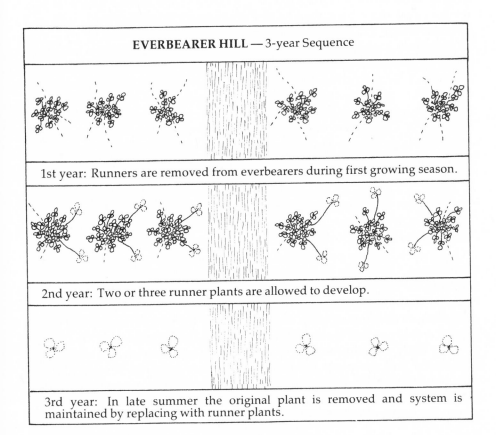

EVERBEARER HILL — 3-year Sequence

1st year: Runners are removed from everbearers during first growing season.

2nd year: Two or three runner plants are allowed to develop.

3rd year: In late summer the original plant is removed and system is maintained by replacing with runner plants.

STRAWBERRY VARIETIES FOR THE PACIFIC NORTHWEST

VARIETY	TYPE		BERRY SIZE[1]	TIME OF CROP[2]	USE				HARDINESS		DISEASE RESISTANCE		REMARKS
	Everbearing	Single			Fresh	Canned	Frozen	Dried	Good	Fair	Good	Fair	
Benton		X	A	M/L	X	X	X	X	X		X		
Gem	X		C		X				X		X		soft fruit
Hood		X	A	M	X	X	X		X		X		tolerates Red Stele, runners freely
Linn		X	A	M	X	X	X	X		X		X	runners freely
Marshall		X	A	E/M		X	X	X	X			X	susceptible to virus
Northwest		X	B	M	X	X	X	X	X		X		runners freely
Ogallala	X		B		X		X		X			X	good for short season areas
Olympus		X	B	M	X	X	X		X		X		few runners
Ozark Beauty	X		B		X				X			X	runner plants may fail
Puget Beauty		X	B	E	X		X			X		X	susceptible to virus, runners freely
Quinault	X		A		X				X			X	
Rainier		X	A	M/L	X	X		X	X			X	moderate runner production
Rockhill	X		B		X			X		X		X	
Shuksan		X	B	L		X			X		X		runners freely
Totem		X	B	M	X		X		X		X		moderate runner production, upright fruiting clusters

[1] A – large, B – medium, C – small   [2] E – early, M – midsummer, L – late summer

The most common pests affecting strawberry plants are root weevil, aphid and spittlebug. Root weevils feed in the plant crowns, thus killing the plant. Any or all of these insects can injure foliage, flowers and fruit. Timely treatment is required to kill the pests before they cause serious damage. A number of pesticides are available to home gardeners and currently include diazinon, malathion, pyrethrum, rotenone, etc.

Virus diseases may be brought to the strawberry planting in plants or by marauding insects. Typical virus symptoms will include leaf distortion, discoloration of foliage, stunting of the plant and deformation of the berries. Whatever the virus symptom, the disease is incurable and infected plants should be removed and burned.

Botrytis fungus disease attacks ripening fruit and can convert a luscious, juicy, sweet berry to a gray, furry one in a matter of hours. Remove infected fruit, dead leaves, and plant debris from the beds. Pick ripe fruits before they become infested and avoid watering during warm nights.

Canefruits

The name "Canefruits" is used to identify the berry plants which grow woody canes or stems. The canefruits include red raspberries, the blackberry group, and black raspberries. In the blackberry group will be found boysenberries and other trailing types. All of these fruits belong to the genus *Rubus* and all have similar fruiting habits. Fruit structure differs between the blackberry types and raspberries. The raspberry has a berry-core (receptacle) which remains on the plant when the fruit is pulled away. The blackberry fruit has a solid core attached to the small parts of the fruit and the entire structure is eaten.

TRAILING BERRY IDENTIFICATION CHART

Loganberry: essentially a red blackberry (Judge Logan, Cal. 1881); cross of red raspberry and western trailing blackberry, i.e. *Rubus idaeus* and *Rubus ursinus* (or *R. vitifolius*); *R. idaeus* also is known as the European Red Raspberry; *R. vitifolius* is also known as Aughinbaugh.

Boysenberry: cross of Logan and Lucretia, *R. procumbus* (also known as the Eastern Trailing Blackberry)

Nectarberry: a mutation of Boysen or a seedling of Youngberry; the fruit is slightly sweeter and less acid than Boysen.

Youngberry: result of crossing Cuthbert Red Raspberry, Western Trailing Blackberry, the Texas Dewberry and another eastern trailing blackberry, i.e. *Rubus idaeus* + *R. ursinus* + *R. villosus* + *R. trivialis*.

Olallieberry: result of cross of Black Logan (a selection from the Western Blackberry) and Youngberry.

Chehalem: cross between Himalaya (our native upright blackberry) and Santiam, i.e. *R. procercus + R. ursinus.*

Marionberry: cross between Chehalem and Olallie.

Cascade: cross between Loganberry and Zielinski (a selection from the wild Oregon blackberry).

Santiam: selected seedling from wild blackberries.

While canefruit plantings require more space than strawberries, the different quality, landscape potential, and flavor make the caneberry planting an important part of the garden. If garden space is not available, try to fit some of these plants into the landscape design where they can be trellised, trained against a fence or be used as a screen between parts of the yard. Most of the caneberries are quite vigorous, so plant them where they will not invade other plantings.

Canefruits demand fairly specific environmental conditions to thrive. None of the caneberries will live in poorly drained soils. Root rot, a fungus disease, is one of the main causes of red raspberry death. Avoid planting raspberries in soils where tomatoes or potatoes have grown within the past two years.

Full sunlight is needed by all caneberries. If planted in shade, they will become spindly and seldom bear fruit.

While air circulation is necessary to keep foliage and fruit diseases to a minimum, avoid windy sites. Red raspberries and trailing berries need to be trained onto trellises and wire supports. Hard and frequent wind will damage plants by beating them against their trellis or pulling the canes from their supports. Select an area of the yard or garden where air movement is constant but gentle.

The varieties mentioned in this chapter are those which have proven successful in Northwest conditions. Yet, not all of them will be successful in all areas. Rely on your local Extension Service and Experimental Stations for advice on varieties best suited to your particular region and soil.

Once the proper place is found for caneberry planting, prepare the soil for a long term plant. Caneberries can be expected to live for many years if they are placed in the right soil and given sunlight and protection. If drainage is a problem, install a drainage system to remove excess winter water. Blackberries, and their related Boysens and Logans, will last longer in wet soils than raspberries but they too weaken and die after several years of wet feet.

The area where caneberries are to be planted should be free of noxious perennial weeds. Quackgrass, thistles, wild morning glory and sorrel are invasive and compete for water and minerals. So give the new planting a fair chance, and save yourself some hard work later by getting rid of these weeds before planting. See Chapter 4 for suggestions on coping with weeds.

Caneberries like a moderately rich and fertile soil with lots of organic matter. If you are blessed with a sandy loam soil two feet deep your caneberries will take over the neighborhood. If yours is a typical clay loam soil it can be improved by adding manure or other organic matter and some mineral amendments. Heavy applications of well rotted manure will increase the soil's fertility, aeration, drainage capacity, and microorganism activity. Work four to six inches of manure into the soil before planting. If it can be spaded or tilled into the ground several months before planting, so much the better. But if time does not allow, get it in before placing the young plants.

While preparing the soil, supply calcium and phosphorus by working one pound of 10-20-20 fertilizer and five pounds of ground limestone into 100 square feet of planting area. This amendment will get the new plants off to a fast start and develop the canes necessary for fruiting the following year.

Once the site is selected and the soil prepared you can start the new planting. Caneberry plants are purchased and planted in early spring. Early planting (late February or early March) gives the new plants a full growing season to produce three to five strong canes which will bear fruit the following year.

Caneberry plants are dug from established fields and are either plants which have grown from roots of healthy plants or from tip layering of vigorous canes. In either case the new plants will have from one to five short stems attached to a fibrous root system. Raspberries generally come with a single cane while blackberries may have five or more canes ready to grow.

New plants should be kept damp and cool until you get them planted. The sooner the plants can be set in place the better their growth will be. Do not let the roots dry. If you must keep the plants for awhile before planting, heel them in a shallow trench where the roots can be covered with damp soil and new root growth may begin. However, to give your caneberry planting its best chance, have the soil ready and plant the caneberries as soon as you get them home.

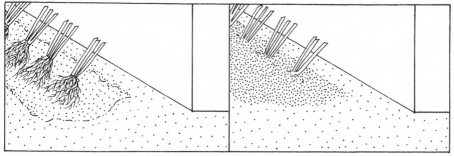

"Heeling In;" temporarily placing the root system of soon-to-be planted plants in soil as a way to prevent drying. The spot selected should be protected from drying winds and hot sunlight. Trench soil should be kept damp. Remember, this is temporary storage only.

When setting new plants, plant them so they will be about an inch deeper than they were in the field. Usually a soil line will show on the lower end of the canes. Plant them so the soil line is covered by an inch of soil. It will be easier to handle the plants if you prune back the tops to about 6". This pruning will also stimulate new canes to sprout from the crown.

The planting hole should be large enough to spread the roots outward in all directions without binding or circling. Firm the soil around the roots as you fill the planting hole. Water the newly set plant at planting time and again several weeks later if spring rainfall is not sufficient to keep the soil damp.

A word here about spacing. A minimum spacing for planting red raspberries is 3' apart in rows 6' apart. Closer spacing will only produce a jungle of weak and unproductive canes. Black raspberries need a little more room as they are more like a bush and therefore similar to blueberries. Plant black raspberries four feet apart, in rows eight feet apart. In the home landscape give them a space with four feet of freedom on all sides. Blackberries can be planted from three to ten feet apart depending on the training or trellising system to be used. Remember, give these plants room to grow. If you use them in the landscape, place far enough away from other plants that they don't become a competitive nuisance. All caneberries are vigorous and invasive growers so they can take over a small yard in short order.

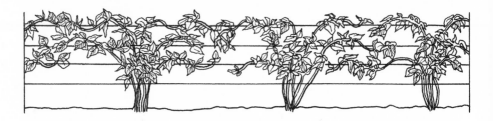

The frst year your management objective should be to assist the caneberry in establishing itself and grow vigorous canes for making fruit the following year. A "baby crop" of berries may be produced but you should not count on much being harvested until the second year.

To promote growth in the first year, control weeds by hoeing, pulling or by applying one of the soil residual herbicides which can be safely used around caneberries. Check Chapter 4 for more details. Mulches can be used to smother new annual weeds. When the new canes have grown out six or eight inches from the crown, use a 2" layer of bark or sawdust as a surface mulch.

Irrigate often enough to maintain a damp soil around new caneberries. In sandy soils it may be necessary to water once per week during dry periods. Clay soils may only need water once every two weeks. The yield of fruit is directly dependent on the growth of husky, vigorous canes the previous year, so assist this growth by adequate watering and weeding.

You can expect red raspberry canes to grow 8–10 feet long in their first year. Most of the berries develop on canes ½'' in diameter with short internodes.

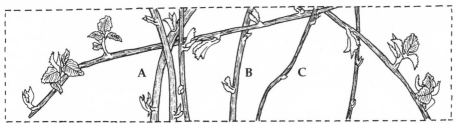

Husky canes **A** and short internodes **B** produce more and larger fruit than do weak, spindly shoots **C**.

In good soil, with adequate water a red raspberry will develop 3 to 5 strong canes. Some sucker plants may come up between plants or between rows. If you like the caneberry variety and want to increase the planting, take some of the sucker plants for this purpose. If you don't need any more plants, remove the suckers to keep the planting from becoming overgrown.

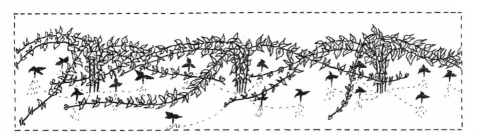

Black raspberries will grow 6 to 10 strong new shoots the first year. These should be tipped (the tips pinched off) to stimulate side branching when they are about knee-high.

Vigorous, new blackberries will send up 5 to 12 new shoots the first year. After growing upward for a foot or so they turn down and grow along the ground. To keep them out of harms way, train them in a narrow row until late summer.

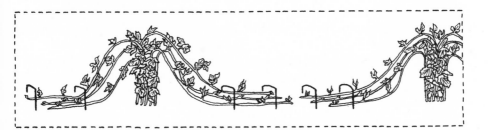

In September or October of the first growing season, raise the blackberry canes onto trellis wires. Usually 8–12 vigorous canes must be trained onto supports.

Red raspberries and blackberries need some form of trellis support when they enter their second year. During the first year the shoot and canes can scramble about on the ground but by the second year they need to be raised and supported. Most often trellises are made of #10 or #12 galvanized wire stretched between posts. The canes are either tied to the wire(s) or are wound and braided through several wires.

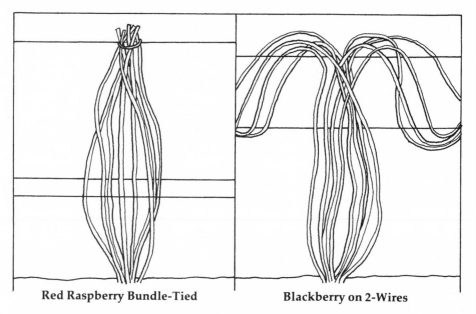

Red Raspberry Bundle-Tied   **Blackberry on 2-Wires**

Stiff cane plants such as Red Raspberry are trellised by support to a single crop wire. Trailing berries are normally wrapped around several wires.

Plant losses in the first year are largely attributable to inadequate water. Make sure the new plants are watered often enough to maintain dampness in the top foot of soil around their roots. Eliminate the use of water by weeds with frequent hoeing, pulling and mulching. If your new caneberry plants make it through the first year you can look forward to a payoff in the second and subsequent years.

Caneberries are unwilling hosts to specific pests and are victimized by environmental excesses. Red raspberries are most often killed by excessive soil moisture arising from inadequate drainage during the winter. The first symptom is usually dieback of fruiting canes, just before the berries ripen. New canes will survive for a summer but eventually succumb to root rot. Good soil drainage is the solution to this problem.

The crown borer is an insect pest throughout the Northwest. It burrows into the lower stems and crowns of the plant. Usually the damage is done during late winter and early spring. As the weather warms and the plant begins to grow, damaged and stressed canes begin dying. To control this pest, drench the crown with diazinon in late winter. Crown borers are particularly fond of red raspberries but also attack blackberries and their relatives.

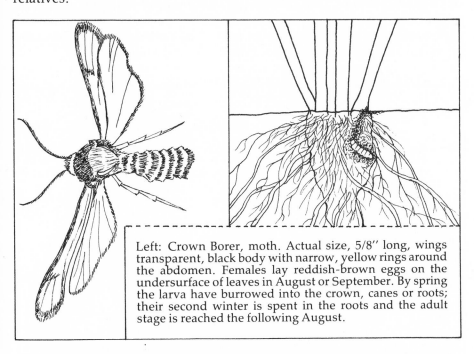

Left: Crown Borer, moth. Actual size, 5/8" long, wings transparent, black body with narrow, yellow rings around the abdomen. Females lay reddish-brown eggs on the undersurface of leaves in August or September. By spring the larva have burrowed into the crown, canes or roots; their second winter is spent in the roots and the adult stage is reached the following August.

If the blackberries were not trellised the previous fall, raise them to their support in late winter. Blackberry canes trellised when they were one summer in age will be cut out after harvest the following summer. The new canes laying on the ground will be trained upward for the next crop.

Fertilize during the spring as new growth appears. While it is helpful to have a soil analysis as a guide, a good rule of thumb is a 5-10-10 fertilizer, or something similar, at 2 pounds per 100 feet of row. A suggestion here on fertilizing — not all caneberries need fertilizer every year. In fact, you will find that members of the blackberry group seem to do wonderfully well with no fertilizer for several years. Watch the amount of growth your canefruit is making. If eight to ten feet of strong cane is being made and numerous canes are arising from each crown, cut back on fertilizer. Too often we tend to overdo the feeding and get so much growth that the planting becomes unmanageable.

When fertilizing a row planting, apply the fertilizer in a shallow trench a foot away from the plant. For single plant spacings, as used for black raspberries, apply the fertilizer in a broad, scattered ring around the drip-line of the plant. Water or rake fertilizer into the soil immediately.

TRELLIS SYSTEMS

From top to bottom: Individual cane 4-wire training system for Red Raspberries; Spiral Weave, Serpentine, and 4-Arm training systems for trailing berries.

Manure can be used in place of commecial fertilizers. Here again, base the amount on the growth being made by the plant. A 2″ layer of barnyard manure, applied around the plants and over the row will generally be sufficient.

The moisture needs of the plant are most critical at the time the berries are developing and ripening. Irrigate with enough water to soak the soil a foot downward. Particularly watch water needs as the weather turns hot and dry. Water once a week or every ten days as needed to maintain dampness around the root systems. Mulches will slow surface evaporation of water. Weeds must be controlled to keep them from using moisture.

Irrigation equipment designed to apply water to the soil rather than sprinkling the foliage is best. Foliage diseases become more troublesome during periods of warm temperatures and high humidity. Ground soaker hoses, drip systems or an open hose are preferable to lawn-type sprinklers.

Harvesting of caneberries begins in early midsummer with red raspberries. Usually they ripen just as the spring strawberry harvest is finished. Red raspberries should be harvested daily as they ripen, as raspberries tend to loosen and drop quickly once they are ripe. A hot, dry summer will ripen the fruit within two weeks, while harvest will continue for a month or more in mild, cool years.

Black raspberries follow on the heels of reds, starting to ripen by early August. Blackberries will be the last to ripen and generally start with Santiam, Cascade and Aurora, followed by Marion, Logan, Boysen and Olallie, and end with Thornless Evergreen.

Pick in early morning for best flavor and keeping quality. Keep the berries cool and handle them carefully to prevent bruising. Most varieties should be picked every second day once they have begun ripening.

The crowns of blackberries (and red raspberries) are perennial, so send new canes up each year, but the canes are biennial, growing one year and fruiting the next. After a single crop the canes no longer produce fruit.

Pruning is the way to keep the caneberry planting productive. The major pruning for the year is done immediately after the berries are harvested and mostly involves cutting out the vines which bore fruit and selecting the new strong canes for next year's fruit. This pruning stimulates new productive canes, provides air circulation to minimize foliar diseases, and affords the gardener control over the invasive traits of canefruits.

Red raspberries should be pruned right after harvest. Cut out all second-year canes (the ones which bore the fruit) so sunlight can reach the young canes which will bear fruit next year. Also remove any weak, spindly or damaged canes. All pruned canes should be cut to the ground, leaving no stubs. Tie the new canes to the trellis. In November cut these newly trained canes to 8" above the top trellis wire.

Everbearing raspberries form fruit on the new canes in the fall and may set another crop on the same canes the next spring. So cut half of the canes back to the ground in the fall or winter. Leave the other half to set fruit next spring. Those that were cut back will stimulate new canes for the following fall crop. Everbearing types generally develop more and shorter canes and may not require trellising.

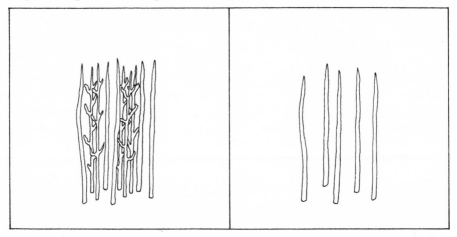

Black raspberries are also given their main pruning after harvest is completed. Remove canes that bore fruit. Trim the newest canes back to 18" from the ground. During the winter cut out any weak canes and cut the side branches on the strong canes back to 8" lengths.

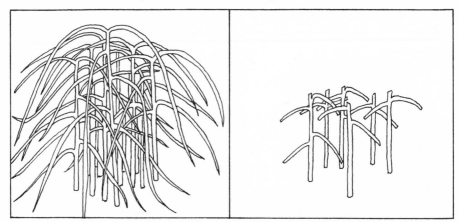

CANEFRUIT VARIETIES FOR THE PACIFIC NORTHWEST

TYPE/variety	Single	CROP Fall/Summer	Fresh	USE Frozen	Canned	FRUIT SIZE[1]	SEASON	REMARKS
RED RASPBERRY								
Canby	X		X			M/L	Long	sensitive to heavy, wet soils (avoid these), winter hardy
Fairview	X		X	X		M	Long	will tolerate heavier soils
Haida	X			X	X	M		
Heritage		X	X		X	M		
Indian Summer		X	X			M		low yields
Meeker	X		X		X	L	Short	winter hardy
Newburgh	X		X	X		L		
Puyallup	X		X		X	L+	Short	
September		X	X			S		quality poor
Sumner	X			X	X	M	Short	intense flavor, winter hardy, tolerant of wet soils
Willamette	X			X	X	L+		ripens early
BLACKBERRY								
Aurora			X			L	Very early	coloration: black
Boysenberry (Nectar)			X	X	X	L	Midseason	ripens early July to late August
Cascade			X	X		M	Early	coloration: dark red
Chehalem				X		S		coloration: bright black
Loganberry					X	M	Midseason	coloration: dark red, good juice berry
Marion			X	X	X	L	Midseason	coloration: bright black
Olallie			X	X		L	Midseason	coloration: bright black
Santiam			X	X	X	M	Early	
Thornless Evergreen					X	M	Late	ripens in August to September
BLACK RASPBERRY								
Cumberland			X	X	X	M	Midseason	
Munger			X	X	X	M	Midseason	
Plum Farmer			X	X	X	L	Early	

1S—small, M—medium, L—large

Blackberry canes are pruned away after harvest in the fall. Cut the old canes which bore the fruit back to the ground. Leave 6 to 12 of the strongest new canes to bear fruit next year. The number of canes to leave depends on the type of trellising, i.e. how many it takes to fill the trellis. Depending on the severity of your winters, the new canes may be placed on the trellis as soon as the old canes are removed or they may be left on the ground until late winter. Leaving them on the ground gives them a better chance of surviving a hard winter. If you are in an area of mild winters, tie the canes to the trellis as soon as pruned as they are likely to be damaged by insects, rodents and disease if left on the ground.

After pruning out the old canes, rake and remove old leaves and berries as they are harbors for both disease-causing organisms and insect pests. Remove weeds which may have eluded your previous efforts.

Bush Fruits

Bush berries include currants, gooseberry, elderberry, huckleberry, and the most popular, blueberry. They are fruit plants which grow into a permanent shrubby bush, flowering and bearing fruit for many years. They require little in the way of special care. All of the types listed here are hardy in Northwest gardens.

Gooseberries and currants belong to the genus *Ribes*. Both are extremely hardy and will thrive in all parts of the Northwest. In areas east of the Cascades they may be looked on with disfavor because they serve as the alternate host of white pine blister rust disease. However, if you do not have pine forests within a mile feel free to plant them in your fruit garden.

There are two species of elderberry native to the Northwest. One, Blue Elderberry (*Sambucus glauca*), has blue fruit and is edible. It grows into a large shrub or small tree. The other species, Pacific Red Elderberry (*Sambucus callicarpa*), has red fruit which is not edible. The Eastern Elderberry (*Sambucus canadensis*) produces large quantities of fruit in flat topped clusters up to a foot across.

Blueberries and huckleberries belong to the same genus, *Vaccinium*. Both are related to the rhododendron and azalea and can be grown in the same soil and environment as these ornamental shrubs. Better suited to the west side of the Cascades, they need special soil preparation and fertilizing as well as protection from heat and cold in areas east of the Cascades. If rhododendrons grow in your area, blueberries and huckleberries will do well.

The bush berries require less careful attention than do canefruits and are much more permanent than strawberries. They add interest and variability to the fruit diet.

Bush berries, with the exception of blueberries, are much less demanding of perfect soil conditions than are the canefruits and strawberries. Given a foot of topsoil, these plants will grow and produce fruits in places where water drainage is poor. All of the bush fruits like cool, moist growing conditions. So if you have a place in the yard where the soil stays damp and which remains shady for at least half the day, you have a natural spot for bush fruits. Shade is absolutely essential for currants and gooseberries to prevent fruit sunburn. Avoid sites which receive hard wind; and low places which become frost pockets.

Bush fruits require three to five years before they bear a full crop of berries. Currants and gooseberries will have a few berries on two-year old wood but will produce best on growth three or more years old. Huckleberries, blueberries and elderberries will take from four to five years before a full crop is produced.

In order of succession, gooseberries ripen first and will be ripe for picking from mid-June to early July, depending on where your garden is located. Currants come next and are generally ripe the last half of July about the same time as huckleberries begin ripening. Early varieties of blueberry will begin ripening in early to mid-July while the late varieties will not ripen until the end of September. Elderberries ripen in September.

Bush berries make ideal landscape plants and can be used to decorate the yard as well as supply fruit. Since they all develop into good-sized shrubs, give them plenty of room to grow. Currants have an upright habit and will eventually reach four to six feet in height and about four feet in width (but see following page for a warning). They have thornless canes and bear their fruits in clusters, much like bunches of small grapes. Gooseberries have an arching cane habit and will eventually get about five feet tall and five to six feet wide. Gooseberries have thorny canes and bear their fruits singly along the arching canes. (Gooseberry fruits are tart and must be cooked in pies, pastries or preserves to be eaten.) Elderberry plants make attractive, leafy large shrubs or small trees growing to be six—ten feet tall. They bear their fruits in clusters on the outer ends of two and three-year old stems.

Blueberries grow to become attractive shrubs 5—6' tall with an equal spread. They have attractive clusters of white to pinkish urn shaped flowers in late spring. During the summer the berries develop in clusters on shoots grown the previous year. In the fall the blueberry foliage turns yellow to scarlet, ending its growing season in a blaze of color.

There are several varieties of huckleberry, some deciduous (losing their leaves in the fall) and some evergreen. For the home garden the evergreen variety, *Vaccinium ovatum*, grows into an attractive low shrub. Berries are like miniature blueberries. While the yield will not be as good as from a blueberry bush, the huckleberry fruit has a much more distinctive and valued flavor.

Bush fruits are not as easily influenced by local climatic differences as are strawberries so chances are good that varieties from one state will do well in another. If locally produced plants are available, use them.

Currants and gooseberries will do well on most any Northwest soil of average fertility whether acid or slightly alkaline. Select a spot where soil water drainage keeps the roots from being drowned during the winter. Incorporate rotted manure, compost, leaf mold or peat moss into the top

GARDEN BUSH FRUITS: GROWTH PATTERNS		Scale: ¼″=1′
1st Year	3rd Year	5th Year
CURRANT		
GOOSEBERRY		
ELDERBERRY		
HUCKLEBERRY		
BLUEBERRY		

eight inches of soil to speed the root growth. Neither plant demands high soil fertility. In rich soil or in soils which have received annual fertilization with complete fertilizers, the bushes may grow so fast and lush as to become unmanageable. Generally, these bushes only need to be fertilized every third or fourth year in average soils.

Be careful in selecting the planting spot for currant and gooseberries to provide enough room. Gooseberries grow only from the original crown or cluster of stems and will remain in place as a single bush. Pruned properly each year it will maintain as a 4—6' wide bush. Currants are another matter. Currants send rhizomes (underground stems) outward and within several years you may find you have a thicket of currants. Plant currants in an area where they can be cultivated or pruned to maintain the original plant.

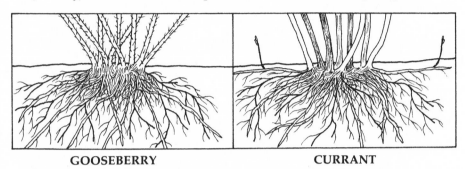

GOOSEBERRY   **CURRANT**

Blueberries and huckleberries need an acid soil to make their best growth. A pH of 4.3 to 5.0 appears ideal. This means that in most soils some annual care must be provided to maintain the proper pH range. If you are unsure of your soil pH, have your state university or local soils laboratory test it for you. Both of these plants have shallow, dense root systems, just like rhododendrons or azaleas in which nearly all roots are in the top eight inches of soil. They both prefer a soil containing lots of organic materials.

Amend soils for blueberries and huckleberries with three to four inches of rotted manure, compost or peat moss to supply humus, aerate the soil. Adjust the soil pH upward or downward to provide the proper range for these plants.

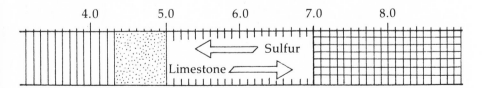

Sulfur, either as finely ground ground sulfur, "flowers" of sulfur or dusting sulfur can be used to bring the pH down. While it is best to have the soil analyzed and to make applications based on analysis, in the absence of a soil test, one pound of sulfur per hundred square feet of area will produce an acceptable if not ideal level of soil acidity. Should tests prove that the pH is too low (highly acidic conditions), ground limestone at one pound per hundred will bring the pH up slightly.

Blueberries and huckleberries will be helped if the three major nutrient elements are worked into the soil at planting time. A complete fertilizer, such as 5-10-10 or similar, at two pounds per hundred square feet of area will furnish the necessary start for these plants.

Elderberries are tolerant of nearly any soil type as long as it is well drained. They can grow in dry areas as well as wet spots providing the soil drainage allows aeration every so often. As with currants and gooseberries, select a place where these plants can grow to maturity. There are some selected forms available from nurseries which are advertised as "dwarf" but given the soil and climate of the Northwest they usually outgrow their description. Give them enough room to grow naturally and they need as much sunlight as your yard can supply. Dense shade makes them grow thin and sparse with resulting poor yields. Soil preparation should be aimed at getting the young plant off to a fast start. Three or four inches of leaf mold, compost or rotted manure should be worked into the soil along with two or three tablespoons of 5-10-10 fertilizer per bush.

While none of the bush fruits are particularly susceptible to soil diseases, it is good insurance to avoid planting these permanent plants in places where tomatoes or potatoes have been grown within the past two years or where woody plants have died out in the last several years.

Purchase and plant new bush fruit plants in early spring so they can grow roots and establish themselves by late spring before hot, dry weather arrives. One and two-year old nursery grown plants are easiest to transplant and will survive better than older plants. Plant them in the spring as early as you can get the soil ready.

Most bush fruit plants are self fertile. That is, they will pollinate their own flowers to set fruit. However, to insure a good crop of fruit it is wise to plant more than one variety. This is especially true of blueberries and to some extent applies to the others. In the case of blueberries, select several varieties to make sure sufficient pollen is available to set a good crop of berries. Cross-pollination gives a larger fruit with more seeds and often

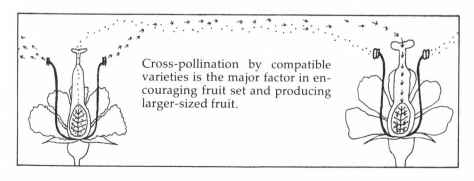

Cross-pollination by compatible varieties is the major factor in encouraging fruit set and producing larger-sized fruit.

promotes faster ripening. As a further dividend, each of the varieties will have different ripening dates, thus extending your harvest period.

Young plants purchased from mail order nurseries will generally come "bare root," i.e. with no soil around the roots. Locally purchased plants are available in containers with all roots intact or bare root. In any case, the root system should be kept damp during the plant's transfer from the nursery to your yard. If bare root, keep the roots covered with damp burlap or damp sawdust. If in a container or burlap-wrapped soil, water the root system frequently enough to prevent dryness which could kill the young roots. Keep them out of hot, direct sunlight, and protect from drying wind. Give the young bush-fruit plants the best chance of growing successfully by keeping them fresh and healthy from digging in the nursery to planting in your yard or garden.

Before planting, trim your new plants to remove damaged canes or broken roots which invite disease. Currants and gooseberries usually come as bare looking plants with two to five shoots. Leave no more than three canes (shoots), clipping the rest back to the crown. Those remaining should be trimmed back to six to eight inches of stem and buds. Prune back thick roots or roots that were broken or damaged in the nursery. Leave as many of the fine fibrous feeder roots as possible.

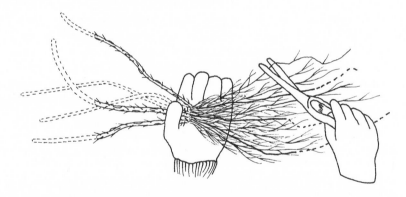

Blue, huckle, and elderberries should have their tops and roots lightly trimmed to remove only broken or damaged parts. Leave as much of the top part of the plant as possible.

When setting bush fruits, give them the room necessary to grow without competition from other plants. Currants and gooseberries should be planted six feet away from any other plant in the landscape. If planting in rows, put the currants and gooseberries four to five feet apart in the row and make the rows ten feet apart. Remember, gooseberries grow with single stems originating from a crown, while currants send out rhizomes to grow new canes. Place currants with enough room for you to cultivate and remove unwanted outlying shoots.

Blueberries should be planted five feet away from other plants in the landscape. If planting in rows, set the plants five feet apart and make the rows five to eight feet apart. Huckleberries should be given the same spacing as blueberries.

Elderberries need lots of room to grow to their mature size, so for economic use of the space they fit better into the landscape rather than as a row crop. They can be planted six to eight feet apart or can be interplanted to supply canopy shade for shade tolerant ornamentals.

Planting depth is important with all of the bush fruits, some because of their naturally shallow fibrous root system and others because of the effect on cane growth. Plant currants and gooseberries deep enough that the lowest branch starts just below the soil surface. This is necessary to help the plant develop into a bush form with the new canes or shoots coming up from the crown each year. Blueberries and huckleberries should be planted shallowly, with the root system covered by no more than an inch of soil. Blueberry and huckleberry planting should be followed with a 3" layer of sawdust or barkdust mulch extending out several feet from the plant stem.

Plant elderberries at the same depth as they were in the nursery row. A line on the stem will indicate the soil line. Plant so that this line is even with your soil surface.

If the soil has been prepared and amended as described previously, there should be no need for fertilizing at planting time. Save the fertilizer for later when new growth appears and the plant may need some mineral nutrition.

After the plants are set at the suggested depth, firm the soil around the roots, then water. The new plants should be watered in to make sure soil is in close contact with all of the roots. Flood the planting hole and add more soil as it settles. Once the plant is in place, set at the proper height, watered in and settled, apply a mulch. Mulches assist the new plant by keeping the soil damp and holding back young weeds. Mulches around bush berries (especially useful to blueberry and huckleberry plantings) need to be re-applied every couple years.

Once the new bush fruits are settled in, several nurturing practices will promote healthy establishment and maximize future production. When new leaves appear and growth has begun, apply ¼ cup of fertilizer in a wide ring around the plant. A complete fertilizer like 5-10-10 or something similar, is adequate. Or, if a source of manure is available, apply a 2-gallon bucketful as a ring dressing a foot away from the plant. These fertilizers can be applied on top of the mulch. Rainfall or irrigation water will carry the nutrients into the root zone.

The new planting requires irrigation and weed control. By using the mulches suggested these requirements will be minimized but not completely eliminated. Water the young plants often enough to maintain dampness in the top six to eight inches of soil. In the heat of midsummer this may mean weekly soakings.

Keep weeds out by pulling or hoeing while the plants are young. Avoid deep cultivation which can damage the roots. After the plants have grown in place for three or four months and are well established, i.e. making new, vigorous top growth and maintaining green leaf color, specifically labeled residual type herbicides can be used to prevent further weed competition.

Pruning Bush Fruits: Bush berries require several years of growing before they bear fruit. During these formative years, pruning should be directed toward stimulating strong, productive shoots. Pruning should be done in late winter before new growth begins. The amount needed will vary by plant and your objective.

Currants and Gooseberries:

These plants will grow and bear well with little or no pruning but will produce larger fruits and be less brushy and easier to harvest if pruned. The second to fourth year are the most productive for each cane.

After they have grown for one summer and before new growth begins for their second year, remove all weak, diseased or damaged parts first. Leave no more than six to eight of the most vigorous shoots. Currants and gooseberries bear their fruits on two to four-year old canes and some fruit will be had the second year they are in the garden. At the beginning of the third summer, prune to leave four to five one-year old canes and three to four two-year old canes. The third summer should be the year you begin enjoying fruits from both of these plants. In succeeding years prune to leave three or four strong canes of each age (one, two, and three-year old wood) and remove anything older than four years.

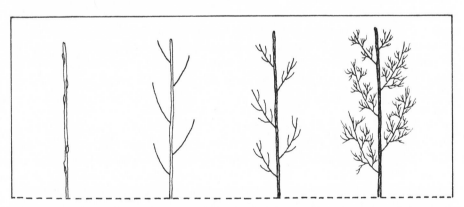

Currant or Gooseberry Cane Growth: from left to right, one, two, three, and four-year old cane.

One and two-year old canes have smooth, light brown bark; canes three years and older have splitting, darker and looser bark. After pruning your bushes you should have some of each age of cane shown above. ⎯⎯⎯⎯⎯⎯⎯⎯

Blueberries and Huckleberries:

These plants need little or no pruning until their fourth year in the garden. For the first three years prune only to remove dead, diseased or damaged limbs or shoots. Heavy pruning is neither helpful nor desirable. Generally the heavier the pruning the larger the berry size but the smaller the total crop will be for that year. By the fourth year these plants may have from ten to fifteen canes or shoots coming up from the crown. Start pruning by taking out any low-spreading branches, leaving only the erect shoots. Cut the low spreaders back to the ground. If the center of the bush is becoming crowded, take out any weak shoots. Do not remove more than one-quarter of the shoots in any year. A healthy, productive bush may have a dozen or more strong shoots arising from the crown. Annual pruning should remove only weak, unproductive wood, and one or two older shoots from the center to allow better air circulation and greater access to sunlight.

Elderberries:

Flowers and developing fruit appear in the second or third year. Flowers are borne on one and two-year old wood after the plant is several years old. Pruning is limited to removal of weak, unproductive shoots and heading back strong growth to keep the plant in bounds.

Once the bush fruits are on their way, growing well, producing fruit and gaining in size, most problems can be kept to a minimum with maintenance fertilizing, irrigation and pest control.

In the spring as new growth begins (if fertilizer has not been applied for two or three years) an application of manure or commercial fertilizer will keep bush fruits productive. The type of fertilizer varies somewhat from one species to another. Currants, gooseberries, and elderberries will do very well with an annual dressing of barnyard manure. If vigor is lacking, i.e. new shoots are few and weak, foliage color is light green or fruit set is minimal, an application of 5-10-10 fertilizer, using one and ¾ cup per mature plant will help. Apply the fertilizer in a broad ring around the outer periphery or dripline of the plant and water it into the soil.

Blueberries and huckleberries need more nitrogen than any other element. This is easily supplied as ammonium sulfate. These plants need an acid-type soil which ammonium sulfate will help maintain. Ammonium sulfate is a water soluble fertilizer which means that if a mature plant's needs are supplied all at once, much of the nitrogen will be leached away before being used by the plant. A serial nitrogen feeding schedule works better on these fruits. Start in the spring as buds are just beginning to open with ½ cup of ammonium sulfate per mature (five years or older) plant. Sprinkle this in a broad ring under the dripline. One month later make another application using ¼ cupful of ammonium sulfate. End the fertilizing program with one additional ¼ cupful, one month after the second. This method provides nitrogen during each of the three months when the blue and huckleberry plants are growing new shoots, blooming, and setting fruit.

While nitrogen is the main mineral requirement of huckle and blueberries, other elements may run short. All will, however, exhibit specific symptoms in the leaves. Nitrogen deficiency is signalled by smaller and narrower leaves than normal and pale green to yellow-green color. Leaves lacking in nitrogen will often turn red in late summer, long before normal, and will usually drop earlier than usual. Phosphorus shortage is shown by purplish tinting of the leaf margins or purple blotches in the center of the leaf. Magnesium deficiency shows on lower leaves causing them to turn yellow while the veins remain green. If phosphorus or magnesium deficiencies occur, supplement the phosphorus level with Superphosphate and use epsom salts to supply magnesium.

Maintain mulches over the root systems of blueberries and huckleberries. Currants, goose, and elderberries will do better with mulches but it is not as critical to their root survival. An additional inch or two of sawdust each year will keep the roots of blueberries and huckleberries blissfully cool and damp in the summer.

Spring rains will usually supply all the moisture that is needed to get plants started for the year. However, dig into the soil periodically to make sure soil is damp six to eight inches downward. If dry, get the irrigation system going. The most critical times for all bush fruits to have water is during the time the berries are developing and as they near ripe. Dry soil at this time will prevent or retard fruit development. The best way to water is by soaker or open hose end so the water is supplied directly to the root system, keeping it off the foliage. Mildew is always a possibility on foliage and fruit of bush berries and it will be encouraged if irrigation water keeps the foliage wet. If overhead irrigation is the only option available to you, water during the early morning. Avoid hot, sunny times of day as water droplets can magnify the sun's rays and burn the foliage or fruit. Less evaporation occurs in the morning, so more effective use of the irrigation water can be made.

Pest problems in the bush fruit plantings are the usual weeds, insects, diseases, and birds. Properly mulched bush berry plantings will seldom be bothered by annual weeds but the invasive perennials are another matter. Wild morning glory, quackgrass, sheep sorrel, and thistles may come in as seed but more likely via invasive underground stems from surrounding areas. Control measures include continual pulling and hoeing or the use of non-selective, systemic herbicides which can be sprayed onto the weed foliage. Check with local garden stores, Extension offices or other gardening authorities before using herbicides.

Insect pests may devour foliage, damage or eat the fruits or may cause injury to the crowns or roots. Watch for the injury and contact your garden store or Extension office for identification and recommended control measures. Injury will show as chewed leaves, dead stems or canes, damaged fruit or even as dead plants.

Birds will be as determined as you to harvest your fruit. Not only are they simply wild about your crop, they also are present at all hours and can have the fruit harvested before you get to the garden. Scarecrows may help, but the best and surest way of protecting your hard-won fruit is by covering the

BUSH FRUIT VARIETIES FOR THE PACIFIC NORTHWEST

TYPE/Variety	VARIETAL DIFFERENCES				HARVEST	GENERAL CHARACTERISTICS			
	BUSH	BERRY size or color	cluster	ripening		APPROX. MATURE SIZE	SOIL PREF.	SUN NEED	COMMENTS
GOOSEBERRY					Late June to Mid July Max. Prod: 2–3 yr. old wood	5' × 5–6'	not fussy	partial shade	Arching canes, usually thorny. Compact bush.
Chautauqua	3–5' thornless	green							
Ore. Champion	few thorns	green							
Pixwell		pink							
Poorman		red							
CURRANTS					July Max. Prod: 2, 3, 4 yr. old wood	4–6' ×4'	not fussy	partial shade	Needs rhizome control.
Perfection	upright	crimson	long/loose	mid					
Red Lake	upright	lt. red	long/loose	late					
Wilder	upright	dk. red		mid					
HUCKLEBERRY					Mid July Begins max. Prod: 4–5 yr. old plant	2–3'	Acid pH 4.3 –5.0 Loam	sun to partial shade	Compact bush, grows to height of 2–3' in sun.
Evergreen	low, compact	blue							
BLUEBERRY					July to September Begins Max. Prod: 4–5 yr. old plant	6' ht.	Acid pH4.3 –5.0 Loam	sun	Long-lived, productive.
Berkeley	spreading med. tall	very large	loose	mid					
Bluecrop	erect tall	large	loose	mid					
Blueray	erect tall	very large	small/tight	early					
Dixi	spreading tall	large	medium/tight	late					
Earliblue	erect tall	large	loose	very early					
Herbert	medium	very large	loose	late					
Jersey	erect tall	medium	long/loose	late					
ELDERBERRY					Late Summer Begins Max. Prod: 3–5 yr. old plant; 1–2 yr. old wood	6–10'	well drained	sun	Leafy large shrub or small tree.

bush with netting. Bird netting, cheesecloth or other small-mesh material placed over the bush just before fruit ripening can save your crop.

Bush fruit harvest extends over a period of several weeks to a month depending on the type of berry. Currants will usually ripen over a two-week period. They are considered ripe when all fruits in a cluster are full color (black or red, depending on the type). If the currant is to be used for jelly, pick when it is slightly underripe and highest in pectin. If the currant is to be used for any other purpose (fresh, frozen, cooked in pies, etc.) wait until fully ripe. Pick by pinching the stem of a cluster from the branch. Pick only the mature clusters, leaving the immature for another day.

Gooseberries are valued for their tart flavor. Pick them when full sized but slightly underripe. The longer they stay on the bush after reaching full size the less tart they become. Gooseberries are picked singly and the bush will need to be picked a number of times over a two to three week period, harvesting the berries when they are at their peak for your use.

Blueberry fruit grows in clusters. The first fruits in the cluster will be the first to ripen. Picking must be done over a three to four week period, harvesting the ripe berries and leaving the immature ones to ripen. The mature berries are a dark blue color at the stem end. A reddish tinge at the stem end means the berry is not yet ripe. A mature blueberry plant may produce from 14 to 20 pints of berries and picking may extend for seven weeks, if the summer is cooler than usual.

Elderberries are the last to mature in the bush berry group and will usually ripen in late summer. The fruit is borne in clusters and harvest is generally delayed until most of the berries have developed full color. At that time the entire cluster is picked and used.

After the harvest, check the bushes for broken branches or dead twigs and prune any damaged parts before winter. In severe winter areas, mulching will insure less root damage. Mulches will also prevent annual winter weed invasion.

Grapes

Grapes are easy to grow in the Northwest; the problem rests in selecting a variety which will ripen in your area. Grapes need many days of sunny, warm weather in order to develop sugars and ripen properly. As much time should be spent finding the warmest spot in your yard as spent in selecting the variety you will grow. Grapes are relatively hardy but in severe weather conditions they can be winter-killed. In the home garden some extra winter care and protection can be given to keep grapes alive through bitter periods but it is better to find the best site, protected and warm, to start with and save yourself the trouble of providing extra winter care.

As a first step, do some research on the climate in your area. Dig out information on the first and last frosts and if the winter temperature dips below 0°F for any length of time. Grapes need a minimum of 160 frost-free days in order to make vegetative growth, flower, and ripen fruit. A growing period of 200 days is better. In the home garden some extra days free of frost can be added by planting near the shelter of buildings or supplying some sort of cover in the spring.

DEGREE DAYS

A key factor in the successful growing and ripening of grapes is the amount of heat available. One way to determine whether your area is warm enough is to calculate "Degree Days." Contact the local weather station for the daily high and low temperatures for your growing season (usually April 1–October 31). Average each daily high and low temperature and subtract 50 degrees F. For example —

Date: June 15
low of 42°/high of 75° =   58.5° average
                    −50.0
                +   8.5   degree days

One degree day is a single heat unit. Negative values do not count. For example —

Date: April 15
low of 37°/high of 58° =   47.5° average
                    − 50.0
                (− 2.5)

Total your plus values for the entire growing season. If the total is at least 1900 degree days, plant grapes. If the total is close but slightly less than 1900 select varieties listed for early season ripening. If under 1750 degree days buy your grapes at your local fruit market.

In locating the site for your grapes, avoid low areas or places where cold air pockets exist. Low areas may also have poor water drainage. Neither condition, cold air pockets or cold, wet, soils, is satisfactory for growing grapes. Choose a spot that provides the most sunlight in your garden or yard. A southerly slope or a place in full sun is best, particularly if yours is an area which barely meets the degree-day needs of grapes.

The planting spot should also have deep, well drained and moderately fertile soil. Grapes root deeply and like three or more feet of soil with considerable moisture holding ability. Shallow soils (less than a foot of topsoil) and soils underlain by heavy clay layers should be avoided. If you have shallow soils and insist on raising grapes build raised planting areas or spend a season preparing deep soil by manuring or trench composting.

If space is limited, grapes can be used in the landscape to cover arbors, trellises, fences or provide a summer screen. As solar energy plantings, the grape makes an ideal summer insulation for the south or west side of the house. Grape vines will provide shade during the summer to cool the house, but allow available winter light to enter after the leaves have dropped in the fall. When planning to use grapes in the landscape, keep in mind that grapes are vigorous growers and a single plant may grow canes fifteen or more feet outward from the main trunk. Do not crowd grapes lest you end up with an impenetrable jungle demanding long frustrating hours to get back into order.

The goal in selecting the right spot is to find a way to provide the growing space, the best requirements for ripening and the winter protection needed to produce ripe grapes. The vines will grow almost anywhere in the Northwest, but unless varieties are selected for speedy ripening and a warm spot in the yard or garden is found, your efforts to produce an edible grape will be futile.

There are basically two types of grapes available to home gardeners in the Northwest: the European types (*Vitis vinifera*) and the American types (*Vitis labrusca*). Hybrids have been developed by crossing the two main groups. However, the hybrids tend to resemble one type more than the other and so will be identified as European or American. Several important differences exist between the two main types, mostly in vigor and hardiness.

American grapes (*V. labrusca*) are generally less vigorous growers and need trellis support to hold the plant erect. On its own, the American varieties tend to sprawl across the ground rather than grow upward. American varieties are hardier, more resistant to pests, and less susceptible to cold injury. They require fewer degree days to ripen and, consequently, yield mature fruit earlier than the European varieties. For the home garden the American varieties are easier to grow and more apt to provide a crop.

The European grapes (*V. vinifera*) are vigorous, upright growers and can dominate a small garden area. To help control the fast shoot growth of European types plant them on poorer soils. European grapes require more heat units to mature their berries and will be the last to ripen in the fall. They are more susceptible to winter injury and in areas where winter temperatures drop below freezing for several weeks or months, trellising must be designed to lay the canes on the ground so they can be covered to prevent winter kill.

With the increasing interest in grapes and the popularity of table and wine grape varieties, almost every area of the Northwest remotely suitable for the plant has an experiment station to test old and new varieties. The varieties listed here are only a beginning, so it would be wise to check with a local, land-grant university experiment station for recent varietal information.

Once the planting spot has been selected, taking into account all of of the plant's needs, i.e. full sunlight, protection from hard winds, deep and well drained soil, there are some things you can do to the soil to help the new grape plants grow. Grapes will overproduce vine growth as a result of a rich soil or an overabundance of nitrogen fertilizer. For this reason it's more important to look to soil drainage and depth rather than try to find the most fertile soil in the yard. Grapes can be expected to grow and yield fruit for

GRAPE VARIETIES FOR THE PACIFIC NORTHWEST

VARIETY	TYPE	SEASON (September)	USE Table	USE Processed	USE Wine	USE Dried	REMARKS
BLUE:							
Barbere	E	Late	X		X		Needs lots of heat to ripen; good win
Buffalo	A	Mid	X	X			Large berry.
Campbell Early	A	Late	X	X			
Concord	A	Late	X	X	X		Needs lots of heat to ripen.
Schuyler	E	Mid			X		
Worden	A	Mid–Late	X	X			Good berry size.
RED:							
Caco	A	Late	X	X			Good juice berry.
Canadice	A	Early	X	X		X	Small berry size; good for raisins, seedless.
Cardinal	A	Mid-Late	X				
Delaware	A	Late	X		X		Small clusters and berry.
Moored	A	Late	X	X			Large berry.
Suffolk Red	A	Mid	X	X		X	Small berry size; seedless.
WHITE:							
Diamond	A	Late	X	X			Large berry.
Himrod	A	Mid	X	X		X	Seedless berry; vigorous vine.
Interlaken	E	Mid	X	X		X	Seedless berry.
Perle de Csaba	E	Early	X		X	X	Seedless berry; very early ripening
Portland	A	Mid	X	X			Concord-like flavor.
Thompson Seedless	E	Late	X	X		X	Very low winter hardiness.
WINE:							
Chardonnay	E	Very Late			X		White wine.
Gewurztraminer	E	Late			X		White wine.
Pinot Noir	E	Late			X		Red wine.
Sauvignon Blanc	E	Very late			X		White wine.
White Riesling	E	Very Late			X		White wine.

A: American
E: European

twenty or more years. They will need three or four years to develop before producing any fruit but once started they should continue bearing for as long as you take care of them. Care consists of providing a few mineral elements every year and pruning to promote fruit development. Before planting, work a complete fertilizer such as 5-10-10 into the planting area. One cupful of 5-10-10 worked into a five by ten foot area will provide the initial minerals necessary for a single grape vine. If barnyard manure is available use three to four inches of manure and spade it into the top six to eight inches of soil.

Proper drainage is a critical requirement of grapes. Grape roots will be killed in a soil that becomes saturated in early winter and remains that way until spring. If drainage is a problem in your garden or yard planting site, either correct the problem with drain lines or plant the grapes on raised beds.

Since the grape planting will be a permanent addition, get rid of perennial weeds before planting to free the young vine from serious competition by weedy plants. Once the vine is established and has made its upper cane growth, several residual soil herbicides can be used to keep weeds under control.

Grape plants should be purchased while they are dormant and be planted before new growth begins in the spring. Generally, the young one to two-year old bare root plants will be available at nurseries in late winter. The plant will consist of one or two short canes and a fibrous root system. Keep the roots damp until you get the plants into the ground. Either keep the roots covered with damp burlap or sawdust or heel them in a trench, if it will be several days before planting. Before planting trim away any broken or damaged roots. Cut the top back to a single strong cane, leaving two healthy basal buds to grow a new top. Place the healthy plants in the ground at the same depth they were in the nursery.

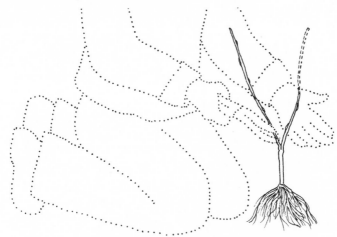

In order to force fast growth and to begin your training system, any grape plant should be cut back to a single strong cane with two buds before planting.

Grapes need room to grow and should be planted at least six feet away from each other or from other plants. If sufficient space exists in your garden, give each plant eight to ten feet on a side. The more space the better the plant can grow and the fewer foliage diseases you will have to contend with. Rows of grapes should be eight to ten feet apart to provide air circulation, access to sunlight, and room for cultivating and picking.

Plans must be made in the spring to handle the spirited growth of the vines that will begin in early summer. If not trained properly the vines take over and become a tangled mass. There are any number of ways of training vines. They can be trained on posts or on wires or can be made to grow to cover arbors, trellises or fences. Make plans now though and be ready to accommodate the plant when it begins making vines. Trellises can be built with posts tall enough to provide a top wire at five to six feet above the ground. A second wire is strung two or three feet lower. Use #9 to #11 gauge wire for the trellis as it must support the weight of the vines and fruit. Posts should be set at convenient distances with one or two plants between posts.

Training methods selected to fit your own garden or yard situation should maximize the amount of sunlight reaching the vines and at the same time reduce exposure to wind. Consider the vines' function in the landscape: they can be trained onto supports to provide shade while utilizing the sun. The illustration shows some of the more popular training systems for grape vines.

Don't expect any fruit for about three years after planting. Grapes take several years to grow enough wood to develop flower buds. During this time pruning should be done annually to develop the upper part of the plant.

While the grape plant is growing to maturity and during succeeding years, the main management effort should be directed toward maintaining the most productive vine growth. The grape plant produces its berry crop from buds produced the previous year. In the following pages we will discuss ways of pruning mature grape vines to stimulate new cane growth in order to maintain annual crops. Now though, let's examine some other factors which influence a vine's fruit production.

Management of the grape vine for the first year or two centers on control of weeds, irrigation during dry periods, and pruning to direct the growth of new vines. Cultivation around new grape vines should be shallow to avoid damaging the numerous feeder roots near the soil surface. In later years the plant's root system will be deeper and less susceptible to damage by tilling or other surface soil disturbances. Mulches will help keep annual weeds under control and conserve soil water. However, grape roots need warm soil as early as possible so don't put mulches over the root system until the soil has warmed in early summer. Irrigation should be thorough, deep and infrequent. Check the soil every two or three weeks during the summer for moisture. If the top five inches is dry irrigate to soak the soil ten to fifteen inches deep. In most soils three or four waterings in a summer will suffice.

SOME TRAINING SYSTEMS FOR GRAPES

Head Pruned: Though not often used in home gardens it is sometimes preferred for its decorative effect. Each year the previous year's shoots are cut back to 2–4 buds which bear the crop and provide canes for next year's buds.

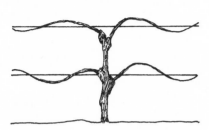

Four-Cane Kniffen: Four fruiting arms are trained on two wires. This is one of the more popular systems for home gardens, partly due to its adaptability and simplicity.

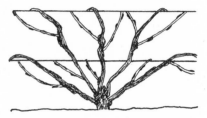

Fan-Training: Permanent canes are developed outward. Previous year's growth must be religiously cut back and thinned to maintain this type of system.

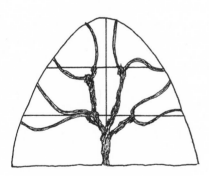

Arbors and Fences: Spread and tie the canes uniformly over the trellis. Each year cut the newest vines back to 2–5 buds to stimulate new growth and fruit.

Cordon: One permanent vine goes each direction on the wire, side canes are pruned back to 2–5 buds each year.

Deep watering stimulates the roots to follow the moisture downward and will result in a plant with a hardy root system.

Normally during the spring and early summer, vines grow rapidly and gradually slow from midsummer to the end of the growing season. When buds are initially developed at the base of each leaf they are all leaf buds. Later, as vine growth slows, the production of plant food reserves exceeds the demand for feeding new shoots and the first formed leaf buds are converted into flower buds. If something interferes with this growth habit, i.e. from fast early growth to slower mature growth, the conversion of leaf buds to flower buds is also affected. Anything which stimulates the plant to maintain continual fast growth into late summer will reduce flower bud development and next year's crop.

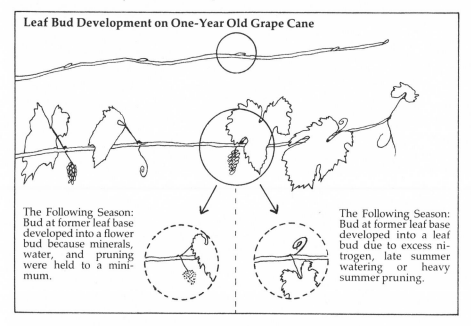

Leaf Bud Development on One-Year Old Grape Cane

The Following Season: Bud at former leaf base developed into a flower bud because minerals, water, and pruning were held to a minimum.

The Following Season: Bud at former leaf base developed into a leaf bud due to excess nitrogen, late summer watering or heavy summer pruning.

For optimum grape production you must balance several factors including nutrients, water, pruning, and size of crop allowed to be borne by the plant. Cultural methods that promote normal growth will stimulate larger crops. Let's look at each factor for better understanding.

Nitrogen fertilizer stimulates leafiness and shoot growth. A shortage results in lighter green leaves and weak growth. An excess causes the grape plant to grow lush, strong vines. For highest grape production avoid nitrogen shortages or excesses. Generally a single application of a complete type fertilizer in the spring as new growth begins will be adequate. One cupful of 5-10-10 spread over a 5 × 10 foot area for each plant will supply the needs for an entire growing season. In fact, if the growth is becoming too rank and vigorous, forget the fertilizer because your soil is probably fertile enough without any additions. Boron is a minor element needed to help promote the development and growth of berry clusters. Boron for grapes can be supplied in borax soap powder or boric acid, using one tablespoon per gallon of water and sprinkling over a 5 × 10 foot area. Apply borax during the dormant season once every 2−3 years.

Generally, mature vines will not need to be irrigated except during long and severe drought. If the vines wilt during hot summer days, obviously they need water and should be watered deeply. If water is needed, apply it to the ground and not the foliage. Mildew is a serious menace to grape leaves and berry clusters and will be worse if they are damp from rain or overhead irrigation. If the vines are not wilting, do not water from midsummer onward. Watering excessively will stimulate growth to the detriment of next year's flowers and fruit. Mulches help by minimizing surface evaporation. In fertile soils with a naturally high moisture content, planting lawn grass between the grape rows will help regulate soil moisture and keep growth normal.

Now, about pruning. Grape pruning can be so baffling that the beginner either prunes nothing for fear of killing the vine or cuts off everything in sight, effectively removing all fruit buds on an annual basis. There have been volumes written on grape pruning, but here we simply give some common sense tips. First of all remember what we said about the flower buds (the ones that will flower, be pollinated, and make fruit). They were formed on vines grown the previous summer. This means we need to leave some of last summer's vine growth in order to get fruit. For the berries to fill properly and for the plant to grow new vines for next year we don't want to overwork the grape plant by leaving too many fruit buds. Our pruning advice is all directed at helping you maintain the proper balance between pruning too heavily, or not pruning enough.

Pruning is best done in late winter, from late January to early March, before growth begins. The canes that will bear fruit are the newest shoots with smooth bark. At each place where a leaf grew last year is a knob or node with a bud. When growth begins, each bud grows into a shoot with leaves and two or three clusters of berries. The more buds that are left after pruning, the more berry clusters. An unpruned vine will set more fruit than it can ripen. The fruit from such vines will be small, sour and poorly colored. Also, leaving too many fruit buds on the plant can severely impede normal growth. One way of determining how many buds to leave on vines of grapes is by weighing the prunings, thereby gaining some idea of the vigor of the plant. This method requires a weighing scale and may seem a nuisance but with experience you can learn to estimate the weight of prunings and feel confident with this system of balancing production of fruit and new growth.

Decisions on how much to prune and what to prune must be based on variety characteristics, vigor, and the type of training system. Some generalities will be made here to be used as a guide. Once you have seen how your particular grape plants grow and respond you can sharpen your techniques to better fit your own situation.

Varieties which grow a dozen or more twelve foot vines each year on a

GRAPE PRUNING: 2-Wire Trellis

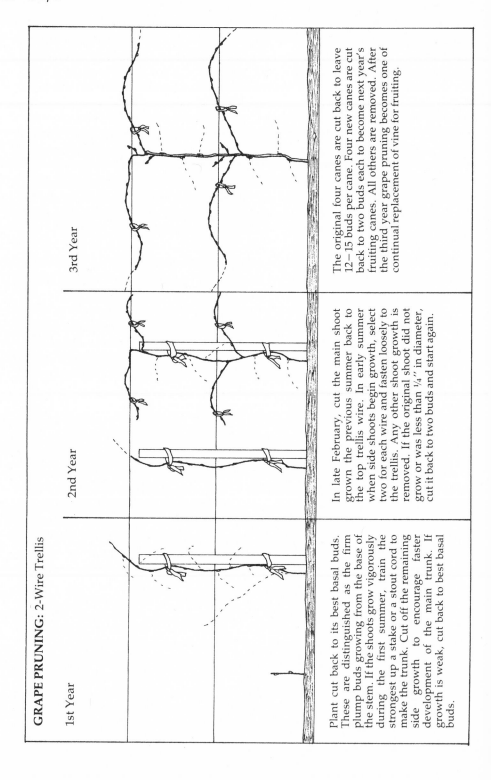

1st Year

Plant cut back to its best basal buds. These are distinguished as the firm plump buds growing from the base of the stem. If the shoots grow vigorously during the first summer, train the strongest up a stake or a stout cord to make the trunk. Cut off the remaining side growth to encourage faster development of the main trunk. If growth is weak, cut back to best basal buds.

2nd Year

In late February, cut the main shoot grown the previous summer back to the top trellis wire. In early summer when side shoots begin growth, select two for each wire and fasten loosely to the trellis. Any other shoot growth is removed. If the original shoot did not grow or was less than 1/4" in diameter, cut it back to two buds and start again.

3rd Year

The original four canes are cut back to leave 12–15 buds per cane. Four new canes are cut back to two buds each to become next year's fruiting canes. All others are removed. After the third year grape pruning becomes one of continual replacement of vine for fruiting.

mature plant are capable of supporting and ripening many more fruit clusters than less vigorous varieties growing finer or shorter vines. Thus, the American varieties, which are usually vigorous plants, are pruned to leave more buds than the European varieties. Concord for example, while not a particularly desirable variety in the Northwest, because it is late ripening, is nevertheless a vigorous plant. For vines of this type leave 40 buds for the first pound of prunings and ten for each additional pound as a general rule. Using this method of balancing the crop with the vigor of the plant, a mature vine could have up to 60 or more buds to produce next year's harvest. On the four-cane Kniffen system, each of the four canes growing outward from the central trunk would have 15 buds, each of which could be expected to have an average of two fruit clusters.

Varieties producing 6−8 healthy canes, less than six feet in length, should be pruned to leave 25 buds for the first pound of prunings and 10 for each additional pound. At first glance this seems a lot of buds to leave on a plant, but grape prunings do not weigh very much, as you will learn with experience. These varieties might end up having 45 buds to produce their crop of fruit.

European varieties are usually grown for wine production and have extremely large clusters. These types of grapes require more severe pruning to leave shorter canes and fewer buds. Leaving too many large clusters will result in few of them ripening and few or none reaching the sugar content needed for quality. For these varieties, a general rule of six buds remaining for the first pound of prunings and two additional buds for each added pound works well.

WEIGHING GRAPE PRUNINGS

An example of how to use the idea of balancing vine growth with fruit production follows. Given a grape plant with 3.5 pounds of prunings, here is what one would strive for:

Weight of Prunings/	Vigorous	Less Vigorous	European/Wine Grapes
1st pound	40 buds left	25 buds left	6 buds left
2nd pound	10 additional	10 additional	2 additional
3rd pound	10 additional	10 additional	2 additional
0.5 pound	5 additional	5 additional	1 additional
3.5 pounds	65 buds left	50 buds left	11 buds left

One arrives at the number of buds to leave by starting with some basic pruning cuts. Take a look at your system of trellising. A fruiting cane (last year's growth) with from 3−15 buds will need to be left to grow each arm of your trellis. You will also need to leave one or two canes pruned back to two

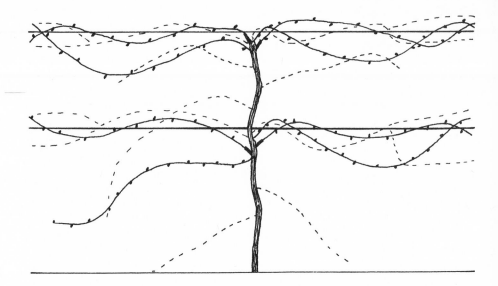

Pruning a Grape Plant: example — a moderately vigorous plant trained to the 4-cane Kniffen system.

Start pruning by cutting off any unneeded canes to conform the vine to the training system you have planned. Leave a surplus of buds. Start weighing the prunings and counting how many buds are left. Using previous chart, find out how many buds can be left for maximum fruiting without overloading the plant. In this example we have 2 lbs. of prunings; a total of 35 buds can be left. This process does get easier with practice; eventually routine judgments will eliminate the weighing step.

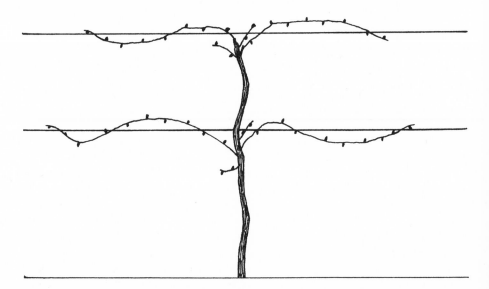

buds at the base of each arm or fruiting cane to make growth for next year's crop and are not included in your bud count.

Start pruning by cutting off any unneeded canes to conform the vines to the training system and trellis you have planned. Leave a surplus of buds. Follow this with a detailed weighing of prunings and counting of buds. With a little practice, routine judgments can be made and only an infrequent weighing will be needed.

As you gain some experience with your own varieties and growing success, bud and growth balancing becomes the art of determining how many pounds of fruit you will produce. For example, if the variety produces two clusters of grapes per bud, and each cluster in past years has weighed about ¼ pound, then each bud could be expected to yield ½ pound of fruit. So, if 60 buds remain on the plant after pruning, you can expect 30 pounds of grapes as a result of your careful planning and management.

All pruning cuts should be made with shears having two cutting edges to avoid damaging tissue near the cuts. Prune ½ to ¾ inch outward from the topmost bud being left on the cane. Don't worry about "bleeding." Grapes pruned in late winter and early spring will flow sap for several days, but this loss does not hurt the plant. Do not prune grapes in freezing weather as the vines are brittle and may be damaged.

During the first two or three years of the grape vine's growth some pruning during the summer will help stimuate the growth of canes selected to develop onto the trellis. Removing unneeded side shoots will direct the energy of the plant into those canes selected for permanent trunks or arms. Once the vine is mature avoid heavy pruning during the summer as this may delay ripening of the berries. Some light thinning of side shoots may be needed where vine growth is so rank that sunlight and air movement are restricted.

Watch for the appearance of powdery mildew, one of the most common but serious diseases of grapes. This is a sign that air circulation is not the best. Powdery mildew forms a whitish-gray coating on the leaves and fruit. Usually, it will be found first on leaves toward the inside of the foliage canopy. If the weather is unusually mild as new growth begins and when flower clusters are opening, mildew may destroy or deform the plant tissues and prevent berry formation. Mildew is most prevalent during warm periods of high humidity with no air movement. In late summer powdery mildew attacks the fruit and covers the berries with a white to gray fungus which causes the berries to crack and shrivel.

If and when mildew appears, try to provide more sunlight and better air movement. Prune out or pick and destroy leaves coated with the mildew. If the problem persists, which is likely, dust or spray at weekly intervals with sulfur.

The grape berry progresses through several stages from early to late summer. In its green stage, the berry grows from pinhead size to nearly full size. In this state it is hard. When it reaches the ripening stage, usually mid to late August, the berry begins to change color, soften slightly and reaches its full size. Next sugars, primarily glucose and fructose, develop and acidity decreases. This is a time of rapid change in the berry. At this stage sample a berry every so often to test if the berries are ripe enough for use.

The grape plant is easy to propagate by using a "cutting," an eight to twelve inch piece of stem with 3–5 buds. If you can't find the particular variety you want at a garden shop, try to find the plant and propagate it. Also, use cuttings to multiply your own grape planting. Grapes can be propagated in mid-winter to furnish new plants by spring.

Grape cuttings from the middle portion of the previous summer's growth will root easiest and make the best plants. Take cuttings that have a node or bud near the bottom end. The cutting should have a total of three to five buds the length of the cutting piece. From one average shoot of the previous summer's growth three to five cuttings can be taken. Cuttings should be 8–12" long and no less than pencil size in diameter.

For easier handling tie the cuttings in bundles with all buds pointed in the same direction. Make sure a plant name tag is attached so you can identify the variety in subsequent years.

Grapes will root quite well by simply poking the cutting into the ground, leaving the uppermost one or two buds exposed. They will root even better though, and your chances of success are increased, if you store them for six to eight weeks in a cool, damp place. The vegetable section of the refrigerator works well or better yet, store the bundles of cuttings outdoors covered with sand or sawdust. Cover the bundles with about eight inches of sand or sawdust and keep the pile damp but not saturated. Storage allows the cutting to develop callus tissue and a few roots before being planted. Storage also keeps the buds dormant while the roots are forming, thus giving the cutting a better chance to establish itself when planted out in the soil.

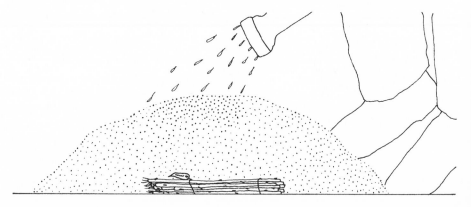

After they have been stored for six to eight weeks the individual cuttings can be planted outside in a temporary row where they can grow for one or two years. In a year or two they should grow at least two strong canes which can be used to develop trunks and arms. Wait until the plants are dormant before moving them to a permanent location.

Grape growing in Northwest gardens is more challenging than most gardeners realize. The vines grow well and the plant remains vigorous for many years, making trellis growth, providing arbor shade, sun screen, and generally beautifying the yard. The challenge is one of selecting varieties which can ripen their fruit in our climate. We hope the foregoing information will assist grape enthusiasts meet and beat this challenge.

Chapter 7: Food Crops: TREE FRUITS

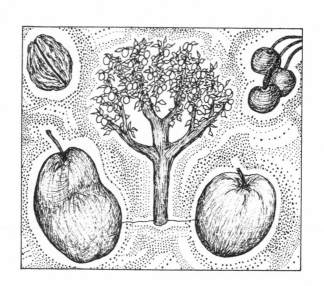

Introduction

Overview:

The wide selection of fruit trees suitable for Northwest conditions, allows gardeners to add a plant or two which supplies both fruit and interest to their garden or landscape. Part of the value of tree fruit growing is the production of your own choice of fruit. In the apple group for example, there are more than 6,000 varieties. Most of these are not commercially grown for any number of reasons, but each has some unique quality which the home gardener may wish to incorporate in his own yard. Have you ever heard of or seen a *Cortland* apple in your supermarket? Eaten a baked *Mutsu* or some *Northern Spy* applesauce? Not likely, yet these are only three of the superb apple varieties suitable for Northwest gardens. This chapter will cover the general principles of fruit tree cultivation but you will have to decide which fruits and varieties fit your palate and your needs.

Central to successful fruit gardening is an understanding of the environmental requirements of fruit trees. Tree survival is not enough. The climate and local microclimate must be such that the fruit tree can bloom; be pollinated; and the fruit ripen on time and with a normal sugar content. Further, fruit trees need enough cold weather during the dormant period to chill the buds for growth the following spring. All of this may sound a bit complicated, but we hope to have made the proper means for growing good fruit clear by the end of the chapter. For the moment suffice it to say that carefully selected apple and sour cherry varieties will grow and fruit in all areas of the Northwest, on either side of the Cascade Range. Plums and sweet cherries do well in all but the coastal areas where high humidity promotes stone fruit disease. Pears, peaches, and walnuts do best in valley areas and along rivers on both sides of the Cascades. Apricots are relatively hardy trees so grow well in most areas but we have problems with their bloom time — typically, a crop will mature only about once every six years.

One of the major outcomes of recent horticultural research has been the development of dwarf fruit trees. Dwarf trees are smaller versions of regular sized (standard) trees which make them not only more easily managed but better suited to the size of most home gardens. They produce full sized fruits typical of the variety and generally begin bearing at a younger age. However, not all tree species can be dwarfed. Some, such as walnuts and sweet cherries, are not available in reliable dwarf types. There are a few genetic peach and cherry dwarfs but they have not proved sufficiently productive to be of value in the home orchard. Apples and pears are dwarfed by grafting onto a special type of root system.

Fruit trees serve a multiplicity of purposes: as yard shade trees, hedges or screens, living sculpture (espalier forms), and, of course, fruit for eating. Sweet cherry and walnut are marvelous shade trees. Both of them grow thirty to fifty feet in height with a nearly equal spread. In a smaller yard, peaches and filberts that grow to about twenty feet are more suitable.

Many can be pruned and trained into patterns. "Espalier" means the training of limbs by pruning to grow in a nearly two-dimensional form against walls, fences, and trellises, or into free standing single-plane figures. While espaliering is not recommended for the casual gardener, it is a very useful means for growing a good fruit crop in limited space and once developed, espaliered trees are easy to maintain. Chosen for variety and rootstock, two espaliered apple trees may be grown and provide abundant fruit along a fifteen or twenty foot fence.

ESPALIER: A plant is restricted to growing in a pre-determined pattern. New shoots are trained and pruned to limit the size and shape of the plant. Pruning and training is a continuous process and requires considerable time and attention.

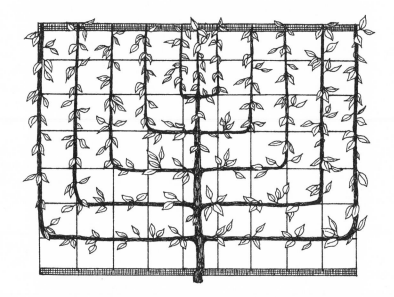

For this design start with an unbranched one-year old nursery tree. After planting cut the top back to 18", just above a bud. Select the three most vigorous shoots that emerge below this pruning cut. Bend two horizontally in opposite directions and tie them to the lowest supporting wire or fence. Use soft but durable tying material to avoid damaging limbs. Continue tying the new growth horizontally to form the bottom tier of limbs. Allow the third shoot to grow vertically 15–18" and remove the tip. Select the three best shoots that follow. Train two horizontally and one up the center. Repeat the process in succeeding years until five or more tiers are attained. During the training process all side shoots that appear on the laterals should be cut back to their lowest leaf when they reach 12" in length. Pruning and training continues for the life of the plant.

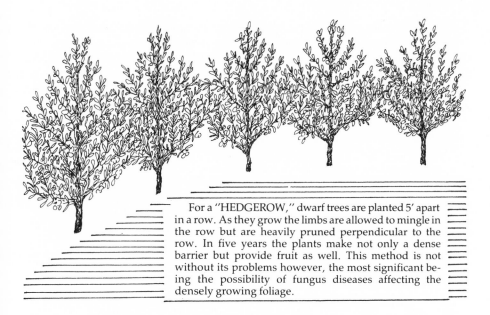

For a "HEDGEROW," dwarf trees are planted 5' apart in a row. As they grow the limbs are allowed to mingle in the row but are heavily pruned perpendicular to the row. In five years the plants make not only a dense barrier but provide fruit as well. This method is not without its problems however, the most significant being the possibility of fungus diseases affecting the densely growing foliage.

There are many pests which enjoy fruit crops as much as you, which can make home production discouraging. However, if pest control is reduced to a regular schedule it is not an overwhelming chore. Some pests will need to be attacked periodically. For these you can plan and develop routine control methods and materials that are easily and economically applied. Other pests appear irregularly, but routine inspection of your plants will usually provide early warning so control measures can be invoked. Learn which insect and disease pests are a part of your environment and plan accordingly. A call to your nearest Extention Service office will provide a wealth of information on local pests.

Listed here are some of the more common pests of specific tree fruits.

TREE FRUIT PESTS

Fruit	Pest	When Most Likely/*Where
Apple	Scab	spring, early summer, B, D
	Codling Moth	early summer, D, E
	Apple Maggot	early summer, D, E
	Powdery Mildew	early spring, B, D
Pear	Fire Blight	early spring, B, C, D
	Scab	spring, early summer, B, D
	Codling Moth	early summer, D, E
	Pear Slug	summer, G

(Fruit)	(Pest)	(When Most Likely/*Where)
Peach	Leaf Curl	dormant, A
	Fruit Worm	early summer, D, E
	Aphid	spring, early summer, B, D
	Brown Rot	spring, summer, B, C, E
	Root Borer	midsummer, F
Apricot	Brown Rot	spring, early summer, B, C, E
	Coryneum Blight	spring, fall, A, B, D
	Bacterial Canker	fall, A
Cherry	Brown Rot	spring, early summer, B, C, E
	Leaf Spot	early summer, B, D
	Cherry Slug	early summer, G
	Bacterial Canker	fall, A
	Fruit Fly Maggot	early summer, D, E
Plum	Brown Rot	spring, early summer, B, C, E
	Root Borer	midsummer, F
	Aphid	spring, early summer, B
Filbert	Filbert Worm	midsummer, D, E
	Aphid	early summer, B, D
Walnut	Husk Fly	midsummer, D, E
	Blister Mite	early summer, B, D

*WHERE: A — dormant bud   E — full sized fruit stage
              B — leaf emerging   F — upper roots, lower trunk
              C — bloom   G — foliage
              D — small fruit stage

Diseases are markedly influenced by weather and will usually be worse during humid, warm periods. Choosing a planting site which provides good sunlight, ample air circulation and soil water drainage will reduce the probability of disease outbreaks. Good garden practices help ward off mildews, leaf spots, and blights. Spray schedules and materials recommended by your local Extension Service office will help you cope with severe outbreaks of disease.

Home gardeners are often disappointed by expecting too much, too soon. Fruit trees must make a certain amount of growth, develop mature growth buds, and store sufficient reserves before they can bloom. Remember, no fruit can be formed until the trees bloom. The time required for this development ranges from three or four years for a fully dwarfed apple tree to ten or twelve years for an English walnut.

POSSIBLE YIELDS OF TREE FRUITS IN THE NORTHWEST*

Fruit	Dwarf	Standard	1Approx. years to Bearing	2Space per tree
Apple	2–6 bushel	10–25 bushel	5–10 years	5–40 feet
Pear	2–4 bushel	8–15 bushel	5–7 years	10–20 feet
Peach	1–2 bushel	4–6 bushel	4–5 years	12–15 feet
Apricot	– – – –	50–70 lbs.	4–5 years	30 feet
Sour Cherry	– – – –	40–120 lbs.	5–6 years	14–20 feet
Sweet Cherry	– – – –	50–160 lbs.	6–7 years	20–35 feet
Plum	15–40 lbs.	30–120 lbs.	5–6 years	10–20 feet
Filberts	– – – –	15–20 lbs.	6–8 years	15–20 feet
Walnuts	– – – –	50–100 lbs.	8–10 years	50 feet

*Note: higher yield figures represent the most productive varieties, in their productive, mature years, grown on proper sites, and properly cared for.

1begins when the tree is planted in its permanent location.

2lower figures represent dwarf varieties if available; if unavailable, lower figures represent pruning to upright forms.

How will you know when to pick your fruit? Look at the color, are fruits dropping? Check for ease of picking, feel for softness, taste. These are the indicators of maturity. Fruit color is the least reliable indicator unless one knows exactly what the fruit of that particular variety is supposed to look like. Sour cherries come loose from their stems when ripe. Peaches and apricots become soft and more aromatic when ripe and, as with plums, the greenish look changes to a yellow undercolor. Walnuts and filberts simply drop to the ground when mature.

The crop of most tree fruits ripens over a period of several weeks, which gives the home fruit grower a longer time to enjoy tree-ripened fruit unobtainable in any other way. Harvest often enough to collect the fruits at the peak of their perfection and to prevent loss of overripe fruits that will fall from the tree and be eaten by something else.

Some fruits store well for many months, others will only keep for a week or two before becoming compost material. Apples are the long-term keepers, but all varieties are not equal in this respect. Peaches, apricots, plums, and cherries are poor keepers and should be processed within several weeks of picking. Pears, for the most part, need to be stored for awhile and then be ripened for eating. An unheated basement, a dugout underground space or insulated box are good storage places for apples and pears. Dry fruits such as filberts and walnuts, prefer a cool and dry storage spot.

Do not store any fruit that has been damaged during picking or been injured by insects. These culls should be used immediately because they break down rapidly and will spread rot to any fruit stored with them. Do not store fruit near strong-flavored vegetables (onions, etc.) as the fruit will absorb their distinctive odors. The storage spaces used for all moist fruits should be maintained between 32–45°F with high humidity. Within this range fruits stored at 45°F will not keep as long as those stored at lower temperatures. Sound fruit can be stored in clean, airy containers, perforated plastic bags, wood or paper boxes. Do not wrap fruit as they need fresh air for gas exchange.

Damage to fruit trees in the Northwest seldom results from low temperatures. Perhaps, once in ten years a cold spell will be cold enough and last long enough to damage a few trees. Usually fruit trees are simply damaged by neglect — neglect in pruning and training, sanitation, soil and water management, rodent control or other cultural and mangement practices. Most of a tree's needs should be attended to during the dormant, winter season. During the fall, dead and disease-injured twigs and limbs must be removed to prevent the unseen spread of fungus. During the winter, dormant spray must be applied to check disease spores and destroy overwintering forms of insect enemies. Wire collars should be placed to protect young fruit tree trunks from rodent damage. In late winter, pruning should be done to direct the growth of the fruit tree and renew its wood. And of course, during the annual winter downfall of rain you must make sure excess water is draining away. (This problem should have been dealt with before the trees were planted, but never take drainage for granted.) In areas of cold and sunny winters, paint the trunks with white latex paint to prevent sunscald on dormant trunks.

The general management and cultural practices covered in this chapter are applicable to all tree fruits. However, related species have specific and similar needs and habits, so we have grouped apples and pears; peaches and apricots; cherries and plums; and filberts and walnuts into separate sections for more detailed exposition.

We will deal first with the general management and culture practices and then address matters relating to specific groups of fruit trees.

Siting Fruit Trees:

When deciding where to put fruit trees in your yard, consider the basic requirements for tree growth (sun, soil and space) and minimizing pest problems (in particular, good air circulation). All fruit trees require full sunlight for at least eight hours per day during active growth. Trees planted in shade will be weak, easily done in by fungus diseases and insects, and seldom bear fruit. Find a sunny spot to aid healthy tree development and ensure fruit ripening.

SPACE REQUIREMENTS: HOW MANY FRUIT TREES WILL FIT*

| | Apples and Pears | | | | | Cherry | | | | |
	dwarf	semi	stand.	Peach	Apricot	sweet	sour	Plum	Filbert	Walnut
Sq. ft. Needed -	64	150	900	225	900	900	225	300	300	2500
Size of Yard:										
10 × 40	6	2	—	—	—	—	2	2	—	—
20 × 20	6	2	—	2	—	—	2	2	1	—
30 × 30	14	6	1	4	1	1	4	3	3	—
40 × 40	25	11	2	7	2	2	7	5	5	1

*Read chart as an "or" situation; for example, in a 10 × 40 yard a person could put in 6 dwarf apple or pears, or 2 semi-dwarf apple or pear, or 2 sour cherry trees, or 2 plum trees.

Soil fertility is not as important a consideration as soil depth and drainage. Fruit trees are inherently long-lived residents of the garden, so to reach a ripe old age they must have a situation that allows roots to grow deep. At least three feet is ideal. Adequate drainage is equally important. Fruit trees cannot be expected to thrive in a marsh or even in heavy clay soils that remain saturated for most of the year. Neither can they grow in bone dry soil. A dry site can be moderated (with proper irrigation) more readily than a wet site.

Fruit trees need space not only for normal growth without crowding or shading, but also "breathing space" for good air circulation. This is particularly important in Northwest gardens where our spring weather is conducive to the development of fungus problems.

Avoid sites where cold air collects and heavy winds occur. This caution is especially important in siting the earlier blooming fruits, i.e., peaches and apricots. If your local topography offers no frost-free or windless areas, plan to utilize microclimate effects. A south facing fence, for example, collects heat and re-radiates it at night. A sheltering, inner corner of house walls or shrubbery will give a measure of protection. Take time to find the best possible spot for your fruit trees. The time you spend in sound observation and reflection before planting will be more than offset by the time gained in avoiding wind losses, cold damage, extra spraying or years of concerned effort without a pear or peach picked.

If you are buying property for the specific purpose of growing tree fruits, look for southern slopes and avoid bottom land which contains frost pockets. The ideal site for fruit trees is sunny, sheltered from severe wind, with deep and moderately fertile, well drained soil. The following table will assist you in your site assessment for a fruit orchard.

RELATIVE TOLERANCE OF FRUIT TREES

Type:	Shade	Severe Wind	Soil			Late Spring Frost
			Low Fertility	Poor Drainage	Depth Less than 3'	
Apples	2	2	2	5	4	2
Pears	3	2	5	8	3	1
Peaches	0	0	0	2	4	0
Apricots	0	0	0	2	2	0
Cherries	4	3	0	0	2	5
Plums	4	3	10	8	8	5
Filberts	2	2	4	2	1	10
Walnuts	2	3	4	0	0	7

0 = intolerant, 10 = acceptable

Pollination and Yield:

Fruit tree production is somewhat chancy and ought to be viewed philosophically. Enjoy the trees, and if the gods are smiling, count your blessings when your trees bear a great crop of fruit. But whatever the vagaries of nature in any particular year, there is one aspect of yield which you must understand and carefully observe. This is the pollination characteristics of the trees planted. There are fundamentally two classes of trees — self-fertile or self-sterile. Self-fertile means that the pollen produced by a single tree will fertilize the flowers of that tree. Self-sterile means that the pollen produced by a single tree will not fertilize the flowers of the same tree. As a practical consequence, the home gardener may plant only one self-fertile variety but must plant two or more trees of the self-sterile varieties.

Pears, sweet cherries, and filberts are self-sterile or only partially self-fertile, so more than one tree is needed in the garden for pollination. Some varieties of apples and plums are self-fertile while others require nearby pollinators. So, before buying young trees determine whether the varieties you select also require pollinator trees.

When selecting pollinators it is important to use those known to have both "good" pollen and bloom at the same time as the variety to be pollinated. The varieties and pollination requirements of the fruit trees best adapted to the Northwest are identified in each of the specific sections which follow.

Fruit production is dependent on several other factors as well. First of all, the trees must grow for several years before they are sexually mature and bear flowers. Once the age of bearing is reached, blossom set varies with weather conditions, pruning practices, fertilization, and the size of the previous year's crop.

Most fruit trees are pollinated by insects which physically move the pollen from one variety to the flower of another. They do this accidentally as they search out the pollen grains and nectar of the open flowers to satisfy their own nutritional needs. As they pass a receptive flower stigma (female part) some of the pollen rubs off and pollinates the flower. Bees are the most common pollinating insects, but any insect drawn by the odor of the open flower can do the job. Do not use insecticides in or near the fruit trees while in bloom. The insects you kill will not offset the loss you will sustain by killing the pollinators.

Fruit yield is directly dependent on flower pollination. Rainy or cold weather at blossom time keeps the bees and other insects from doing their job. This is a factor of the climate that is out of the control of the gardener, but is one to be acknowledged.

The ovaries of the common fruit trees must be fertilized for seeds to develop. The development of normal fruit is the direct result of seed production. Pears and cherries will often make nearly normal growth without seed development but the fruits drop before reaching full size. Apples and pears need at least three and sometimes five seeds; peaches, apricots, cherries, plums, filberts, and walnuts need only one seed fertilized.

A way to check fallen fruit for pollination is to cut the core or pit horizontally and see if seeds have formed. In the above illustration the two on the left show complete pollination; the three on the right show incomplete pollination. If no seeds are present you may need to add a pollinator to your tree fruit planting.

The pollination requirements of self-sterile varieties can be met in several ways — i.e. by planting two different varieties, by grafting several varieties on a single trunk or by placing a bouquet of blooms from another variety in the tree needing to be pollinated. Pollinator trees must be planted within fifty feet of each other for best effect. Bees are the common carriers of pollen and a greater distance might be a distraction.

While a single trunk with four or five varieties grafted to it can be grown to insure pollination, there are problems involved. The distinct varieties, even though grafted on a single tree, have different rates and styles of growth. These differences make tree shaping difficult so the tree never seems to quite look like what you expect. One variety will grow quickly, another stay bushy, while the others are crowded out by the more vigorous.

Many fruit trees tend to bear fruit erratically, heavy one year and light the following. A mature apple has thousands of blooms in an average year. If all the flowers were pollinated the tree would yield an enormous amount of marble-size fruit. The fruits would be small because they compete with each other for the food materials manufactured by the leaves. The tree itself would suffer by having to put all its reserves into growing fruit, so no reserves would be left for the growth of fruit buds for the following year. The tree would become a "biennial bearer," i.e. bearing a heavy crop one year and none the following. Luckily, we get some help from Mother Nature. Fruits that are not completely pollinated will fall. Usually this fruit shedding occurs in early summer and is referred to as the "June Drop." This helps, but the tree is still left with too many fruits to mature and continue its normal growth. Here is where your management skills can shine. After the June Drop, do some thinning of apples, pears, peaches, apricots, and plums. Remove enough so that the remainder have a sufficient number of leaves to supply their food needs. Here is a table with suggested spacing and leaf and fruit ratios either of which can be used as a guide to thinning.

THINNING FRUIT

Type	Spacing	Optimum Number of Leaves per Fruit*
Apples	1–2 per cluster	30–40
Pears	1–2 per cluster	20–30
Peaches	6–10" apart	80–85
Apricots	5–6" apart	40–50
Cherries	— — no thinning necessary — —	
Plums	1–3" apart	30–40
Filberts	— — no thinning necessary — —	
Walnuts	— — no thinning necessary — —	

*reflects the number of leaves needed to ripen fruit while maintaining tree integrity.

Selection and Purchase:

The first step in being certain of a crop of fruit is to select types specifically adapted to the Northwest and within those types, choose the varieties whose fruits will mature in your specific growing season.

Fruit trees should be selected for the length of your local growing season, the space available for growing the trees and the varieties which you like. Select from among varieties you like, those whose bloom period and ripening dates fit the growing season in your area. The bloom period is the most critical in the fruit growing cycle. Select varieties which will bloom after the average date of your last hard frost. Trees blooming earlier usually suffer from frost-killed blossoms or failure of pollination due to lack of interest from cold weary pollinizing insects. Rootstock determines the ultimate size of a tree, while the characteristics of the fruit grown are determined by the grafted top. To make a particular variety of fruit or nut tree, the nurseryman buds or grafts the desired variety onto a rootstock that will control tree size. A *Gravenstein* apple for example will be grafted or budded onto a Malling 27 root for extreme dwarfness, or if a standard sized *Gravenstein* is desired it is grafted onto a rootstock selected for its vigorous root system. So size suitable for your space and variety to tickle your palate are interrelated factors which can be readily varied to meet your needs.

Do not attempt to grow named variety fruit trees from seed. Few seedlings will resemble their parents (be true to type) and will generally yield only small, poor quality fruit. This happens because fruit trees are open pollinated (that is, pollinated by any other compatible varieties nearby) so the resulting seed carries the genetic characteristics of both parents. The parent trees have been selected over many generations for specifically desired qualities. These selected characteristics are seldom successfully transmitted to offspring. The offspring will differ in growth habit, size, quality of fruit, size of leaf, etc. To avoid this uncertain outcome, fruit trees possessing desirable characteristics are propagated clonally (asexually) by budding, grafting, layering, or rooting of cuttings. By growing a new tree from a piece of the parent tree, given the same rootstock and growing conditions, we produce a tree identical to its parents.

Fruit trees are most often purchased and planted from November until late February while they are dormant. During dormancy they can be dug, shipped, and sold bare-root. This means that they are handled with no soil surrounding the roots. Bare-root trees must be planted before growth begins to avoid severe transplant shock, so get them into the ground as soon as possible and definitely by early March.

All varieties suitable to your area may not be available locally so you may need to order by mail. It is important that you buy the proper tree from a reliable nursery. Nursery catalogs and listings give a lot of information about varieties and planting. Study them carefully. Medium size one or two-year old trees are preferable to three-year or older trees. Keep in mind that peach and apricot trees are somewhat temperamental and mail order buying is not always successful with them. For unusual, rare or old varieties, check with the nearest experiment station, the Home Orchard Society (*Home Orchard Society*, c/o Marion Dunlap, 2511 S.W. Miles Street, Portland, Oregon, 97219), or local extension agent for sources.

Generally fruit trees are available bare-root as one-year "whips" or two-year branched trees. Either is acceptable, although whips suffer less transplant shock. The best trees are one-year old plants, three to four feet tall with trunks ½'' or more in diameter. Select trees with sound, un-damaged bark, firm and plump buds, and roots free of knobs. Bark damage may allow fungus or bacteria to enter the tree. koot knobs may indicate crown gall disease or nematodes. Unbroken tops and roots indicate careful handling in the nursery.

Fruit trees are now commonly available in containers. Container grown trees have the advantage that they may be planted in your garden at any time of the year which will give you more flexibility in preparing the planting site.

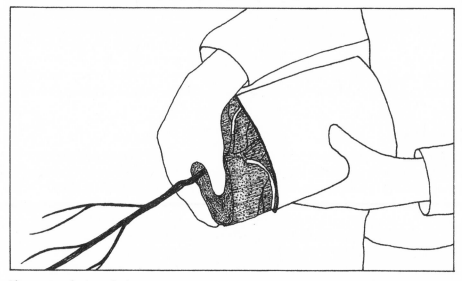

If you purchase a fruit tree growing in a container, avoid those having long roots coming from the drain holes. Check the root activity by lifting the plant from the container. If the tree has been growing in the container for more than a year, roots may be circling the ball of soil. These will need to be straightened to grow outward at planting time. If the soil ball is so rootbound that straightening is impossible, leave it and find a better specimen.

Do not buy a tree that is simply labelled "dwarf." Insist on positive identification of the specific rootstock, (this is covered later) with that information check the listings in this chapter to learn whether the "dwarf" you are about to buy is truly a dwarf or more nearly the size of standard tree. There are many degrees of dwarfness, identifiable only by knowing the rootstock.

Quite often fruit trees will bear a few fruits the first year in the home garden from flower buds developed during the tree's life in the nursery. This excites the gardener who believes the tree is on its way to an exceed-ingly fruitful life. But, because of transplant shock and the consequent need of the tree to establish roots and leafiness to rebuild its reserves, the tree does not bear again for three to five years. Dwarf varieties are not as susceptible to such interrupted growth and generally will continue to bear fruit once started.

Don't spend too much time worrying about the aesthetics of the bare-root plant. The top will be pruned at planting time anyway. Do look at the root system — the tree should have at least four strong roots fairly equally spaced around the crown and should have lots of fibrous, smaller roots growing from the larger ones.

The slight offset of the whip or trunk of a one or two-year tree indicates the graft union. It is usually slightly larger than the adjacent trunk and can be used as an indicator for planting depth.

When you bring your new trees home be sure to keep the roots damp. Cover the roots with damp soil, wet burlap, wet newspapers, or wet anything to prevent drying. It's best to plant immediately, but if the weather isn't cooperating or there's some other hitch, heel the plants in. If the planting will be done within a day, set the tree's roots in a bucket of water.

Planting:

To give the new tree the best chance to live and grow quickly prepare the planting site with a little extra care. If the tree is to be planted in a lawn or in an area that is frequently mowed, give it a break by removing the grass for two feet outward from the trunk. Mowers bumping into young trunks destroy bark and can provide an entrance for diseases. Given that you have located the best available site as recommended earlier in this chapter — one with adequate drainage and air circulation, reasonably deep and moderately fertile soil, in full sunlight, plant the trees in the following way:

Dig a hole about twice the spread of the root system and about three feet deep. Make sure that the roots will have enough room to lay straight outward from the trunk. If the roots are forced into an undersized hole, the roots will grow in a circle and eventually girdle and kill the tree.

To the soil removed from the hole add 1/3 by volume organic matter. Composted material, peat moss or leaf mold are all fine additions and will stimulate new root development. Do not add any commercial fertilizer as this can damage young roots. Mix the organic matter thoroughly with the dug soil. This amended soil will be best for your tree since it will initiate adaptation to your soil type.

Loosen the soil on the sides and bottom of the hole and start backfilling (filling the hole up again) with the amended soil. Fill the hole about half-full, firming it lightly.

Before setting the tree in the hole do some work on its roots. Trim away any broken, cracked or frazzled roots, cutting back to the live, healthy white tissue. Damaged roots allow easy entry of wood rotting fungus diseases. Sound, healthy roots will begin growing soon after planting and easily heal over any pruning cuts. Unusually long roots, those more than 12–15 inches long, should be shortened or the hole should be dug larger to accommodate them.

The amended soil in the planting hole should be mounded. Mounding will direct the roots outward and downward, giving the tree better anchorage. Center the tree in the planting hole on top of the soil mound with the trimmed roots straightened and spread outward. Add to or dig out some of the soil to set the tree at the correct planting depth. Dwarf trees should be set so that the graft union is two to three inches above ground level. Should your new tree be a seedling without a graft union junction, the original line of soil on the trunk should be even with the soil surface.

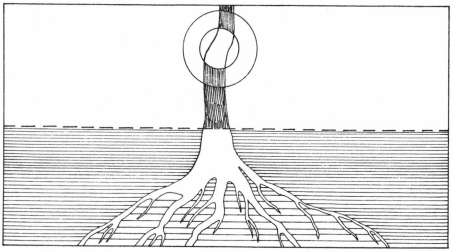

If the graft union is buried, roots from the topstock may develop. When this happens the benefits of the grafted root system are lost. If the graft joined a desirable variety to a dwarfing root, the dwarfing characteristic will be lost and the tree will grow to a standard, normal size, perhaps too large for the selected spot. Also, remember we are planting a tree, not burying one. Newly planted trees are often killed by planting too deeply.

Once the tree is set to the correct depth continue backfilling with the amended soil, tamping lightly to firm the soil around the tree roots. Water as you fill to eliminate air pockets. If the tree is branched, point the lowest permanent limb into the prevailing wind. To encourage better anchorage you can also direct the strongest upper root toward the prevailing wind. After the soil has settled in the planting hole finish filling to a final grade that is level with the surrounding soil surface. In dry areas or in soil that tends to dry out quickly leave a 2–3″ basin to facilitate watering. Also, before final filling determine if staking will be needed for your site and tree variety.

Notice we have not advised using any fertilizer during the planting sequence. The trees themselves have enough inherent vigor and reserves to grow through the first year. Many new trees are injured by adding fertilizer to the planting hole. If you feel your soil is too poor to support growth or simply feel an undeniable urge to feed your new plant, use a quarter cupful of an organic fertilizer such as tankage, blood meal, fish meal, or a mulch of manure. These fertilizers act slowly enough that the tree will not be damaged. However, you will find the tree is very self-sufficient and would prefer no fertilizer the first year.

Transplanting shock is a poorly understood phenomena of all woody plants. The process of digging and moving a tree from one location to another invariably means that some of the roots are lost. Roots keep the top alive. This root loss creates an imbalance that encourages the tree to die back until a new balance is developed. Resulting dead tissue, stems, buds, etc., can allow entry of diseases. To avoid this cycle prune the top of your trees at planting time. Trees pruned to balance root loss will outgrow trees left to fend for themselves. This pruning and next year's pruning are actually part of a training system. The goal is to develop a sturdy tree capable of producing and supporting the weight of a beautiful crop of fruit.

PRUNING TREE FRUITS AT PLANTING TIME

Type:	Starting With: Whips	2-year Branched Tree
Apples and Pears	Cut about ½ off.	Reduce height by about ½; completely remove limbs and shoots that are unnecessary for the training system you've decided on; the limbs that look like they'll fit the plan should be cut back about ½.
Peaches	Cut to 24" height.	Select 3−4 side limbs and remove the rest.
Apricots	(seldom available)	Cut to 24−30" height; remove any side branches that are closer than 12" to the ground; trim the others back to 4−6".
Plums	Cut to 24−30" height.	Prune out all but four equally spaced side limbs.
Cherries: Sweet	Cut to 24" height.	Leave 4−7 side branches.
Sour	Cut to 24" height.	Select 5−6 side limbs; the lowest one should be about 15" above the ground.
Filberts	Cut to 30−36" height.	Cut lateral branches back to 2−3 buds. If branching is sparse, remove all laterals and treat as whip.
Walnuts	Cut ½ off.	Remove any limbs below three feet; save 3−5 good scaffolds, cut them back halfway and remove the remainder.

*Note:
all pruning cuts should be made just above a bud.

In windy sites or areas where seasonal wind storms could dislodge the tree, supporting stakes may be needed for the first summer. Dwarf varieties and peach trees grafted onto a brittle root system such as *P. besseyi* may need permanent staking. In these cases use metal or cedar stakes for longevity.

Staking of trees should be a temporary measure, for a tree trunk must flex in the wind to develop strength and grow normally. If your site or tree seems to demand staking, drive the stake about six to eight inches on the upwind side while the planting hole is open. Stakes should be durable, preferably treated with copper rot-proofing compounds (not penta or creosote compounds) and tall enough to give several feet of support height. Connect the stake and the tree with a simple wire loop passed through a section of garden hose to avoid damaging the tree trunk.

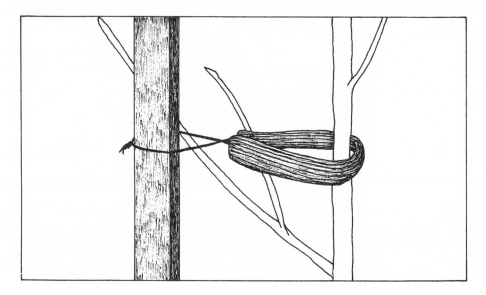

Protect the trunk by wrapping with chicken wire netting or hardware cloth. Rodents, rabbits, dogs, cats, and kids with hatchets seem to prefer the trunks of newly planted trees. Rodents can be especially bad in areas surrounded by native brush or fallow fields. Hungry rodents eat the bark away from trunks or upper roots, thus girdling and killing the tree. Cats sharpening their claws on trunks can damage the bark and open areas to infection. A cylinder of mesh wire extending from an inch or two below the soil surface to a foot above will discourage all but the most ardent small animals. When the tree is four or five years old and the bark corky, the wire can be removed. If you live in an area where rodents are a continual problem, leave the protective cylinder permanently.

The bark of some young trees (especially filberts) sunburns easily and the exposed side of the trunk may be killed from the damage inflicted. If you live in an area where the sun might damage your young tree, paint the lower part of the trunk with white latex paint.

After the planting is completed and the trunk protected, mulch the soil with bark, sawdust, chips or whatever else is handy. Organic mulches will help control weed growth and conserve soil moisture, thus giving the tree a better chance. Mulches should be one to two inches thick and extend several feet away from the trunk to protect the young roots.

PLANTING A TREE

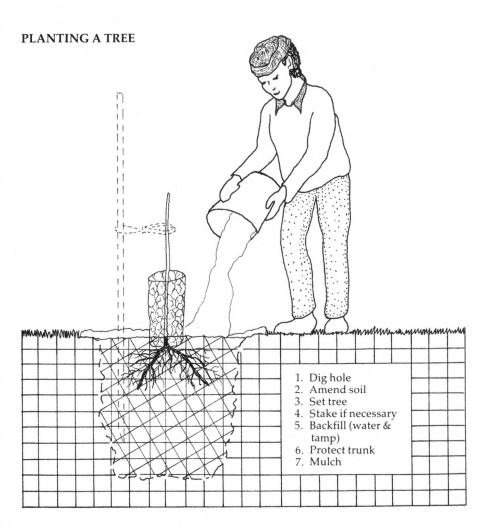

1. Dig hole
2. Amend soil
3. Set tree
4. Stake if necessary
5. Backfill (water & tamp)
6. Protect trunk
7. Mulch

Fertilizing:

As mentioned previously, most new fruit trees can grow quite well for at least a year without fertilizing. The exceptions are peaches, apricots, and sour cherries, all of which are heavy users of mineral elements. As soon as new growth appears after planting they'll need about ¼ pound actual nitrogen. (Nitrogen is the element which promotes growth of fruit trees.

Phosphorus and potassium levels in Northwest soils are generally sufficient.) Nitrogen can be supplied as ammonium sulfate (1 pound), ammonium nitrate (¾ pound), 10-10-10 (2½ pounds) or manure (10 pounds). Spread the fertilizer in a three foot circle out from the tree trunk. Water in or let the rain carry it in. Make a second application in early June. Do not fertilize again or buds and wood will not ripen properly to endure the winter. Peaches, apricots, and sour cherries require an annual application of nitrogen in early spring after the first year.

All the fruit trees other than those just mentioned should not be fertilized the first year. In subsequent years base fertilization on leaf color and annual growth. If the leaves are a good dark green and the annual growth being made is within the ranges given in the chart below, do not fertilize. Too often home orchard trees are overfertilized which reduces fruit formation while keeping you busy pruning away lush, but excessive, shoot growth.

ADEQUATE GROWTH RATES FOR FRUIT TREES

TYPE	Shoot Growth	
	Young Trees	Mature Trees
Apples	18-30"	8-12"
Pears	18-30"	8-12"
Peaches	20-30"	12-15"
Apricots	20-30"	12-15"
Cherries:		
Sweet	22-36"	8-10"
Sour	12-24"	8-10"
Plums	18-36"	8-10"
Filberts	18-30"	6-9"
Walnuts	18-30"	10-14"

If growth is not adequate or leaf color not right, a little nitrogen fertilizer should be used. A good rule of thumb for fruit trees is ¼ pound actual nitrogen per year of age. For practical purposes aging begins when the tree is planted. This means that a tree which has spent one full year in the garden and is showing a need for fertilizer, apply ¼ pound of actual nitrogen. This amount can be obtained from approximately ½ pound urea, ¾ pound ammonium nitrate, one pound ammonium sulfate, 10 pounds manure, or 2½ pounds 10-10-10. The 10-10-10 complete fertilizer also adds some phosphorus and potassium which, while not necessary, will not hurt the tree.

Fertilizer (except for peach, apricot and sour cherry that require nutrients added in spring) should be applied between the beginning of the dormant season (just as the leaves drop from the tree in the fall) and spring growth. Scatter the fertilizer in a wide band under the dripline of the tree. If the tree is growing in a lawn area, bore a number of holes 12–20 inches deep under the dripline so the fertilizer is not all used up by the grass. If you're in the habit of regularly fertilizing your lawn chances are good that the fruit tree is getting all it needs.

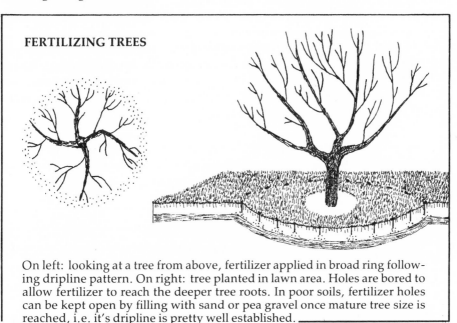

FERTILIZING TREES

On left: looking at a tree from above, fertilizer applied in broad ring following dripline pattern. On right: tree planted in lawn area. Holes are bored to allow fertilizer to reach the deeper tree roots. In poor soils, fertilizer holes can be kept open by filling with sand or pea gravel once mature tree size is reached, i.e. it's dripline is pretty well established.

Mature trees in the home orchard seldom need complete fertilizers, usually only nitrogen, but some potassium and one or two minor elements on occasion. To avoid potassium shortage supply the trees' nitrogen need with a fertilizer such as potassium nitrate. If you suspect a mineral deficiency a soil test is in order.

Boron is commonly deficient in Northwest soils but since it can cause extensive damage to trees do not use except on the basis of soil or leaf analysis. Boron deficiency causes "cork" development in the fruit of pears. In severe cases the skin becomes rough and scabby and will sometimes crack. However, the same symptoms may be caused by pear scab fungus so carefully analyze the situation before assuming a boron deficiency. Generally less than 1/10 pound of boron per tree will correct any deficiency. Boron can be applied using borated fertilizer or by applying borax in any form. Do not apply boron to young, non-bearing trees. Mature trees may need boron once every third year.

Magnesium is deficient in some Northwest soils and will need to be added to maintain healthy foliage. Signs of a magnesium deficiency are yellowing of tissues between green veins followed by browning, reducing the photosynthetic capacity of the leaf. Symptoms usually appear in late summer and are more noticeable on older leaves. Magnesium can be supplied by epsom salts at one pound per 100 sq. ft. If you can work the ground, dolomitic limestone at five pounds per 100 sq. ft. in early winter will give a long-term supply.

No matter how much rain we get during our Northwest winter and spring seasons, fruit trees need summer watering through their first two years at least. The exception again is peaches and apricots which will benefit from a deep watering every several weeks during the hot summer even when mature. When the peaches or apricots are about two weeks away from ripening hold back on watering to get a sweeter crop of fruit.

Young trees need to be watered deeply every two weeks during their first couple of summers. Moisture loss to evaporation can be minimized by using a 2" mulch three or four feet around the tree.

Training and Pruning:

A good hand pruning shear is the only tool you will need for the first several years. Later, when large branches have grown, a pair of loppers (long-handled pruning shears) or a pruning saw will be required. When you are pruning diseased parts use a household bleach, denatured alcohol, or some other type of disinfectant on the pruning tools to avoid spreading diseases. Always disinfect tools when pruning cherry, peach, apricot, plum, and filbert.

There are several steps which make any pruning job simpler —

1.   Remove all dead wood. Dead wood should be taken off anytime it is found because it harbors diseases.

2.   Take off broken or damaged wood.

3.   Remove any watersprouts along the trunk or any sucker growth sprouting from the base of the tree.

4.   Remove limbs that cross and rub against other branches.

Now, stand back and see what the structure looks like after you have taken off all of this non-essential wood. Then, if you're shaping a mature tree, prune out a few of the old limbs which have fruited for four or five years in order to stimulate a few new ones.

Pruning is not a one-time-per-year activity. Though most of the pruning to form, shape or replace is done in the dormant season (preferably in February in the Northwest) when limbs are more visible, summer pruning is also done to improve air circulation and sunlight penetration or correct the direction of growth.

Always make pruning cuts clean and just above a healthy bud or side branch. Never leave stubs, for they simply decay and cause trouble. Cut larger limbs back to the trunk, just outside the collar surrounding the limb. The collar is a slightly thickened area of growth which will heal over much more quickly than a cut made flush against the trunk.

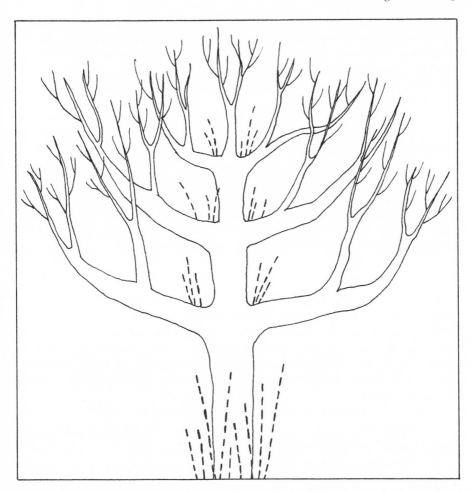

Watersprouts and Suckers: Both types of growth should be removed when noticed as they interfere with training and management. Pull them off if you can catch them while still small; older ones will need to be clipped.

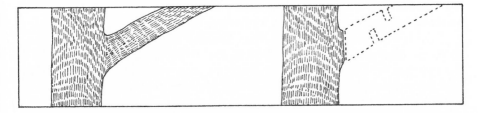

Collar Cuts: Large, heavy limbs need to be cut off in three stages to avoid dropping and tearing damage. Begin by making an undercut on the limb to be removed. Follow with another cut further out and on top to remove the limb. The final cut, removing the stub, is made to the collar of the limb to encourage faster healing of the pruning wound.

Pruning cuts on most fruit trees do not need to be "dressed," i.e. left to dry and then covered with one of the special polyvinyl acetate wound paints. Filberts are an exception; all pruning cuts more than an inch in diameter should be covered.

Severe pruning is as detrimental as none at all. Pruning is considered "severe" or *hard* when one third or more of the limbs and leaves are removed. This upsets the balance between growth and reserve. Hard pruning forces the tree to put all its efforts into staying alive by growing new shoots and leaves, so the tree never has the energy to bear a crop of fruit.

Young trees need careful pruning during their first years to develop a strong system of limbs. This limb system or **scaffold system** establishes the main structure of the mature tree. A properly trained fruit tree will grow to maturity and bear heavy crops of fruit without trouble. Pruned improperly or not at all, the tree may be broken by the weight of its crop. Since a young tree has only a few limbs and shoots, very little removal of wood will be needed to direct its growth.

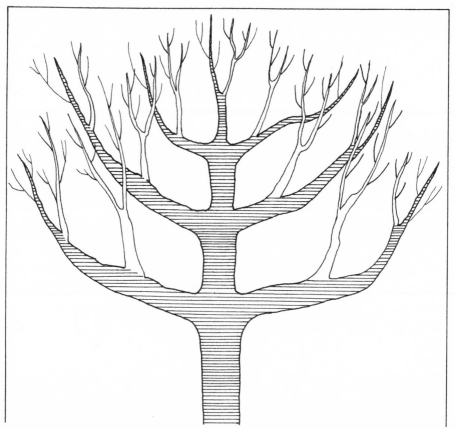

A well-established Scaffold System of a mature fruit tree: *Primary* scaffold is the main branches and trunk. *Secondary* scaffolds (also referred to as laterals) arise from the primary structure.

Two kinds of pruning cuts are used to train fruit trees, heading and thinning. Heading cuts are those where a limb is cut back to a side limb or healthy bud to make it branch and form the secondary set of scaffold limbs. Heading cuts remove the terminal or outermost bud of a limb. This bud produces a hormone that prevents lower buds from growing. When it is cut off, the buds below the cut will grow into shoots.

Thinning cuts are used to completely remove a branch, "thin out" the tree to make it less bushy, and direct the tree's growth into a selected scaffold system.

Both types of cuts are needed at various times to produce sound trees which will yield good fruit. Thus, in a new whip thinning cuts will be used to remove unneeded branches. Heading cuts will remove the tops of selected shoots to make them branch.

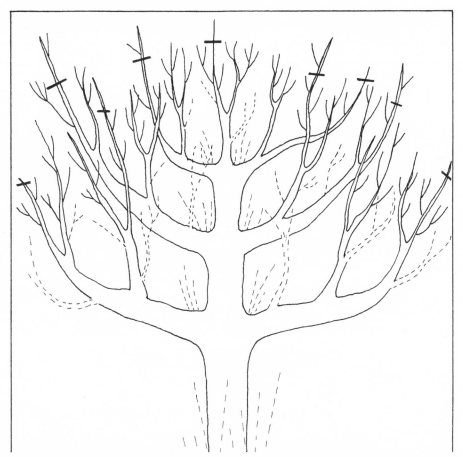

Heading and Thinning Cuts: Heading cuts remove the end of a branch (the terminal) and stimulate lower buds to sprout. Heading is done in the early training years to develop the secondary scaffolds; in maturity some fruit trees are headed to manage their height. Thinning cuts are used throughout the life of the tree for suckers and watersprouts, excess branches or nonproductive limbs.

Orchardists use specific scaffold systems adapted to their particular fruit type. **Central leader, Modified Leader,** and **Open Center** systems are each suitable for a certain type of fruit tree. The central leader system is used on trees where an upright form is desirable. Apples, walnuts, and apricots are frequently trained this way. The modified leader system allows more up-

TREE FRUIT TRAINING SYSTEMS

Tree Fruit:	Central Leader	Modified Leader	Open Center
Apple	1	2	3
Pear	2	1	no
Peach	3	2	1
Apricot	2	1	no
Cherry — Sweet	2	1	no
Sour	3	2	1
Plum	2	1	no
Filbert	2	1	3
Walnut	1	2	no

#1 indicates the preferred system for that type of tree based on growth habit and fruiting characteristic. #2 would be second choice, #3 third choice, and "no" means that we're not recommending it for this specimen.

right primary scaffolds, resulting in a lower tree head and somewhat wider spread. The modified leader system is usually used for plum, sweet cherry, filbert or pear. The open center system gives all of the laterals an equal chance to elongate; no center upright shoots dominate and fruiting wood gets more sun and air circulation. Peaches and sour cherries trained to the open center system remain relatively low, spreading, and productive.

The central leader system involves growing a main trunk (the leader) with scaffold branches growing out more or less at right angles. If your new tree is a whip, head it back to a good bud 24−36" from the ground. If a two-year old is being planted, select three or four side branches for scaffolds, head them back halfway and cut off the rest. Head the leader to about 12−14" above the uppermost side branch. When side shoots are about a foot long and show signs of making a narrow crotch angle, pull them to a horizontal position and hold them by tying with cloth, plastic or use clothespins with weights. The position ties must be left for about a month to establish a strong crotch, i.e. a right angle. Limbs with narrow crotch angles split and break easily from wind or from the weight of their fruit.

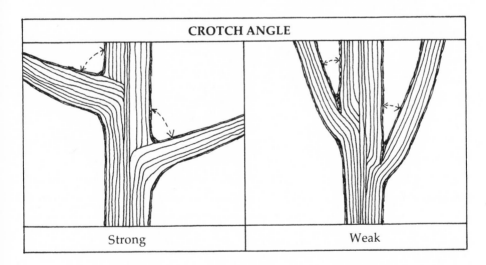

CROTCH ANGLE

| Strong | Weak |

A tree should have scaffold limbs evenly spread around the central leader and 6−8" above one another. If the tree has too many limbs, make thinning cuts in July and August to remove crowded limbs. In the following late winter (second year), head back the leader to 12−14" above the uppermost side limb and develop another group of limbs as before. In the third year of training, some fruit may develop on the lower scaffold limbs which is all right. If the upper portions of a central leader tree are allowed to fruit in the early training years however, the tree will be bent out of shape by the weight of the fruit. Keep fruits picked off the upper part of the tree until the desired shape is obtained.

The modified leader system involves developing several upward growth limbs which become equal leaders. Select three to six primary limbs around the trunk and head them to about two feet from the main trunk. Remove all others. By the next dormant season the primary scaffolds will have grown three or more shoots. Thin these out to a single shoot on each scaffold limb and head it lightly.

After the third year prune as little as possible. By this time the basic structure should be formed and the only pruning needed would be some light thinning to keep the tree from becoming too dense for good air circulation. The lighter the pruning from now on, the sooner the tree will bear fruit.

Peach trees and sour cherries can be pruned and trained to an open center system which will promote new growth and better sunlight penetration, both of which are necessary to develop and ripen these fruits.

If purchased as a one-year whip, cut it back to about 24" from the ground. Cut just above a healthy bud. The pruning at planting time will stimulate three to six buds below the cut to grow shoots the first year. Around the latter half of the following February, select three or four of these new limbs to become the scaffold system of the tree. Select branches that make the widest angle at their point of attachment to the trunk. The wider the angle, the stronger the attachment so the less chance of the limb breaking in its bearing years. Remove any extra limbs by cutting them back to the limb collar. Trees purchased as 2-year olds should be handled in a similar way — cut back the main trunk to just above a strong, well angled side branch, select two or three scaffold limbs below the side branch to fill out the system. Scaffold limbs should be four to six inches apart vertically down the trunk and evenly spaced around the tree.

In the next dormant pruning season the primary scaffolds should be headed to about 24–30" from the trunk. If the scaffolds have grown less than 30" but have branched freely, thin the secondary shoots to leave two or three on each primary limb. Cut off any side branches closer than 15" from the trunk. In this thinning operation, side branches which grow toward the ground, toward the center of the tree or straight toward the sky should be the first removed. Side limbs which grow up and outward are the most desirable. If pruning cuts have been carefully thought out, the tree's framework for the open center system should be well formed by the third or fourth year. From this point onward pruning will consist of thinning to keep the center open.

Mature apples and apricots need to be pruned for spur renewal. Peaches need to be pruned hard every year to grow new and fruiting wood. But filberts and sour cherries need very little pruning once their framework is established. Details on pruning the mature tree will be covered in the specific sections.

Apples & Pears

Apples are probably the most versatile home orchard fruit. They are a natural for the Northwest gardener because they thrive in our soils and climate. Pears will do nearly as well. Both species are attractive in bloom, their soft foliage providing a touch of exuberance to the general greenery in a home landscape. Characteristic shapes of apple and pear trees range from upright stiff to spreading-willowy.

Growth habits of apples are such that the trees can be grown into various forms, i.e. espalier or hedgerow plantings, and they are available in many dwarf, semi-dwarf, and standard sizes. With the dwarfing rootstocks used for growing dwarf apple trees, a tree can be virtually tailormade to fit a particular spot in the yard — for height by selecting the proper rootstock and for spread by selecting variety characteristics.

Unless you have twenty or thirty feet of space for a standard sized apple or pear tree, the best choices for the average yard are the dwarf or semi-dwarf forms of these trees. Apple trees growing on regular seedling roots, called standard sized, may grow to thirty feet and spread over 20−30 feet of space. Standard sized trees yield more fruit than do individual dwarf trees but take up almost three times the space. A mature standard sized pear tree may reach 25−50 feet in height. Dwarf pear varieties generally grow twelve to fifteen feet.

Apples are mostly dwarfed by grafting onto a rootstock called a "Malling." The name Malling refers to the East Malling Research Station in England which has played a leading role in developing dwarfing rootstocks. These varieties are identified by a number such as Malling 9 (M 9) or Malling 26 (M 26). Here is a listing of current dwarf apple and pear rootstocks:

APPLES —

Malling 9 (M 9)   This is the most dwarfing of the commercial apple stocks. Varieties grafted onto this rootstock will usually mature at around nine feet tall. The roots of this understock are brittle and the tree needs supporting. Do not plant M9 trees in windy areas. Varieties on this root may begin bearing fruit within two or three years after planting and should reach full production in their fifth year.

Malling 27 (M 27)   This rootstock is as dwarfing as the M9 but is a little less brittle. Varieties on this root system will often begin bearing in the third year after planting. The tree at maturity will be around nine feet tall. Staking or supporting will be helpful in directing the trees' growth during the first five or six years.

Malling 26 (M 26)   This understock produces a tree nearly as small as M9 but with stronger, more pliable roots. Trees on this rootstock need staking and support in areas where wind might be a problem. Varieties on this root tend to bear early and heavily. To keep the young tree from becoming stunted in its early bearing life some fruit thinning is needed.

Malling 7 (M 7) Less dwarfing than M 26, yet is like M 9 and M 26 in that varieties would do better if given some support during the first several years in the garden. This rootstock tends to grow a lot of suckers which will need to be removed whenever they are seen.

Malling-Merton 106 (MM 106) This is a semidwarf rootstock that is a little more vigorous than M 7. Here we begin to get to trees that will mature at around fifteen feet. This is a vigorous root and will promote early bearing. Roots are strong and well anchored, so the tree will need less stake or trellis support.

Malling 2 (M 2) This rootstock makes about the same size tree as MM 106. It is another strong rootstock and will provide good anchorage but it is not tolerant of soil moisture extremes. It will not withstand poor drainage nor droughty soils. If your soil tends to be bone dry in the summer or remains marshy most of the year, forget this one.

Malling-Merton 111 (MM 111) This is less dwarfing than MM 106 or M 2. Well anchored and reported to be heavier bearing and earlier than M 2. This rootstock is more drought tolerant than others.

Malling-Merton 104 (MM 104) This rootstock develops trees only sightly smaller than standard. It facilitates heavier and earlier crops than standard trees, is well anchored and intolerant of wet soils.

PEARS —

Pear varieties are grafted onto two different dwarfing rootstocks:

Old Home X Farmingdale clones (OH X F). There are several clones (selected types which are vegetatively propagated) of this cross which give smaller than standard pear trees. Trees on these clones will be about half to three quarters as large as standard trees. All of the major varieties of pears are compatible with this group. Clones are given numbers and the following lists them in order of decreasing mature size: OH X F 217, 9, 87, 333, 69, and 51. The first five clones give trees from 75% to 50% standard size. OH X F 51 gives a pear tree that matures at about ten feet in height.

Quince. Quince rootstock gives a nearly true dwarf (ten feet high at maturity), however it is not compatible with all pear varieties. Those compatible are grafted directly onto quince roots and others can be grafted to an interstem piece compatible to variety and root. Quince is shallow rooted and requires good fertile soil and adequate soil moisture. Quince root systems don't anchor as well as the clones mentioned above and trees will need some support if planted in windy sites.

Dwarfing effects from the various root systems mentioned can be altered by variety of fruit, soil condition, early fruit production, and pruning. Apples and pears vary in size regardless of the rootstock they are growing on. Some varieties are very vigorous and will outgrow less vigorous varieties no matter what the rootstock. *Yellow Newtown* and *Gravenstein* apples will outgrow *Red* and *Golden Delicious* which in turn will make larger trees than *Winesap, Rome Beauty* or *Jonathon*. Among pears, *Comice* and *Anjou* are the most vigorous, followed by *Bosc, Bartlett, Packham Triumph, Forelle,* and *El Dorado.* What this means is that on any given root system, differences in growth rates and eventual size occur. Also, apples and pears will grow vigorously on fertile soils and less so on poor or shallow soils. To obtain a true dwarf tree on good soil, one should use a dwarfing root with a naturally smaller topstock variety. On poor soils an M 9 root and a *Jonathon* top, for example, may make too small a tree.

Apples and pears are sometimes dwarfed by grafting a stempiece of one of the dwarfing rootstocks onto a seedling root system. This is referred to as using an "interpiece graft." A desirable variety is then grafted onto the dwarfing stempiece. This method requires an additional year in the nursery, but it is a way to get by root and topstock incompatibilities.

Some varieties are budded or grafted onto seedling roots to produce standard sized uniform trees. Depending on the vigor and inherent growth type they may grow from 25 to 60 feet tall. Obviously in a small yard a standard fruit tree could be the dominant plant.

To complicate apple variety selections even further, there are distinctions in fruiting wood and growth habit. Apple trees such as *Golden Delicious* bear their fruits on short growths called spurs. Each spur on a standard type apple tree may remain productive for about five years. A new type whose spurs remain productive for seven or more years has recently been developed. Called a "spur-type" tree it is smaller, more conical in shape, and branches lower. Watch for the availability of these new spur-type trees and be aware of their advantages for home orchardists.

Early fruiting is a powerful dwarfing force itself. The earlier a tree bears, the more dwarf the tree will generally be. However, heavy fruiting in the early formative years of the tree is not entirely desirable because it may be hard to draw the line between stunting and dwarfing. Pick off the flowers and prevent fruit setting for the first two or three years to give the tree a better chance to develop.

Pollination from a second nearby variety is needed for setting a crop of fruit on most apples and pears. *Red Delicious* will not pollinate itself but does a good job setting fruit on *Golden Delicious* and vice versa. We have listed some varieties as self-fertile, but even they will set a better crop with pollen from another variety.

Pears are complicated. *Bartlett* and *Anjou* will set seedless crops from their own pollen under certain conditions. The degree of fertility using their own pollen depends on the weather and the vigor of the tree. Warm temperatures at blossom time and immediately following, coupled with high vigor will generally allow these normally self-sterile varieties to set a near-normal crop. However, in all cases, cross pollination gives a better chance at getting the highest yield.

A major requirement for successful crop set is in selecting varieties so that their bloom periods are the same or are known to overlap in your area. Pears have a longer bloom season so even though *Anjou, Bartlett,* and *Bosc* are considered early, mid and late bloomers respectively, their bloom periods overlap enough to provide each other with viable pollen. A *Gravenstein* apple tree would need another early bloomer, such as *Lodi*, for a pollinator. A late bloomer, such as *Red Delicious* would need another such as *Jonathon* or *Golden Delicious*. Pollinator trees should be within 50 feet of each other.

See the table at the end of this section to assist you in making selections.

Now, if all the information about the need for several varieties in your small garden space worries you, simply borrow a bouquet of blossoms from a variety which will pollinate your tree. Place the blossoms in a bucket of water and hang it in your tree. The bees will do the rest for you.

Bloom and earlier fruiting on apples and pears can be induced through several techniques. However, these should not be used until the trees have made several years of growth and are strong enough to bear a crop of fruit. One method is to bend and secure the side branches down to 40−50° from vertical to stimulate flower bud development along the adjusted limbs. Blossom development of *Anjou* and *Comice* pears can be helped along by pruning 2-year old shoots back to just above a blossom bud at flowering time or by removing the tips of rapidly growing shoots in May and June. Scoring apple and pear trees induces them to bloom more the following year. Scoring is usually done by circling the trunk or major scaffold limbs with a pocketknife. Score by carefully cutting through the bark, but not into the wood, within three to four weeks after the normal bloom time.

Once the hurdle of pollination is passed, the next potential problem is that too many fruits have been set. An overabundance of fruits may break the tree and/or cause the tree to become a biennial bearer. It is better for the tree, and more productive to you, if you thin the heavy crops and allow only a certain number of apples or pears to remain. Wait until the natural event of June Drop has occurred before thinning.

Both apples and pears bear their fruits in clusters of from three to five or six on each fruiting site. If the set of fruit on the entire tree is excessive, reduce these clusters to one or two by removing the smaller fruits. If in doubt as to how much fruit to safely leave, see the chart on page 234.

In young apples and pears the balance between fruit development and vegetative growth is easily upset. Too much pruning causes shoot growth and may prevent a tree from making flower buds. Make as few pruning cuts as possible after the structure is established. If the tree is growing too large, remove entirely (i.e. thinning cuts) some of the one-year old shoots. Both apples and pears bear fruits on spur growths and some varieties also bear fruit along the two-year old limbs. After spurs are four or five years old replace with a new limb. Watersprouts arising at convenient places along an old limb can be saved to replace the old wood. Do not take out more than two or three old limbs in any single year. When cutting, cut back to a branch point to avoid leaving stubs. Any corrective pruning for apples and pears, such as for reducing height, removing excess limbs or balancing leaning trees, should be done over several years to minimize the stimulatory effect of pruning.

The presence of serious apple and pear pests will depend somewhat on the proximity of other fruit trees, but most are universal enough to pop up in any yard or garden. Some natural predatory insects will help control a few of the insect pests but may be too slow to prevent fruit damage. Consider the implications of treating versus not treating the trees for pest damage. Seldom does an insect or fungus disease completely kill an apple or pear tree. Yet, the infestation or infection can be damaging enough to interfere with normal growth and affect the fruit so adversely that it is of low quality. Pest control efforts should be carefully planned. Check with local agricultural experts for acceptable pest control methods.

Besides the common pests, others may appear in various areas of the Northwest. Check with local authorities for identification and treatment advice. Given the proper growing sites, soil conditions, and regular maintenance, apples and pears can be expected to live fifty or more years. For a long-lived tree keep in mind its ongoing needs: water, adequate drainage, minerals, pruning, sunlight, and pest control. Make sure changes in the surrounding environment are not harmful to the tree.

Some special problems of apples include **watercore** and **bitter pit**. You can detect watercore by cutting the ripest fruit equatorially and look for areas in the flesh that appear watersoaked. Usually it occurs on fruits of advanced maturity, but similar symptoms appear on fruits that have been sunburned. If you find watercore, pick and use the fruit but don't count on storing any. Watercore is considered to be a physiological disease (no known causal agent) and varieties differ in susceptibility. Varieties most likely to develop watercore include *King, Gravenstein, Winter Banana, Jonathon, Delicious, Stayman, Arkansas*, and *Winesap*. There is no known prevention.

Bitter pit is another non-parasitic disorder affecting the fruit of apples. This problem is characterized by small, circular sunken spots on the fruit surface, beneath which are brownish areas in the flesh. It has been related to a shortage of calcium. Apparently, vigorous leaf growth which uses available calcium supplies can bring on the problem in susceptible varieties. *Delicious* and *Winesap* appear to be resistant while *Northern Spy, Gravenstein,*

COMMON PESTS: APPLES AND PEARS

APPLE MAGGOT eggs are laid just under apple skin. Larva feed on the flesh. Pupa are usually found in upper 2" of soil under the tree.

Larva: ⅛ – ¼" long

Adult: ¼" long

APPLES — PEST	EFFECT	TREATMENT
Codling Moth	Wormy Apples.	Spray, sanitation, trap, predators, accept.
Scab	Fruit and leaves distorted.	Spray, sanitation, accept.
Powdery Mildew	Leaves, new growth deformed.	Spray, sanitation, prune.
Apple Maggot	Fruit mined.	Spray, trap.
Aphid	New growth deformed.	Spray, predators.
Leafrollers	Leaves rolled.	Spray, trap adults.

SCAB is a fungus disease; it overwinters on fallen infected leaves. Generally it first appears as spots on leaves; spots gradually darken and spread.

PEARS — PEST	EFFECT	TREATMENT
Fireblight	New growth killed.	Spray, prune.
Psylla	Leaf and shoot growth reduction.	Spray, predators.
Codling Moth	Wormy pears.	same as for apples.
Scab	Fruit and leaves distorted.	same as for apples.

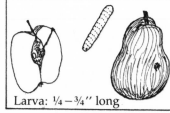

CODLING MOTH eggs are laid on foliage and fruit. Larva move into developing fruit core, feed, grow and then emerge. Pupa usually cocooned just beneath bark scales.

Larva: ¼ – ¾" long

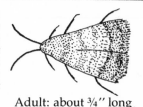

Adult: about ¾" long

Grimes Golden, and *Baldwin* are most susceptible. Hot, dry weather in midsummer seems to aggravate the problem. Irregular soil moisture supply, heavy dormant season pruning, overthinning, or excessive nitrogen fertilization all may promote bitter pit. Some prevention or control can be achieved by careful and light pruning, avoiding excess nitrogen fertilization, maintaining consistent soil moisture during summer, and by temporarily shading trees during periods of excessive midsummer heat. Foliage and fruit sprays of calcium chloride or calcium nitrate may help but won't eliminate this condition. Use about 1½ tablespoons per gallon of water and spray about five times during the summer. Bitter pit affected apples are edible but will not store for very long.

Finally the harvest arrives, the end product of much planning and hard work, so handle it with care. For most varieties of apples the change of skin and pulp color from green is an indication of maturity. The exceptions here are *Granny Smith* and *Yellow Newtown* which are greenish colored when mature. How readily the fruit separates from the tree is usually the best indicator of maturity in both apples and pears. A slight twisting movement will easily dislodge the fruit at the stem attachment, it if is mature.

Pick the largest and ripest fruits first, leaving smaller ones to gain a little more size and maturity. Lopsided and deformed fruit is usually the result of uneven distribution of the seeds, a result of poor pollination.

Bartlett and Oriental type pears are picked when ripe on the tree. *Anjou* and *Comice* pears will not ripen until they have been stored in a cool area for 4−8 weeks, or exposed to ethylene gas (a commercial practice). For the storage-to-ripen varieties of pears, pick when their widest diameter is at least two inches. After the cold storage (32−45°F) take them as needed and place in a warm room for three to ten days. By the time they are ready for eating the fruit skins will have lost most of their green color.

Store apples and pears in clean, ventilated wooden or cardboard boxes. Do not line boxes with paper or individually wrap the fruit. An old but still serviceable refrigerator makes a good fruit storage place. Ideally, storage temperatures should be from 30−32°F, but such conditions are hard to achieve at home. An unheated garage, shed or basement may be satisfactory if temperatures below 30 or above 45 can be avoided. An insulated box, storage cabinet or dugout underground room which can be ventilated at night for cooling makes a good storage unit. Humidity is not often a problem in the Northwest, but if storage places are too dry shriveling begins. Place the fruit in unsealed or perforated plastic bags or dampen the floor or the boxes. Shriveling of apples can be avoided by storing them in loosely tied plastic bags.

Store apples and pears immediately after they are picked. Do not store with onions, potatoes or other strong smelling produce as the fruit will absorb flavors from them. Inspect the fruit regularly for mold, flesh breakdown, freezing or excessive ripening. Storing ripe fruit with pears may cause them to ripen faster than expected. Avoid freezing the fruits. Partially frozen pears can be salvaged if thawed slowly, but freezing usually ruins apples.

APPLE VARIETIES FOR THE PACIFIC NORTHWEST

[1]VARIETY	BLOOM SEASON	[2]P.R.	FRUIT SIZE	[3]HARVEST PERIOD	STORAGE AT 32°F	COLOR	COMMON USE: Fresh and
Arkansas Black	mid	2	medium	late	5–6 mo.	dark red	process
Baldwin	mid	2	large	late	3 mo.	red mottled	cider
Beacon	late	3	medium	early	1/2 mo.	red stripe	
Cortland	early–mid	2	large	mid	4 mo.	red stripe	process
Early McIntosh	early	3	small	early	1/2 mo.	red stripe	
Golden Delicious	mid–late	3*	medium	late	5 mo.	lt. yellow	process
Granny Smith	mid	1	med–lg.	very late	6 mo.	green	
Gravenstein	early	1	large	early	2 mo.	yel/red stripe	sauce
Grimes Golden	mid	2	small	mid	4 mo.	yellow	process, sauce
Idared	early	3	large	mid	6 mo.	red	process
Jonadel	early	3	medium	mid	6 mo.	red stripe	process
Jonagold	mid–late	1	medium	mid	4 mo.	yellow	process
Jonathon	mid	2*	small	mid	3 mo.	red	sauce
King	early	1	large	late	4 mo.	red stripe	cider
Lodi	early	3	large	very early	-0-	yellow	pies
Macoun	mid	3	large	mid	5 mo.	red	
Macspur	early	2	small	mid	1 mo.	red	
Melba	early	3	medium	early	1/2 mo.	red stripe	
Melrose	mid	3	medium	late	7 mo.	red stripe	
Mutsu	early	1	large	mid	4 mo.	yellow	
Northern Spy	late	1	medium	mid	4 mo.	red	cider, process, sauce
Prima	mid	2	med–lg	early	4 mo.	red	process
Red Delicious	midseason	1*	medium	late	5 mo.	red	
Red Wealthy	early	3	medium	mid	2 mo.	red stripe	
Rome Beauty	late	3*	large	very late	5 mo.	red	process
Ruby	late	3	large	late	7 mo.	red	process
Sandow	mid	1	medium	very late	3–4 mo.	red stripe	
Spartan	early	2	small	mid	4–5 mo.	red	
Stayman	mid	1	medium	late	6 mo.	red	process
20 oz. Pippin	mid	2	very lg.	late	2 mo.	yellow	process, sauce
Tydemans Red	early	3	medium	mid	2 mo.	red	
Wayne	late	1	medium	late	2–3 mo.	red	process
Winesap	mid	1	small	late	6 mo.	red	
Winter Banana	late	2	large	late	4–5 mo.	yellow	
Yellow Newtown	mid	3	medium	very late	6 mo.	yel/green	process

[1]These are only a few of the 6,000 or more apple varieties available to gardeners.

[2]P.R. — Pollination Requirement: 1. self sterile
2. partially self fertile
3. self fertile
* denotes best pollinators.

[3]Early = August;   Mid = September;   Late = October.

PEAR VARIETIES FOR THE PACIFIC NORTHWEST

*VARIETY	BLOOM SEASON	DAYS FROM BLOOM TO MATURITY	FRUIT SIZE	HARVEST PERIOD	STORAGE AT 32°F	COLOR	USE	STORAGE REQUIREMENT BEFORE RIPENING
Anjou	early	130–152	medium	late Sept.–early Oct.	6 mos.	gr. yellow	fresh	2 months
Bartlett	mid	112–135	med–large	mid Aug. to early Sept.	3 mos.	yellow	fresh, canned	none
Bosc	late	125–140	large	late Sept.	5 mos.	tan russet	fresh	none
Clapp Favorite	mid	112–135	large	early Aug.	3 mos.	yellow	fresh, canned	none
Comice	late	140–150	medium	late Sept.	5 mos.	yel. green	fresh	1 month
El Dorado	mid	140–155	medium	late Sept.–early Oct.	6–8 mos.	gr. yellow	fresh	1 month
Forelle	early	135–155	med–large	late Sept.	5 mos.	red blush over yel.	fresh	1 month
Kieffer	early	125–140	med–large	late Sept.–early Oct.	3 mos.	gr. yellow w/red blush	fresh, canned	none
Max–Red Bartlett	mid	112–135	medium	mid Aug. to early Sept.	3 mos.	red	fresh	none
Packham Triumph	mid	140–150	med–large	late Sept.–early Oct.	6 mos.	yel. green	fresh	1 month
Seckel	mid	125–140	small	late Aug.–early Sept.	3 mos.	yel. green w/red blush	fresh	none
Winter Nelis	late	140–150	med–small	early Oct.	6 mos.	dull green or yel.	fresh, canned	1 month
ORIENTAL TYPES: Ripen on the tree and are crisp like apples —								
Chojura	early	140–150	medium	September	5 mos.	tan russet	fresh	--------
Nijisseike (20th Century)	early	140–150	medium	September	2–3 mos.	pale yel.	fresh	--------
Shinseiki (New Century)	early	125–150	medium	August	5 mos.	yellow	fresh	--------

* Plant two varieties with overlapping or coinciding bloom seasons to insure a fruit crop.

The storage times listed in the varietal charts are based on the best of storage conditions. Actual storage life varies by variety and by storage temperature. Pears held beyond their normal storage life will not ripen when removed from storage. Apples held too long will become soft and mealy, or deteriorate internally to the point that they become unusable.

Peaches & Apricots

Peaches and apricots will be more of a challenge to the Northwest gardener due both to growth problems and susceptibility to disease. Given the time required in cultivating these trees, and their questionable yield, they do not rank as the most profitable venture for the home orchardist.

Peach trees tend to be relatively short-lived. One that is productive after twenty years could be considered an old timer. Apricots remain vigorous and productive for thirty or more years, if given proper care. Without care neither may make it past their fifth birthday.

What about nectarines? Nectarines are actually fuzzless peaches. Their culture, growth, and harvest are the same as for peaches. If you live in the southern part of the Northwest and want to try growing your own, we suggest *Le Grande* and *Sun Grand*. Other varieties may be developed that are equally good, so give them a try if you have the inclination and space available.

Peach and apricot trees make good landscaping choices. Their spreading growth habit can provide shade in the yard. Their interesting leaf shapes, texture, and fall color rival some of the deciduous ornamentals.

A standard peach or apricot tree is naturally smaller than a standard apple or pear and can fit nicely into almost any average size yard. A standard apricot tree needs 15 to 25 feet of open space and will mature at about 30 feet high. Standard peaches need 12–15 feet. A standard peach tree matures at around 8–10 feet high but its growth habit is such that it can be kept lower. Genetic dwarf peaches are attractive plants used more for their decorative quality than for fruit.

If you want to experiment with seedlings, peaches and apricots offer better odds than the other tree fruits covered in this chapter. Many of the peaches and apricots on old farmsteads were a result of seed plantings and produce relatively good fruit.

An important characteristic of both species is that they bloom in the mild days of late March and early April. At that time of year warm temperatures and high humidity favor fungi that can kill the flowers, new leaves and twigs, or cause leaves to curl on peaches. Fungicides may prevent extensive damage as long as wet weather doesn't persist. If you get past the fungi, clear weather may mean frost-killed blooms. A discouraging tale, but one that needs to be understood by the newcomer to peaches and apricots in Northwest gardens. Careful site selection may allow you to circumvent some of the climatic problems.

A related matter is that bees and other pollinating insects do not like to work in rainy weather. While there is not much you can do about the rain, place the trees close together so an easy flight from one tree to another can be made.

Peaches and apricots are available as dwarfs. Grafted onto *Prunus besseyi* and *Prunus tomentosa* rootstocks they are reliable producers and result in a tree about half as large as a standard tree. Dwarf varieties can be planted eight to ten feet apart. The following table lists the characteristics produced by the more commonly used rootstocks:

Prunus besseyi	This rootstock is somewhat brittle so trees should be permanently supported. It is compatible with nearly all varieties of peaches and apricots. Trees will be 6–8 feet tall.
Prunus tomentosa	More dwarfing than *P. besseyi* but you may have trouble finding trees grafted onto this rootstock. It is not compatible with all varieties.
Siberian "C"	This is a hardy rootstock that will easily withstand any of the winters in the Northwest. Varieties on this root may come into bearing a year earlier than normal and will be about 8–9 feet tall.
St. Julian "A"	This is likely the strongest of the dwarfing roots in the Northwest and the one most widely used. It is a semi-dwarf system and trees would mature at less than ten feet. The best feature of this rootstock is its tolerance of wet, poorly drained soils and ability to grow a productive tree in nearly any soil type.

Most peach varieties are self-fertile and will set good crops with their own pollen. Like all other fruit trees classed as self-fertile, two varieties to pollinate each other will yield larger crops. *J. H. Hale* and *Alamar* varieties are self-sterile and definitely need another variety nearby to supply pollen.

Apricot varieties are a mixed bag, some need pollinators while others do the job by themselves. Again, if space is available, better crops will be forthcoming if two varieties can be planted in the home orchard.

Yields will vary from year to year. Both apricot and peach trees require substantial bud chilling so in mild winters fruit buds may drop long before bloom. In a cooperative year you can expect to get about 150 peaches off of a six or seven year old peach tree. A mature productive apricot tree will yield about 60 lbs. of fruit.

For the first two years after planting, no fruit should even be allowed to develop. For the health of the tree pick off all fruit to allow more time for the tree to develop reserves.

With care, an apricot tree reaches peak productivity at about 12 years of age, and should bear fruit for twenty or more years. Peaches will usually reach top production in 8–10 years. Beyond this point, production will remain high if the tree is managed right.

Both of these fruits develop on wood grown the previous year — peaches on the new shoots, apricots on short spurs of second-year growth. It is absolutely essential to prune these trees radically every winter to grow the necessary young wood. If they are not pruned hard there will be no crop and Mother Nature takes over . . . after six or seven years the trees mature and then begin to die. If pruning is done correctly, these trees can live to thirty years and produce a crop of fruit every year.

Peaches grow on the shoots that grew last year. Long, vigorous shoots produce more fruit than the shorter ones. The object is to do some thinning to keep the tree from getting dense and brushy and a lot of heading cuts to stimulate new shoots. Cut away about half of last year's growth, thinning out the smaller shoots and heading the larger, healthier shoots to about half their length. Prune hardest in the tops of the tree and near the ends of the major limbs. Cut top limbs back to side shoots to reduce tree height and to stiffen the upper growth.

Apricots grow on short spurs of second and third year wood. Head back the new shoots by about half. This will stimulate new shoots for next year and cause the half that is left to grow fruit spurs. Also thin out any shoots that are making the tree brushy or dense.

As the fruit is developing on your peach and apricot trees install supports to bear the limbs. Even large limbs can break from the weight of the fruit. Prop the limbs with 2 × 4's, posts, or with whatever is handy and strong. Supports should be long enough to hold the limb at its normal height. Place a pad of rubber or other soft material on top of the support so that the bark isn't damaged. After the crop is harvested remove the supports and stow them away for next year.

Apricots are among the earliest tree fruits to ripen and will usually be ready to eat by mid-July. The earliest varieties of peaches and nectarines begin ripening in late July while the late varieties ripen into September. If you plant *Cardinal* (an early variety) and *Elberta* (a late variety) you can have fresh peaches for two months.

There should be no doubt about when these fruits are ready for harvest. Peaches reach full size and the skin color becomes a deeper red. If you gently squeeze the ripe fruit you will know it is just right to sink your teeth into.

Apricots almost glow with goodness as they ripen. Usually the crop will ripen over several weeks. A few falling to the ground is a strong hint that some are ready for picking. Ripe apricots are firm but not hard, and separate easily from the tree.

Neither peaches nor apricots store long after picking. At the most, they will remain fresh for several weeks if refrigerated. Can, dry or freeze them soon after picking to avoid excess loss of flavor and texture.

PEACH AND APRICOT VARIETIES FOR THE PACIFIC NORTHWEST

PEACH VARIETY	SIZE	SKIN COLOR	FUZZ	FLESH COLOR	TEXTURE	PIT	APPROX. HARVEST
Alamar	large	red	light	yellow	firm	free	September 1–10
Cardinal	small	80% red/yellow	heavy	lt. yellow	stringy	cling	July 25–August 5
Early Elberta	medium	20% red/yellow	light	yellow w/red pit	melting	free	August 25–September 5
Elberta	medium	10% red/yellow	medium	yellow w/red pit	slightly stringy	free	September 10–15
Fairhaven	med–large	50% red/yellow	light	yellow	med. fine	free	August 15–20
Herb Hale	medium	20% red/yellow	medium	yellow w/red pit	melting	free	August 15–25
J. H. Hale	large	20% red/yellow	light	yellow w/red pit	slightly stringy	free	September 1–10
July Elberta	medium	40% red/yellow	medium	yellow	slightly stringy	free	August 15–20
Pacific Gold	medium	30% red/yellow	medium	yellow w/red pit	firm	free	August 15–20
Ranger	medium	65% red/yellow	light	lt. yellow	med. firm	free	August 5–10
Red Haven	medium	75% red/yellow	medium	yellow	melting firm	free	August 5–15
Redglobe	large	80% red/yellow	light	yellow w/red pit	light	free	August 15–25
Veteran	medium	10% red/yellow	medium	yellow	slightly stringy	free	August 20–30

APRICOT VARIETY	FRUIT SIZE	APPROX. HARVEST/JULY	POLLINATION REQUIREMENT
Brooks	medium	late	self fertile
Jannes	large	late	self sterile
Moorpack (Wenatchee)	large	midseason	self fertile
Perfection	largest	early	self sterile
Riland	medium	early	self sterile
Royal	medium	midseason	self fertile
Tilton	medium	midseason	self fertile

Now, what about problems? We have suggested that peaches and apricots are hard to grow. Yet, there are some fine peach and apricot trees in the Northwest, not only in carefully tended orchards but also in home gardens where the owner follows a few simple management practices. Peaches and apricots contract some of the same diseases — **coryneum blight, brown rot,** and **bacterial canker.** Peaches are also subject to **peach leaf curl**. These diseases can be mitigated, if not totally prevented, by proper site selection, sanitation and the use of fungicides. Without such help from you the tree will not become a long-lived inhabitant of the yard.

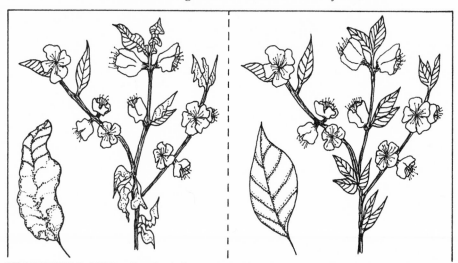

PEACH LEAF CURL: On the left, symptoms on new growth; on the right, normal development. Watch for this disorder when leaves start to unfold in the spring; remove any that show curling and fertilize the tree with nitrogen to stimulate new healthy leaves. Unattended, peach leaf curl will slow the growth of new shoots, affect young fruit, and cause leaves to drop with warm, dry weather. A mild infection will allow fruit to mature normally except for one or more wartlike growths and a lack of fuzz. Peach varieties vary in susceptibility though none seem to be immune.

Preventing or minimizing these diseases involves pruning for air circulation, faithfully following a dormant and early season spray schedule, and pruning away diseased parts when they become evident. *Coryneum blight* carries over from one year to the next. It is identifiable by small reddish-colored sunken spots on infected twigs. This disease kills twigs, causes round holes in the leaves, and spots on the fruit. *Brown rot* hits the trees just as the blooms begin opening and will kill the flowers and nearby leaves. *Bacterial canker* infects the twigs and limbs, gradually working its way downward to infect the entire tree. Bacterial diseases are spread by pruning tools and rain water so always disinfect pruning tools after several cuts. Infections from bacteria enter through wounds in the wood. *Peach leaf curl* fungus disease infects the buds during their dormant period, but symptoms aren't evident until the leaves begin to grow several months later. Here are suggested treatments for these problems.

COMMON DISEASES OF PEACHES AND APRICOTS

Name	Effect	Treatment
Coryneum Blight	Leaves/shot hole effect; Fruits/spots and gumming; Twigs/sunken, red spots	Dormant and early season fungicide spray; prune away infected parts. (Do not sprinkle water on leaves during the summer months.)
Brown Rot	Flowers/killed; nearby twigs and leaves also killed; ripening fruit rotted.	Spray with fungicide at early bloom stage; prune away dead material; reduce the humidity; spray with fungicide again, just ahead of fruit ripening.
Bacterial Canker	Cankers on limbs and trunk; exudation of gum; dieback of limbs.	Prune away infected parts; fall and winter bactericide sprays; sterilize pruning tools.
Leaf Curl (Peach)	Leaves/deformed; Twig/dieback.	Dormant fungicide spray in December and February; pick off and burn affected leaves; fertilize the tree.

As some consolation, insect pests are seldom as damaging to peaches and apricots as to other tree fruits. Occasionally, aphids and spider mites may build up; a few worms, such as leafrollers and climbing cutworms may appear; and scale insects sometimes become a problem on older, untended trees. Generally, a carefully managed peach or apricot in the home orchard will not have a serious bug problem. Earwigs love the ripening fruit of both, and so do ants, which might necessitate placing a sticky band around the trunk to trap the critters. Several borers can cause trouble, either by boring into and killing young twigs or by mining into the base of the tree. The twig borers can be detected by the "flagging" or wilting of affected twigs and, trunk borers by the appearance of fresh sap and expelled borings near the base of the tree. In the first case, prune the affected twigs out and in the latter dig out the trunk borer with a pocketknife. Sprays are seldom effective because the damage was done before we knew the pest was present.

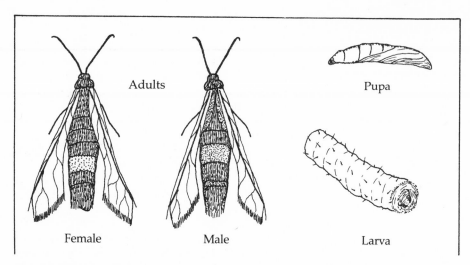

Adults   Pupa

Female   Male   Larva

PEACHTREE BORER: Insect pest of peach, apricot, cherry, and plum trees. Larvae are about an inch long and feed on the roots and the base of the tree just under the bark. This is the damaging phase; it is frequently fatal for a young tree. Larvae feed from late summer to fall and overwinter in their burrows. In the spring, they begin feeding again until the pupal stage is reached. The pupae cocoon themselves in the upper inch of soil near the tree. Adults emerge around June; the female can be recognized by her broad orange band, the male by yellow stripes, on black bodies. Eggs are laid on branches, the trunk, and in the soil as much as two feet from the trunk of the fruit tree. The larvae hatch, move to the tree, and begin boring and feeding.

Cherries & Plums

Cherries and plums are much more easily managed than peaches and apricots. Both the sweet and sour cherry types do well in Northwest gardens. Should the name "sour" deter you, bear in mind that "red," "tart," and "pie" are synonyms for sour cherries. Standard sweet cherry trees are large and can dominate an average sized yard. Sour cherries are a naturally smaller tree, seldom growing more than 12' tall. Plums are one of the most productive and dependable of the tree fruits and, given a minimum of care, they will provide juicy fruits for many years. Plums are generally small trees and are prolific growers; if left untended they will develop into rather dense thickets. Plums and sour cherry trees are small enough at maturity that they make good patio shade and can be closely planted to form a medium-height screen, or can serve as accent trees to emphasize a particular part of the yard.

Dwarf varieties of sweet cherries and plums are available but they don't produce fruit reliably. Plums being a naturally small tree, a dwarf variety is seldom needed. Sweet cherry dwarfs are mostly planted as ornamentals.

Plum varieties are of two types, European and Oriental. European types have a dense, firmly fleshed fruit with a rich flavor, and tend to bloom and mature later than the Oriental types. Practically all prunes are made from European varieties because their high sugar content allows them to dry without fermenting. Oriental varieties generally have larger-sized fruits, often heart shaped, bright yellow or red in color (seldom blue) and are much juicier than European types. Oriental types may fail to set fruit either because they were not pollinated or because of fungus problems associated with our weather conditions.

Cherries and plums ripen at times different than other stone fruits and so can fill gaps in the summer fruit supply. If you like to preserve fruit, the addition of cherry and plum trees to your home orchard can keep the canners, dryers, and freezers busy throughout the summer season. Sweet and sour cherries are generally ripe by mid-July. In some of the warmer areas of the Northwest, cherries will begin ripening by the end of June. Oriental plums begin ripening in early August and extend into September, depending on the variety and the climate in your area. European plums are a little later, beginning to ripen in early September, extending into October.

Site selection is more critical for sweet cheries than for the sour varieties and both are more particular than plums. Sweet cherries can be expected to live for forty or more years and attain a size rivaling that of the native big-leaf maple if given the site and care needed. Deep, fertile and well drained soil is a must for sweet cherries. Plant them in a well drained spot where you have good soil at least three to six feet deep. This may seem like a big order but take a look at some mature sweet cherries in your area. They are probably forty feet tall with a thirty foot spread. They have nearly as much root system below the ground as branches above. For such a root system to grow properly, the tree needs plenty of good soil. Planting a sweet cherry in poor or minimal soil conditions sentences the tree to a short, non-productive life.

Sour cherries and plums are not as demanding. Sour cherries need good drainage but can survive and produce fruit on shallower soils with a little assistance from you by way of fertilizer. Plums seem to do well in almost any soil type and depth, however like all tree fruits, drainage and soil aeration is needed for root growth. In fact, plums only require ample moisture through the summer, oxygen in the soil during the winter, and a little nitrogen now and then to keep them happy. Indeed, one of the problems with most plum varieties in the home orchard or yard is that they grow too well and become dense, brushy trees even in the poorest of soils.

Do not plant in windy sites. Cherries and plums are relatively strong trees and can tolerate more wind than apples and pears but grow better in calm areas. Oriental plums bloom early and are subject to damage from late spring frosts, more so than the European plum or the cherries. Avoid low terrain which might be a frost pocket in the spring.

Sweet cherries need about 30 feet of space for their development. In the home yard they can be planted near low-growing shrubs but should be far enough from large trees to avoid branch interference. Sour cherries can be planted 15—20 feet apart or interspersed with other small trees or large shrubs. Plums need from 12 to 15 feet of space and are well adapted to home yard conditions where they can be planted alone or among other, lower plants.

The pollination requirements of cherries and plums are confusing and no general recommendations seem to fit all cases. Check the variety table at the end of this section to learn which varieties pollinate others. Sour cherries will set fruit with their own pollen so a single pie-cherry in the yard or home orchard will do fine by itself. Sweet cherries are mostly self-sterile and need a second variety nearby to pollinate and set their crop. To further confuse things, not all varieties of sweet cherries are compatible and it takes a certain combination of varieties to develop fruit. *Royal Ann* and *Corum* sweet cherry varieties will pollinate each other and make a compatible combination. A *Royal Ann*, *Bing*, and *Lambert* on the other hand is a three-way loser as none can pollinate the others.

Plums are also a confused lot in their reproduction. Most of the European varieties are self-fertile while all of the Oriental types are self-sterile. Pollination requirements noted in the varietal charts at the end of this section should be reviewed carefully before selecting plants.

Remember that pollination can be performed in several ways. If room permits, plant several compatible varieties. If there is not room enough for more than one tree, graft a pollinizing variety onto the tree needing help. If grafting trees is not your forte, hang a bouquet of flowering branches from a compatible variety in your tree so bees can move the pollen to your flowers.

Fruit can be expected on sour cherries in three to five years. Peak production of sour varieties is reached by their seventh year and will continue for thirty or more years with proper care. It is impossible to predict how long a tree can be expected to bear fruit, since the period of effective production is reduced by a lack of care.

Sweet Cherries generally begin bearing in their sixth year after planting, reach their peak at about their twelfth year, and can continue for about forty years if all goes well.

Oriental type plums set a few fruits in their fourth year while European types start several years later. Both types, given responsible care, will bear for fifteen years or more.

The size of your cherry crop is largely a function of your pruning effort and soil fertility management. Moderate pruning to thin shoots and stimulate new fruiting wood is required annually. Enough nitrogen to encourage new productive shoots is required yearly. Unlike other tree fruits, cherries need no manual thinning of fruit.

Plum trees require some thinning of fruits for two reasons: to balance the amount of fruit with the foliage in order to obtain larger and tastier fruit, and to prevent biennial bearing. Thinning not only increases the fruit size but also gives the fruits a more uniform color and reduces the likelihood of breaking limbs. Oriental plums often need more thinning than any other tree fruit. Do not thin plums until after the normal June Drop. After the natural drop has occurred, pick enough fruit so that the remainder have one to three inches of space, with the most space being given the Oriental varieties.

Sweet cherries are usually purchased as one-year whips. Sour cherries and plums may be bought as one-year whips or two-year branched trees. Either size works fine as long as the proper pruning and training procedures are followed. One-year whips usually survive the first summer better than two-year old trees and will establish roots easier due to a better balance between tops and roots. Because they can more quickly get themselves established, they will usually begin bearing fruit as quickly as the two-year old plants. When buying trees, look for healthy plants of ½ to ⅝ inch trunk diameter and, if possible, certified virus-free.

Healthy plum and cherry trees have plump buds, bark free of breaks or open wounds and roots free of galls or knobs (which can be a symptom of crown gall disease). Do not buy trees with shriveled bark, shoots that are oozing sap or that have odd growths on their roots. Shriveled bark tells you the tree has been stressed to the point that the underlying tissue is dead. Sap or gum coming from buds, cuts in the bark or breaks in the wood may indicate a bacterial disease. Crown gall, shown by odd, corky knobs growing on the crown or on the roots of the bare-root tree, is another bacterial disease to which these trees are susceptible and which will infect your soil. Avoid all three of these problems by buying plants free of these symptoms.

As with all tree fruits, plums and cherries should be planted while they are dormant. Generally, nursery-grown plants are available from mid-winter until spring and can be planted successfully through late February. Keep the roots from drying by covering with wet burlap or by heeling the trees in temporary trenches. Plant as soon as the ground can be prepared.

To plant, dig a hole about 2½ feet deep in a well-drained spot and backfill with topsoil so the graft union will remain four inches above the final ground surface. Placement of the graft union is important for two reasons — to prevent rooting of the grafted variety and to reduce the possibility of tree borer attack. Often the tree settles after planting so if the graft union is set at ground level initially it may well subside below ground level. Staking is not needed with these trees, unless they are planted in windy sites. The young trees are generally of a low profile for a year or two and will anchor themselves rapidly.

Pruning and training of young cherry and plum trees are important to the successful management of these fruit plants. Too often trees are purchased, planted, and left untrained. Consequently, trees grow into odd, ungainly forms with weak branch angles. Do not be afraid to use the pruning shears on your new tree. The growth removed at planting time will be replaced many times over.

If sweet cherry whips are purchased, cut back to just above a plump, healthy bud two feet from the ground. In the first year, buds below the pruning cut will grow into branches. The following February, select 4−7 strong branches to save for the scaffold system. If you want the sweet cherry to grow tall, leave only three or four primary scaffold limbs. If you prefer a lower, spreading form, leave up to seven to compete for space and nutrition so none becomes too vigorous and upright. If a branched two-year old tree is planted, select four to seven healthy branches rising not more than 24–30" above the ground line to save as primary scaffolds. Select shoots that have wide angles in relation to the trunk to make a strong tree. Cut the primary scaffolds back to two feet from the trunk and remove any remaining branches.

The limbs of sweet cheries can grow six to eight feet in their first summer. Instead of letting them reach such a size, prune off the outer five inches of growth after a limb has grown 2½ feet. This heading cut makes the limb branch and develop secondary scaffold limbs. Removing less than 5" causes the new shoots to come out at narrow angles, weakening the structure of the tree. Heading cuts should not be made after early August to avoid fall frost damage to new growth.

Sweet cherry trees naturally branch very little and tend to grow long and limber single branches. Often only the terminal or tip bud itself will make annual growth, exerting a strong dominance over lower buds. So, remove new tip growth whenever it reaches two and a half feet. The training done in the tree's first two or three years will make the basic framework of a strong long-lived tree.

After two seasons of growth, the sweet cherry tree should have four to seven strong primary scaffolds. Each scaffold should have three to five secondary scaffolds. In the succeeding dormant seasons pruning can be limited to heading shoots. Shoot growth made the previous season should be headed to 24–36" (36" if you want a taller tree, 24" if you prefer keeping the tree low and spreading).

As the sweet cherry ages it will need less heading. If a tree becomes so dense that some inner limbs die for want of sufficient light, thin out a few branches. When fruiting begins, usually in the fifth or sixth year, begin a program of thinning the secondary scaffolds as needed to arrive at a modified leader trained tree in about the eighth year.

The general pruning rule for sweet cherries is: head everything and don't thin the first two years; head the vertical upright shoots and remove nothing the next two years; and in the fifth year begin to thin out the scaffolds. The fruit on sweet cherries is formed on spurs that form on vigorous two-year old wood. These spurs can live and bear fruit for ten or more years, provided they are not killed or broken away. Pruning of the mature sweet cherry is limited to selective heading back of the tall upper shoots and thinning the excess shoots that develop from heading.

Sour cherries are normally low growing, bushy trees, which in their early years need some training to develop a sturdy framework of permanent scaffold limbs. If purchased as one-year whips, cut the whip back to about 24 inches above the ground. This will stimulate a half dozen or so side branches for selection the next year. Two-year old trees will already be branched and selections can be made for scaffolds just as we will describe for whips. Sour cherries probably need less pruning than any other fruit tree once the structure of the tree has been developed. Start by carefully selecting five or six healthy shoots growing outward from the trunk. These will become the primary scaffolds. The lowest should be about 15″ above the ground, preferably pointing into the prevailing wind. The others should be spaced four inches or so apart vertically and evenly around the tree. If, perchance, your new tree does cooperate and give you the convenient choices of evenly spaced limbs, cut everything back about halfway to force out some branches for selecting next season. Cut the central shoot back about halfway to a healthy bud. Make sure the scaffolds selected do not parallel nor cross one another. Try to avoid having scaffolds emerging from the trunk at the same height. Sour cherries are very brittle so careful selection of wide angled, well spaced primary limbs will give you a stronger tree. By the following year the scaffold limbs will have grown half a dozen or more side shoots which can be selected and trained for the secondary set of limbs. Leave as many of these as possible. The less pruning done on a sour cherry the sooner it begins bearing fruit. Cut out only those limbs which cross and rub against others, or that grow toward the inside part of the tree.

Sour cherry fruit buds grow on one-year terminal shoots and on spurs which grow on two, three, and four-year old wood. Sour cherry spurs do not stay productive for as long as sweet cherries so fertilize a little more and prune moderately to keep the tree productive. Pruning mature trees should be limited to light thinning to keep the tree from becoming so brushy that air and sunlight can't penetrate. Neglected trees become dense; fruit spurs and limbs begin dying in the center and lower sections of the tree.

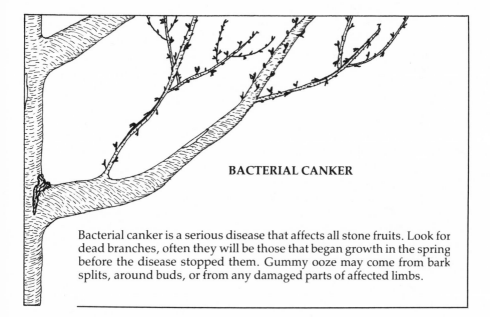

BACTERIAL CANKER

Bacterial canker is a serious disease that affects all stone fruits. Look for dead branches, often they will be those that began growth in the spring before the disease stopped them. Gummy ooze may come from bark splits, around buds, or from any damaged parts of affected limbs.

Plums should be pruned to the open center or multiple leader systems with branches emerging from the trunk about two feet from the ground, scaffolds headed about 30" from the trunk, and excess shoots thinned out. The plum tree will begin bearing a few fruits in its third or fourth year and should be producing well by its fifth year. Fruit is borne on one-year wood and on vigorous spurs on older wood. Mature trees should be pruned every two years to lightly thin the tops, take out the crowded branches, and help air circulation. Every year check the tree over for dead, storm damaged or diseased limbs and remove them.

Beyond pruning, management of cherries and plums involves only fertilizing and controlling the few pests commonly found. Both share some of the same pest problems but differ in their fertilizer needs and responses. Generally, young non-bearing sour cherries should make from 12−24" of shoot growth each year until they start bearing fruit. Non-bearing sweet cherries should make 22−36" of growth during their early years. Mature trees of both should make about 8−10" of growth annually to maintain a proper growth/fruit development balance. Failure to obtain this amount of growth is usually due to a lack of sufficient nitrogen. If the trees make considerably more growth than suggested above, you are probably pruning too hard.

Sour cherries need more nitrogen than do the sweet varieties. Look at the amount of growth made the previous summer to determine if nitrogen will be needed by the tree. Fertilizer, when needed, should be applied between early February and mid-March. Gauge the application time in your area by watching the tree — when the buds begin to open apply the nitrogen. Sour cherries can use as much as ¼ pound of ammonium sulfate per year of tree age. For example, a sour cherry tree that has been in your yard for four years could use one pound of ammonium sulfate. Sweet cherry trees can, generally, get by with half that amount. Apply the nitrogen fertilizer in a wide band under the drip line of the tree so the spring rain can carry it into the soil. Animal manure works as well. An annual mulch of manure, two inches deep over the root area of the cherry tree will likely provide all the nutrients needed.

Several minor elements, such as zinc and boron, may occasionally need attention for cherry trees. Soil or leaf analyses will indicate need and amount required.

Plums do well without any fertilizer for the first two years after planting. Young trees should grow 18−36" annually, mature trees 8−10". If they are making this much or more growth they are being adequately supplied. Should the trees make less growth or show evidence of deficiency, i.e. light green, sparse, or small leaves, one pound of ammonium sulfate per young non-bearing tree, or two pounds per mature tree will usually correct the problem. Manure mulches can also be used to supply the trees' needs.

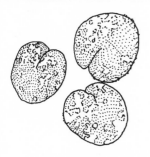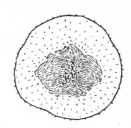

BROWN ROT: A fungus disease that attacks all stone fruits — plums, cherries, peaches (especially nectarines), and apricots. The result is "mummy making" of the fruits, turning them into dry, shriveled lumps. Remove all the mummies since they harbor the fungus. Brown Rot first occurs on blossoms, making them look wet and brown and clump together. Later the fungus appears on the ripening fruit; brownish, powdery pimples develop and cause the fruit to rot. On apricots and peaches and nectarines the fungus may move from the base of the infected blossom into the twig, so prune away infected twigs.

Insect and disease problems of plums and cherries range from those that are serious enough to need annual attention, to others that may never occur. Here are the most common problems with the most serious heading the list.

PEST PROBLEMS OF CHERRIES AND PLUMS

Problem	Affected Parts	Treatment
Brown Rot	Blooms, fruit, twigs	Fungicides in early spring ahead of ripening; pruning out affected parts.
Bacterial Canker	Limbs, trunks, buds; causes death to part or all of tree	Prune away affected limbs; sterilize pruning tools; bactericide treatment during the fall (copper).
*Virus	Leaves, fruit, entire tree affected	Remove tree, no control; buy virus-free trees if available; disinfect pruning tools.
Cherry Leaf Spot	Leaves, fruit; leaves become tattered and full of holes.	Prune for air circulation; fungicide treatment during the blossom period.

(Problem)	(Affected Parts)	(Treatment)
Cherry Fruit Fly	Fruits of cherry	Spray insecticide, early June.
Peachtree Borer	Base of trunks	Dig out borer; preventative insecticide drenches around tree base.
Aphids	Curling of foliage; especially on plum.	Insecticide spray as new leaves unfold.

*There are nearly a dozen viruses or virus-like diseases which affect cherry and plum trees. Symptoms may show as leaf, fruit or growth abnormalities and cause differences in size, shape, and color of nearly any part of the affected tree. There is no control for a virus disease once it has infected the tree. Virus may be spread from an infected tree to another, or from one limb to another on the same tree by way of insects, pruning tools or in any event where sap containing virus from an infected part is carried to another. The best control is to make sure the purchased tree is certified as virus-free. For virus identification take sample of damage to your local Extension Service Office.

Harvest begins in July with the cherries, followed by the Oriental plums in August and European plums in September. There is no question when these fruits are ripe. Sweet cherries will be at their full bodied and brightest coloration when ripe. Sour cherries will have a slight softness when they have reached their peak. Plums also soften slightly when they are ready. Pick a few and sample their flavor. Pick the largest first. None will ripen further once they are picked so let them reach their best and fullest flavor before harvesting. The harvest period for both cherry and plum varieties will normally extend over several weeks.

Filberts & Walnuts

Nut trees adapted to the Northwest are limited to filberts and walnuts. Pecans will grow but set no fruits, almonds grow much like a peach but need a longer growing season than our region usually offers. There are others that may be grown, notably the hickory, Oriental chestnut, and Pinyon pine, but are usually included in landscapes as ornamentals rather than with nut production as a goal. In this section we will discuss the planting and care of the nut trees adapted to the Northwest and which are dependable nut crop producers.

Walnuts (Persian, English or Black) are large trees and unsuitable for the gardener having only limited space for fruit production. The trees reach forty or more feet in both height and spread, which make them suitable dual-purpose trees for shade and nuts if you have sufficient space. Most of the large walnuts seen in Northwest yards are remnants of orchards which have been converted to residential areas. These trees continue to be produc-

CHERRY VARIETIES FOR THE PACIFIC NORTHWEST

VARIETY	BLOOM PERIOD	BEST POLLINATOR VARIETY	FRUIT COLOR	FRUIT WHEN RIPE
SWEET CHERRIES				
Bing	midseason	Chinook or Black Republican	black	midseason
Black Republican	early	Royal Ann or Bing	black	late
Chinook	midseason	Bing	black	midseason
Corum	midseason	Royal Ann	yellow	early
Lambert	late	Sam	black	late
Rainier	midseason	Royal Ann or Bing	yellow	midseason
Royal Ann	midseason	Corum	yellow	early midseason
Sam	late	Lambert	black	early
Stella	midseason	self fertile	black	midseason
Van	midseason	Royal Ann or Bing	black	early
SOUR CHERRIES				
Early Richmond			light red	early midseason
Meteor (genetic dwarf)		all varieties listed	light red	midseason
Montmorency		are self fertile	red	late
Northstar (genetic dwarf)			dark red	midseason

PLUM VARIETIES FOR THE PACIFIC NORTHWEST

VARIETY	TYPE[1]	BLOOM SEASON[2]	POLLINATOR REQUIREMENT	SKIN COLOR	FRUIT SHAPE	FRUIT SIZE	WHEN RIPE[3]
Brooks	E	mid	self fertile	blue	long oval	very large	late
Burbank	O	early	Santa Rosa or Elephant Heart	red	round conical	medium	early
Elephant Heart	O	early	Santa Rosa or Red Heart	dark red	heart	large	early
French (Petite)	E	early	self fertile	red/purple	necked oval	medium	early
Green Gage	E	early	self fertile	green	oval	small	mid
Italian	E	late	self fertile	blue	oval, slight neck	large	late
Miller Sweet	E	mid	self fertile	blue	oval	med/small	mid
Moyer	E	late	self fertile	blue	oval	large	late
Nubiana	O	early/mid	Red Heart or Shiro	purple/black	round	medium	early
Parsons	E	mid	Italian	red/blue	oval	med/small	mid
President	E	early	Stanley	blue	oval	very large	late
Queen Ann	O	early/mid	Red Heart or Shiro	blue/purple	round	large	mid
Red Heart	O	early/mid	Elephant Heart	dull red	oval heart	medium	mid
Santa Rosa	O	early	Elephant Heart	dark purple	oblong conical	med/large	early
Shiro	O	early	Red Heart	yellow	round	medium	early
Stanley	E	early	self fertile	dark blue	necked oval	medium	late

[1]E = European, O = Oriental. [2]Early = March 15–April 1; Mid = April 1–15; Late = April 15–30 (dates are approximate)

[3]Early = August 15–September 1; Mid = September 1–September 15; Late = September 15–October 10

tive with minimal care. Information in this section will give you some tips on keeping these old trees alive and well.

Filberts are low-growing, bushy trees seldom becoming more than fifteen feet tall. With their dense foliage they make good low profile shade trees that will fit almost any yard situation. Filberts need full sunlight and prefer about twenty feet of space. If left unpruned, a filbert will grow suckers from its base and become a dense, large shrub.

Walnuts can be expected to produce around 100 pounds of nuts each year after they are ten years old, provided they are kept in good health. Filberts bear a few nuts in their second or third year, reaching a yield of around five pounds by six years and perhaps as high as 15–20 pounds when ten to twelve years of age. Filberts (given the care suggested in this section) live productively for around forty years.

There are no commercially available dwarf trees of either of these two nut types. In the case of walnuts you accept the fact that the tree will be large. With filberts, be happy that a small bushy tree will produce nuts.

Both trees can be grown from seed, but like all tree fruits there is no guarantee that the seedling will bear as good a crop or one with the qualities characteristic of the parent. Because walnuts take so long to bear fruits, seedlings are a long-time risk in the yard. Many of the varieties of filberts presently grown commercially originated as seedlings, so if space and time permit, plant a few seeds. Seedlings will take at least four or five years before you get a nut or two to compare with the parent filbert, and your chances are about 50/50 of the tree being worth keeping. All in all, it is best to buy nursery-grown named variety trees.

The site selected for walnut tree planting should have deep well-drained soil. Filberts can grow on shallower soils but will do much better on the former. Most of the feeder roots (those which take in the greatest amount of water and minerals) of walnuts grow in the upper three feet of soil. Filberts will grow most of their feeding system in the top two feet. This gives you a clue as to what the soil must be like in your yard to support the growth of these trees. Comparatively, walnut trees need much the same soil depth and drainage conditions as required by sweet cherries while filberts can grow in the same soil as plums or sour cherries.

The site should have good air circulation but not hard winds. The filbert, with its dense, bushy head, can be blown over or branches broken by heavy wind. Air circulation is important to hold diseases in check and to slow the development of algae and lichens which often cover the trunks, limbs, and even the twigs of filberts. Lichens and algae are not damaging but during heavy snowfall or ice storms the lichens absorb water and add weight to already strained limbs.

Walnuts are generally self-fertile so will set crops providing the male flowers shed pollen when the female flowers are receptive. As the previous sentence implies, flowering time is a tricky characteristic of walnuts, in that the male flowers sometimes open and shed pollen too early or too late for the female flowers. Commercial orchards try to eliminate this gamble by planting several walnut varieties in the hope that pollen shedding and female flower receptiveness will overlap with varietal differences. In the home orchard, where space limitations commonly dictate a single tree, hope for the best but do not be too disappointed if no crop occurs until the tree reaches 12–15 years. The older the tree, the better the male and female blooming times overlap so the better the chances of a full walnut crop.

Filberts need pollinators to set a crop of nuts. Unfortunately, not all filbert varieties can pollinate all others. Filberts do not share the walnut's problem of receptiveness. The female flowers in the filbert are receptive from the time they first appear as a tiny red dot at the tip of the flower bud until they extend to their maximum length, wither and fade. In mild winters this period extends from late November through February. If this sounds like an odd time for flowering, let us have a quick look at nut tree flower anatomy. The female flower of both filbert and walnut is a tiny little thing scarcely resembling a flower. Female flowers on filberts are reddish colored and greenish on walnuts. They will be found where a leaf attached to last year's growth in filberts but be scattered over one to three-year old wood in walnuts. Walnuts generally bloom in early spring, from around early March to mid-April; filberts usually are in full bloom in January and February. The male blooms are called *catkins* and are the two or three-inch long, dangly things that you see hanging from the tree twigs from mid-winter to mid-spring. The reason for this side trip into botany of the nut flower is that certain pest control measures must be scheduled to either avoid or coincide with flowering.

Filberts are usually sprayed with lime sulfur or copper fungicides during their dormant period to control algae and lichen. This treatment must not coincide with the blooming time else you may kill the flowers and have no crop. Walnuts are subject to a blight disease that must be treated just before and soon after open bloom. If you grow a nut tree you will soon learn to recognize these important features of your tree and can dazzle your friends with worldly discussions of catkins, stigmas (the female flower tip), and pollination.

And, for a real dazzler, here is an interesting facet of the filbert's sex life. At the time of pollination, i.e. when the pollen grain grows its tube down to fertilize the ovary of the female flower, the female flower has not yet developed ovaries but has a tiny bit of tissue at the base of the flower. Within a few days following pollination the tip of the pollen tube containing the sperm becomes walled off and enters a long resting period of about five months. At the end of that time the ovary will have developed to make the young nut and when the nut kernel is about a third of an inch in diameter the resting sperm reactivates, grows toward the egg and fertilization takes place. This lapse of time between pollination and fertilization makes the filbert an oddity in the plant world. (In most plants fertilization takes place within a few hours, or at most several days after pollination.)

Nut trees should be planted as early in the winter as you can get them. Most other fruit trees can be planted in late winter and be expected to grow enough roots before growth of the tops begins, to keep the tree alive. Nut trees are slow to develop roots in their first year so the longer they are planted before the top growth begins, the better your chances will be. Root growth occurs during the winter whenever the soil temperature is above 41°F.

Follow the same planting suggestions as for other tree fruits. Prune off broken and damaged roots. Many filberts are grown from layer or stool beds. With the layering process, a young growing tree is bent over and covered in a trench. New shoots arising from the horizontal trunk grow upward and make new trees, forming roots above the parent trunk. In stool beds a young tree is cut back heavily and earth is mounded around its trunk. Suckers stimulated by the pruning come through the earth from the trunk and form roots. In either method a part of the parent may remain attached when you buy the tree. Prune away the layered wood that may be found below the main root system. Walnuts are generally grafted so you will see a graft union, filberts are not. Both should be planted so their uppermost root is only about two inches below the soil surface. Point the strongest root into the direction from which your prevailing wind comes.

Both walnuts and filberts are generally bought as one-year whips and at planting time are cut back to about 30–36″ from the ground. New walnut trees are long whips, as much as ten feet in length, while filberts are more likely to be four to five feet tall. Cutting back (heading) the whip stimulates side branches from the remaining trunk of the whip. Filberts may also be sold as two-year old trees in which case the laterals can be selected, cut back to two or three buds from the trunk and the remainder cut off. If the existing side branches on the two-year old filbert do not meet your branch needs, cut them all off and treat the trunk as a whip.

A word about pruning filberts. The wood of a filbert tree is especially susceptible to fungus organisms that rot wood. Do not leave any pruning cuts of more than one inch diameter uncovered on this tree. Make pruning cuts flush with the collar (tapered area at the junction of the limb and trunk) or cut to just above a limb or healthy bud. When the pruning cut dries, usually within a day or so, cover the pruned area with the polyvinyl acetate paints sold especially for this purpose. Most other fruit trees will heal themselves satisfactorily without a covering but filberts need this bit of extra care.

Pruning after planting should proceed as described for other trees. Walnuts are generally trained to a central leader system with three to five scaffolds spaced a foot apart vertically and evenly distributed around the central trunk. Filberts are trained to an open center system or to a modified leader system depending on how low you want the tree to be.

Avoid heavy or severe pruning with nut trees. When the main scaffolds have been selected and excess limbs cut away, leave filberts alone for several years. Heavy pruning of the filbert delays maturity while stimulating a lot of sucker growth which only makes the tree brushier.

Walnuts need some training through the first three or four years to develop strong, large trees. If shoot growth is more than four or five feet, head the terminals. Especially watch the lower scaffold branches and keep them from becoming too long and limber. If extra long scaffolds low on the tree are not headed they will droop to the ground when they bear a crop of nuts.

In the formative years, avoid large pruning cuts on walnuts by pruning when the shoots are small. Once the training system is developed and you know which limbs are needed, intruding growth can be taken off whenever it is noticed. Rubbing off or pruning away a shoot just after it has begun growth causes much less shock to the tree than cutting it after several years of growth have been made. The secret to success with walnut training is constant surveillance with the pruning shears handy. Walnuts should be left alone for several years once they begin bearing. When mature, walnut trees shold be cut back severely every four or five years to renew the fruiting wood. Heading most of the outer limbs back three or four feet to strong side limbs allows more sunlight to enter and invigorates growth near the cuts.

Filbert trees should be left alone once the training system has been developed. Other than removal of suckers, no pruning should be needed for eight to ten years. When the annual growth averages four or five inches and the tree has numerous dead twigs in the center or the limbs are covered with moss and lichens, get out the pruners and work the tree over. Some trees may not reach such a state for twenty years. Others, depending on their surroundings and general vigor, may need pruning within six to eight years. Remove as much of the unthrifty, moss-covered wood as possible. Prune out the center part of the tree for air and sunlight, shorten the lateral branches a little, then let the tree go for several more years. Filbert trees have a tendency to sucker profusely and if not given regular pruning attention they can soon become a large, multi-trunked bush rather than a single trunked, well-trained tree. Remove suckers whenever they are seen, either by pulling or pruning.

Walnuts formerly were grafted onto black walnut seedlings but a problem known as "blackline" sometimes developed ten to twenty years after planting and killed the trees. Many of the old dying walnut trees in the Northwest are the victims of blackline disorder. It is a non-reversible process. Once blackline starts it is only a matter of time before the tree dies. It was once thought that blackline resulted from a physiological incompatibility between the black walnut root and the English walnut variety. Recent research indicates that blackline may be transmitted much as a virus disease from one diseased tree to another. This possibility means that a blackline infected tree should be removed to prevent spreading. Blackline is characterized by a separation or groove forming at the graft union. More often though, identification is made by cutting away some of the bark covering the graft area and looking for the thin black line marking the area where the two varieties meet. Mature walnuts die for a variety of reasons but blackline is the cause of the greatest percentage. Nowadays nurserymen graft walnut varieties onto other, compatible root systems to avoid this problem. Rootstocks now used include *Carpathian* and *Manregion* varieties, neither of which have shown susceptibility to blackline disorder.

Staking should not be necessary unless the trees are planted in windy areas or their tops are so bushy in their first two years that wind could push the tree over. When necessary, stake on the upwind side with a sturdy stake about a foot away from the trunk. Tie loosely, so the tree can move freely in all but heavy winds. Mulching newly planted walnut and filbert trees pays off by maintaining soil moisture for root development. Irrigation during the tree's first year in the home orchard is important and should be done often enough to keep the soil damp 12–14" below the surface.

Newly planted nut trees do not need fertilizer. Soil fertility in the home orchard may be high enough to preclude the need for fertilization in later years. Observe the amount of growth the trees are making and the color of the foliage. Young trees making 18–30" of new shoot growth annually do not need fertilizing. If less growth is forthcoming or if the leaf color is pale instead of dark green, apply from ¼ to 1 pound actual nitrogen per tree. Use the lower amount for young trees and the higher for trees more than ten years old. Potassium is sometimes deficient causing smaller than normal leaves. If both nitrogen and potassium need to be supplied, apply a mixed fertilizer, such as potassium nitrate (13-0-44) or something similar in late winter. Spread the fertilizer in a wide band at the drip line of the tree. If the tree is growing in a lawn area, punch holes 12–20 inches deep around the dripline and divide the fertilizer.

Boron is sometimes too low in the Northwest for walnuts and filberts. The most usual sign of a shortage in both species is a reduced number of nuts. However, this symptom can result from many other factors, so do not assume your trees need boron. A striking symptom of boron shortage in walnuts is the appearance of new shoots, nearly leafless, mostly in the tops of the trees. Deficient shoots become twisted and flattened at their tips, resembling the head of a snake. These shoots usually die the following winter. Use these symptoms only as clues to the level of boron in your soil. Only a leaf analysis done by a reliable testing laboratory will provide a trustworthy guide. Boron is easily overdone and if overdone can damage your trees. A single application usually remains effective for three or four years.

FILBERTWORM: Insect pest unique to filbert nuts. Adult moths emerge in early summer and lay eggs through mid-July. Eggs are usually laid singly on the upper surface of the filbert husk. In eight or nine days the eggs hatch and the larvae bore inside to feast on the meat of the filbert.

Left: adult moth; wingspread is about ½". Two gold bands mark each forewing. _____

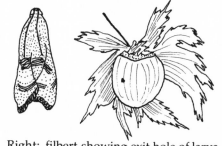

Right: filbert showing exit hole of larva.

Pests affecting nut trees are not nearly as numerous as those affecting other tree fruits. A few diseases may affect the walnut crop or the growth of young filberts and several insects damage the crop of both. Here are some of the more commonly seen problems:

PESTS OF FILBERTS AND WALNUTS

FILBERT

Problem	Affected Parts	Treatment
Eastern Filbert Blight	Affects young twigs first; may move downward and kill trunk in spring.	Prune and burn diseased parts; dormant and early sprays of copper may help.
Filbert Aphid	Sticky residues on leaves; nut size affected; damage cumulative to harvest.	Spray when seen.
Filbertworm	Larva feed inside and destroy kernels.	Early and mid-July, spray insecticide.
Lichen & Algae	Covers old limbs, contributes to limb breakage in ice storms.	Dormant spray, copper or lime sulfur; avoid spraying fungicides while trees are blooming.

WALNUT

Problem	Affected Parts	Treatment
Walnut Blight	Leaves, stems and fruit; black slimy spots on nut husks.	Copper sprays just before and immediately following bloom.
Blackline	Graft union.	Avoid planting English or Persian walnuts grafted to black walnut roots.
Walnut Huskfly	Nut husk tissue is destroyed and shells are stained, quality is lowered.	Early August insecticide sprays to prevent egg laying.

When the crop of walnuts or filberts is mature the nuts fall to the ground, usually in October. Walnut husks will loosen and allow the nut to fall. If hard winds blow the nearly mature nut from the tree the husks will generally split after a week on the ground. Walnut husks do a good job of staining hands and clothing, so let the husks loosen before you begin harvest. Pick up the husk-free walnuts within a day or two after they drop. Nuts allowed to lie on wet ground will discolor. This does not affect the flavor but if you want an attractive nut, pick them up early.

Filbert husks also open and let the nut fall when mature. Filberts can lay on the ground for months without losing quality. When most of the nuts have dropped, give the tree a shake to loosen the holdouts before winter rains start. The usual method of harvesting filberts is by raking them into a pile and separating the nuts from leaves, old husks and various other trash found under the tree.

Once the nuts are harvested they must be dried. Fresh nuts have too much moisture in their kernels to be stored without molding or becoming rancid. Walnut drying should begin as soon as they are picked up because once you bring them indoors for storing they may begin molding inside the shell.

Nuts can be dried either in the shell or the shell cracked and only the kernels dried. Either way works equally well. Drying the kernels after they are shelled will take less heat and time.

At any rate, the nuts must be dried for about a week. The best drying temperature is between 90—105°F with air circulating around and through the nuts. Put the nuts on screen-bottomed trays or mesh bags and set them above a furnace vent or hang them in the furnace room. At this temperature range, with air circulating, the walnuts will generally be dry in four to seven days, filberts in three or four. Lower temperatures are acceptable but the drying time is longer. Temperatures above 110°F will reduce the quality of the nut.

There are several ways to check if the nuts are properly dry. In-shell walnuts have a thin divider between the halves. Crack a walnut after three or four days of drying. If the divider is still rubbery continue drying. If it breaks with a snap, the nut is ready for storing or using. Kernels dried out of the shell will be firm and the papery outer cover will be crisp.

Filbert kernels are firm at the beginning of drying, become spongy as they start drying, and firm again when dry enough for storage. The color inside the kernel is the best indicator. During drying the internal color changes from white to a creamy color beginning at the outer part of the kernel. When the color change reaches the center the filbert is dry.

Once the nuts are properly dried, store them in a cool place in closed containers. Walnuts stored under average conditions in mesh bags or other open-type containers may soon be infested with Indian Meal Moth. The best way to avoid this pest is to either store the walnuts in tightly closed containers or shell the kernels and store them in the deep freeze.

FILBERT AND WALNUT VARIETIES FOR THE PACIFIC NORTHWEST

FILBERT VARIETY	NUT		POLLINATOR	PRODUCTIVITY
	SHAPE	SIZE		
Barcelona	round	medium/large	Davianna, Butler	moderate
Brixnut	round	medium/large	Butler	heavy
Butler	oval	medium/large	Barcelona	moderate
Davianna	oval	medium	Barcelona	very light
DuChilly	long	large	Barcelona	heavy (tends to bear biennially)
Ennis	round	large	Davianna, Butler	heavy
Halls Giant	round	medium	Barcelona	moderate
Royal	oval	large	Butler	moderate

WALNUT VARIETY	HARDINESS	BLIGHT SUSCEPTIBILITY	PRODUCTIVITY	REMARKS
Adams	moderate	nearly tolerant	low/slow	vigorous tree
Chambers #9	moderate	moderate	heavy	large nuts
Franquette	limited	highly	low/slow	
Hartley	limited	highly	heavy	needs Franquette or Spurgeon as pollinator, most susceptible to spring frosts
Spurgeon	very	medium	moderate	a favorite of the walnut husk fly

APPENDIX

VEGETABLE PLANTING INFORMATION
TABLE: UNCOMMON VEGETABLES
MANAGEMENT CALENDAR FOR VEGETABLES
SMALL FRUITS MANAGEMENT CALENDAR
TREE FRUITS MANAGEMENT CALENDAR

VEGETABLE PLANTING INFORMATION

Vegetable	Family[1]	Time to Plant[2]	Distance Apart for Max. Prod.[3]	Yield per 10' Single Row	Length 2' wide Intensive
Artichoke, globe	II.	M	60 inches	12 buds	NA
Artichoke, Jerusalem	II.	M	24	60 lbs.	NA
Asparagus	III.	E	12	50 tips	NA
Beans, bush	IIX.	M	6	12 lbs.	36 lbs.
Beans, pole	IIX.	M	12	15 lbs.	NA
Beets	I.	E, L	3	15 lbs.	105
Broccoli	V.	E, L	18	12 lbs.	NA
Brussels sprouts	V.	E	24	10 lbs.	NA
Cabbage	V.	E, L	18	7 heads	14 heads
Cabbage, Chinese	V.	E, L	6	20 heads	60 heads
Cantaloupes	VI.	M	48	10 melons	NA
Carrots	XIII.	E, L	2	10 lbs.	120 lbs.
Cauliflower	V.	E, L	24	5 heads	NA
Celery	XIII.	E	6	20 stalks	60 stalks
Chard	I.	E, L	8	10–15 lbs.	25–40 lbs.
Chives	IX.	E	clump	NA	NA
Corn	VII.	M	12	10–15 ears	20–30 ears
Cucumber	VI.	M	36	12 lbs.	NA
Dill	XIII.	M	8	15–30 heads	NA
Eggplant	XII.	M	24	30 fruits	NA
Endive	II.	E, L	10	5 lbs.	10–15 lbs.
Garlic	IX.	E, L	3	5 lbs.	30–40 lbs.
Kale	V.	E, L	18	7 heads	14 heads
Kohlrabi	V.	E, L	3	7 lbs.	45–60 lbs.
Leek	IX.	E	2	5 doz.	60 doz.
Lettuce, head	II.	C	10	12 heads	24 heads
Lettuce, leaf	II.	C	6	20 heads	60 heads
Okra	X.	M	18	10 lbs.	NA
Onion, green	IX.	E	1	10 doz.	120 doz.
Onion, bulb	IX.	E	3	40	280

Parsley	XIII.	C	6	3 lbs.	9 lbs.
Parsnip	XIII.	E, L	3	10 lbs.	70 lbs.
Peas	IIX.	E, L	2	2 lbs.	20 lbs.
Pepper	XII.	M	18	4 doz.	NA
Potato, sweet	IV.	M	12	10 lbs.	20 lbs.
Potato, white	XII.	M	12	10 lbs.	20 lbs.
Pumpkin	VI.	M	36	12	NA
Radish	V.	C	1	10 doz.	240 doz.
Rhubarb	XI.	E	30	8−16 lbs.	NA
Rutabaga	V.	M, L	3	3 doz.	20 doz.
Spinach	I.	E, L	3	3−4 lbs.	20−30 lbs.
Squash, summer	VI.	M	24	40 fruits	NA
Squash, winter	VI.	M	48	16 fruits	NA
Tomato	XII.	M	24	10 lbs.	NA
Turnip	V.	E, L	2	5 doz.	50 doz.
Watermelon	VI.	M	48	4−6 fruits	NA

[1]FAMILY: Use as planning factor to avoid planting varieties of the same family in the same garden spot more than two years in a row.

I.	Chenopodiaceae
II.	Compositae
III.	Convallariaceae
IV.	Convolvulaceae
V.	Cruciferae
VI.	Cucurbitaceae
VII.	Gramineae
IIX.	Leguminosae
IX.	Liliaceae
X.	Malvaceae
XI.	Polygonaceae
XII.	Solanaceae
XIII.	Umbelliferae

2.

TIME: See "Weather Data Summary" in Chapter 2 to determine if your locale will have enough growing days for the vegetable to produce a crop.
E = as soon in late winter as ground can be prepared.
M = after all danger of frost is passed.
L = late summer while 50−70 frost free growing days remain.
C = continuous planting from late winter until late summer.

3.

DISTANCE: indicates inches in the row. Check seed packet for row spacings.

TABLE: UNCOMMON VEGETABLES

As your gardening interest increases and as space allows, here are some of the less commonly grown vegetables that you might try:

Name	1Type	Where To Plant	Spacing	Harvest	Winter Hardy	Comments
Amaranth	WS	Sun	18″	6–8 wks.	No	pigweed cousin.
Celeriac	CS	Some Shade	12″	fall	Semi	needs moist soil.
Chicory	WS	Sun	12″	15″ diam.	No	can be a weed.
Comfrey	CS	Sun	24″	as needed	Semi	can be invasive; attracts bees.
Cress	CS	Some Shade	3″	as needed	Yes	quick growing.
Endive	CS	Sun	12″	as needed	Yes	good succession plant.
Fetticus	CS	Some Shade	3″	as needed	Yes	bland— also known as Corn Salad.
Horseradish	CS	Sun	18″	fall	Yes	new plants come from crown.
Leek	CS	Sun	6″	as needed	Yes	needs to be blanched.
Lovage	WS	Some Shade	36″	as needed	No	celery type.
Peanut	WS	Sun	12″	when vines dry	No	curiosity; needs hot weather.
Salsify	CS	Sun	8″	as needed	Semi (store in soil)	also known as "Oyster Plant", taste resemblance.
Shallots	CS	Sun	8″	as needed	No	dry to store like onions.
Soybean	WS	Sun	12″	when pods are full	No	lima substitute

1CS denotes cool season types that can be planted before the last spring frost; WS denotes warm season crops that should be planted after spring frosts end.

MANAGEMENT CALENDAR FOR VEGETABLES

January	Divide rhubarb. Read seed catalogues. Prepare soil for indoor planting.
February	Start seedlings/cool season crops. Turn cover crop if soil conditions allow. Plant garden peas.
March	Harvest asparagus. Plant cool season crops; watch for cutworm damage. Prepare garden soil with organic matter, fertilizer.
April	Continue planting cool season crops. Control young weeds. Watch for aphids on peas.
May	Plant warm season crops (most areas). Harvest cool season crops. Mulch transplants.
June	Watch soil moisture; replenish if dry. Continue planting warm season crops. Continue harvest from cool season crops. Hoe weeds. Mulch. Thin seedlings of newly planted crops. Stake tomatoes. Boost vegetable growth by sidedressing.
July	Continue harvest. Watch water needs. (late in month) Plant cool season crops for fall growth. Watch for tomato late blight.
August	Compost or spade under finished crops. Watch water needs. Watch for spider mites.
September	(late in month) Plant cover crop in empty spaces. Watch water needs. Mulch winter beds. Protect warm season crops from frost.
October	Clean-up garden. Lime soil, add gypsum to heavy or clay soils. Add organic soil amendments. Mulch garden beds with manure. Treat for perennial weeds in empty garden areas.
November	Plant garlic. Analyze soil problems, evaluate garden production.
December	--

SMALL FRUITS MANAGEMENT CALENDAR

MONTH and ACTION	Berry								
	Black *	Black Rasp.	Blue	Currants	Elder	Goose	Grapes	Red Rasp.	Straw
JANUARY Dormant Spray	X							X	
Prune	X						X		
Control winter weeds	X	X	X	X	X	X	X	X	X
FEBRUARY Prune		X	X	X	X	X		X	
Train	X						X		
Tie								X	
MARCH Plant new woody small fruits	X	X	X	X	X	X	X	X	
Treat for crown borer	X							X	
Fertilize	X	X	X	X	X	X		X	
Control weeds	X	X	X	X	X	X	X	X	X
APRIL Plant									X
Disease control			X						
Control weeds	X	X	X	X	X	X	X	X	X
MAY Pick blossoms, new plantings									X
JUNE Harvest								X	X
Maintain soil moisture	X	X	X	X	X	X	X	X	X
JULY Maintain soil moisture	X	X	X	X	X	X	X	X	X
Harvest		X	X	X		X		X	
Mow, single crop									X
Control weeds	X	X	X	X	X	X	X	X	X
AUGUST Maintain soil moisture	X	X	X	X	X	X		X	X
Harvest	X								
Prune old canes		X						X	
Fertilize									X

MONTH and ACTION:	Black	Black Rasp.	Blue	Currants	Elder	Goose	Grapes	Red Rasp.	Straw
Plant runners									X
SEPTEMBER Harvest	X				X		X		
Control weeds	X	X	X	X	X	X	X	X	X
OCTOBER Mulch			X						X
Clean-up	X	X	X	X	X	X	X	X	X
Prepare new planting spot for next year	X	X	X	X	X	X	X	X	X
NOVEMBER Spray for mites	X							X	
Tie								X	
DECEMBER Dormant spray	X						X	X	

*includes Boysens and Logans

TREE FRUITS MANAGEMENT CALENDAR

MONTH and ACTION:	All Tree Fruits	Apple	Pear	Peach	Apricot	Cherry	Plum	Filbert	Walnut	New Plantg's
JANUARY Dormant Spray	X							*		
Prune Winter Damage	X									
FEBRUARY Prune to regulate growth	X									
MARCH Plant, stake if necessary	X									
APRIL Check spray schedules		X	X	X	X	X	X	X		
MAY Fertilize	X									X

MONTH and ACTION:	All Tree Fruits	Apple	Pear	Peach	Apricot	Cherry	Plum	Filbet	Walnut	New Plantg's
JUNE Treat for cherry fruit fly						X				
Harvest						X				
Thin Fruits		X	X	X	X		X			
Prune Suckers	X									
JULY Water										X
Harvest		X		X						
Watch for root borers			X	X	X	X	X			
Check for stake damage	X									X
Treat for filbert worm								X		
AUGUST Treat for walnut husk fly									X	
Water										X
Water if droughty	X									
Harvest		X	X				X			
SEPTEMBER Prune extraneous growth	X									X
Harvest		X	X	X			X			
OCTOBER Compost clean leaves, destroy diseased ones	X									
Fertilize if needed	X									
Spray for bacterial canker				X	X	X	X			
Harvest								X	X	
NOVEMBER Protect trunk from small animals	X									X
DECEMBER Dormant spray, peach leaf curl				X						

*do not spray if catkins are present.

INDEX

Page numbers in *italics* denote illustrations.

THE COMPLETE BOOK OF ROSES
Gerd Krüssman

"A monumental and authoritative work . . . the definitive study of the rose from prehistoric times to 1981 . . ."

Gil Daniels, President, The American Horticultural Society.
"An indispensible and classic work in horticultural literature . . . recommended as a reference for all serious rosarians." Jarold Goldstein, Executive Director,

The American Rose Society

| 436 pages/300 illustrations | 8½x11 | hardbound |

MEDIAEVAL GARDENS
John Harvey

An account of a neglected period in the history of the garden that reveals unexpected insights into the society of the time. Many strikingly beautiful illustrations taken from manuscripts, paintings, stained-glass windows, and other sources.

216 pages/11 color and 95 b&w photos 5 maps & plans 7x10 hardbound

JAPANESE MAPLES
J.D. Vertrees

"Finally, the first comprehensive work on Japanese maples . . . a wonderful job . . ." *Pacific Horticulture.*
"Authoritative . . .enjoyable reading . . . a beautiful and valuable book . . ."

American Horticulturist

| 192 pages/200 color plates | 9x12 | hardbound |

TREES AND SHRUBS FOR WESTERN GARDENS
Gordon Courtright

" . . . pictorial companion to the *Sunset Western Garden Book* . . . a landmark effort and the only book in print to picture so many Western garden plants in color . . ." *Sunset Magazine.*

| 250 pages/800 color plates | 9x12 | hardbound |

RHODODENDRON SPECIES, Volume I: Lepidotes
H.H. Davidian

For each species, a full botanic description as well as a discussion of the plant's discovery, introduction, cultivation, and cultural uses. In addition, a history of rhododendron expeditions, glossaries, and other supplementary tables and sections.

470 pages/97 color plates, 39 line drawings 8½x11 hardbound

THE TERRACE GARDENER'S HANDBOOK
Raising Plants on a Balcony, Terrace, Rooftop, Penthouse or Patio
Linda Yang

" . . . complete, carefully detailed, covering thoroughly and clearly every phase . . ."

National Council State Garden Clubs
" . . .tells how to make the most of cramped quarters . . ." *New York Times Book Review*

283 pages/112 photos, 32 line drawings 5½x8½ softbound

GARDENING IN THE SHADE
Harriet K. Morse

Nearly every garden has some shady spots which need special treatment; city gardeners receive limited sunlight because of surrounding buildings; and indoor gardeners are restricted to plants which grow in little or no light. This book is useful for almost every gardener in almost every situation.

| 242 pages/32 photos | 5½x8½ | softbound |

(Continued on back)

WITHOUT A THORN: A Guide to Rose Gardening in the Pacific Northwest
Stu Mechlin & Ellen Bonanno
" . . .the 'must' rose handbook for the new regional gardener and an excellent review and reference book for the established rosarian . . ." *The Oregonian*
100 pages/300 illustrations   5½x8½   softbound

PENJING The Chinese Art of Miniature Gardens
The first book to come out of China on this ancient horticultural art. The technique of miniaturizing plants and the creation of miniature gardens with water and mountain scenes is graphically demonstrated.
166 pages/80 color plates,   72 b&w photos   30 line drawings   8½x11
hardbound

THE ESSENTIALS OF BONSAI
One of the finest Bonsai books for the beginner to the intermediate enthusiast. It covers all the tools, plant material, and care as well as giving an excellent background.
108 pages/26 color photos, many b&w photos and line drawings 7½x8½
hardbound

HOW TO IDENTIFY FLOWERING PLANT FAMILIES A Practical Guide for Horticulturists and Plant Lovers
John Philip Baumgardt
Learn to analyze flower structure, construct a floral diagram, lay out a floral formula, and so fit a plant into its proper niche.
285 pages/57 color plates   122 illustrations   6x9   softbound

PLANT HUNTING IN NEPAL
Roy Lancaster
A group of horticultural botanists travelled through East Nepal collecting seeds of plants suitable for cultivation in Western gardens. As a result, many of these plants are now found in some of the most famous gardens in Europe.
194 pages/numerous color photos and line drawings   6x9   hardbound

POCKET GUIDE TO CHOOSING WOODY ORNAMENTALS
Gerd Krüssmann — translated by Michael E. Epp
A quick and easy reference for any design situation. A thesaurus of plant material for the professional, serious gardener.
141 pages   4½x7·   flexible binding

ROCK GARDENING A Guide to Growing Alpines and Other Wildflowers in the American Garden
H. Lincoln Foster
This is a book of lasting value for the advanced rock gardener as well as the beginner, whether or not he has a green thumb.
466 pages/many line drawings   5½x8½   softbound

GETTING STARTED WITH RHODODENDRONS AND AZALEAS
J. Harold Clarke
The facts about rhododendrons and azaleas are all here, organized for handy reference in clear, concise, and lively language.
293 pages/73 b&w photos   5½x8½   softbound

Write for our catalogue:
TIMBER PRESS
P.O. Box 1631
Beaverton, Oregon 97075